Spirituality and Theology

Spirituality and Theology
ESSAYS IN HONOR OF DIOGENES ALLEN

Eric O. Springsted, editor

Westminster John Knox Press
Louisville, Kentucky

Scripture quotations from the Revised Standard Version
of the Bible are copyright © 1989 by the Division of Christian Education
of the National Council of the Churches of Christ in the U.S.A.
and are used by permission.

Grateful acknowledgment is made to the following for permission
to reproduce copyrighted material:

The Church Pension Fund, for Percy Dearmer, "Sing Praise to God, Who Spoke through Man,"
from *The Hymnal 1940* (New York: The Church Pension Fund, 1940).

T. & T. Clark, Ltd., from Karl Barth, *Church Dogmatics* (Edinburgh: T. & T. Clark, 1936–72).

Wm. B. Eerdmans Publishing Co., from Charles Péguy, *The Portal of the Mystery of Hope,*
translated by D. L. Schindler, Jr. (Grand Rapids: Wm. B. Eerdmans Publishing Co., 1996).

Book design by Jennifer K. Cox
Cover design by Kevin Darst

First edition
Published by Westminster John Knox Press
Louisville, Kentucky

This book is printed on acid-free paper that meets the
American National Standards Institute Z39.48 standard. ∞

PRINTED IN THE UNITED STATES OF AMERICA
98 99 00 01 02 03 04 05 06 07 — 10 9 8 7 6 5 4 3 2 1

Library of Congress Cataloging-in-Publication Data

Spirituality and theology : essays in honor of Diogenes Allen / Eric
O. Springsted, editor.
    p.   cm.
Includes bibliographical references.
ISBN 0-664-25741-0 (alk. paper)
    1. Theology—Methodology.   2. Spirituality.   3. Spirituality—
History.   I. Allen, Diogenes.   II. Springsted, Eric O.
BR118.S685   1998
291.4—dc21   97-44672

CONTENTS

Part II
Spirituality within Christian Theology

ACKNOWLEDGMENTS

The appearance of a Festschrift is inevitably a collaborative effort, and one in which all contributions are a matter of grace and goodwill. I would therefore like to extend formal thanks to everyone who had a hand in this volume. Deep gratitude goes to all the contributors who gave of their time and energy to honor a colleague. I would also like to thank President Thomas Gillespie of Princeton Theological Seminary for the support of the seminary for this project. Jane and Mary Elizabeth Allen were essential to this book from the beginning, providing helpful suggestions about its shape, matters of substance and information, and ever helpful advice. David Burrell not only contributed to this volume, but also was from the very inception of this project a constant source of advice and help on whom I leaned regularly. Chris Wherley and his staff in the Illinois College Academic Computing Services department and Leah Blake, the ever responsible and dispositionally gifted Chapel secretary, provided invaluable assistance in the manuscript preparation.

WORKS BY
DIOGENES ALLEN

Theodicy, by G. W. Leibniz (editor). Library of Liberal Arts. Indianapolis: Bobbs-Merrill Co., 1966.

The Reasonableness of Faith. Washington, D.C.: Corpus Books, 1968.

Finding Our Father. Atlanta: John Knox Press, 1974. Reprinted as *The Path of Perfect Love.* Cambridge, Mass.: Cowley Publications, 1992.

Between Two Worlds. Atlanta: John Knox Press, 1977. Reprinted as *Temptation,* Cambridge, Mass.: Cowley Publications, 1986. Reprinted as *Temptation,* Princeton: Caroline Press, 1996.

The Traces of God in a Frequently Hostile World. Cambridge, Mass.: Cowley Publications, 1981.

Mechanical Explanations and the Ultimate Origin of the Universe according to Leibniz. Studia Leibnitiana Sonderheft 11. Wiesbaden: Franz Steiner Verlag, 1983.

Three Outsiders: Pascal, Kierkegaard, and Simone Weil. Cambridge, Mass.: Cowley Publications, 1983.

Philosophy for Understanding Theology. Atlanta: John Knox Press, 1985.

Love: Christian Romance, Marriage, and Friendship. Cambridge, Mass.: Cowley Publications, 1987. (Reprint, Princeton, N.J.: Caroline Press, 1997.)

Christian Belief in a Postmodern World: The Full Wealth of Conviction. Louisville, Ky.: Westminster/John Knox Press, 1989.

Quest: the Search for Meaning through Christ. New York: Walker & Co., 1990.

Primary Readings in Philosophy for Understanding Theology (coeditor with Eric O. Springsted). Louisville, Ky.: Westminster/John Knox Press, 1992.

Spirit, Nature, and Community: Issues in the Thought of Simone Weil (with Eric O. Springsted). Albany: State University of New York Press, 1994.

Spiritual Theology: An Introduction to Yesterday's Christian Spirituality for Our Use Today. Cambridge, Mass.: Cowley Publications, 1997.

INTRODUCTION

Within the intellectual climate of much of the twentieth century, theology has found itself continually on the defensive. Diogenes Allen, in *Christian Belief in a Postmodern World,* has described the situation this way, borrowing an image from Basil Mitchell:

> Mitchell pictures traditional Christian theology as a barge going down a river. On one side of the river are shoals which represent the works of David Hume and Immanuel Kant, which enshrine some of the most serious intellectual barriers to Christian belief in modern times. To avoid these shoals, theologians have either jettisoned some of their cargo (Christian claims) to lighten the barge and sail safely over them, or they have swung sharply to the other bank to remain premodern.[1]

It is not just the twentieth century, though, and it is not just a matter of claims. There has been a spirit to the modern world that has been stifling to theology, and to the *spirit* of its claims. One theologian, well versed in the ancient church, has talked about a "dissociation of sensibility"[2] for theology in the modern world. What he meant was this: Theology, which had always lived and moved and breathed in a climate of personal interaction, in the modern world has had to live in a world dictated by scientific method. Not only has it been difficult to make Christian claims in such terms as Mitchell and Allen note; even when those claims have been made, they ring much differently than they did to Gregory of Nyssa, Augustine, or Aquinas. This resonance seems to many to belie the very nature of theology itself, although we have become so accustomed to it that we start reading the tradition (and as Louth notes, it is necessarily a tradition) in ways that utterly mischaracterize it. Michael Buckley, for example, in his *The Origins of Modern Atheism,*[3] has suggested that theologians actually had a hand in contributing to the rise of modern atheism. They did so by treating theological thought as if it were philosophy, and by treating theologians like Aquinas as if they were Cartesian philosophers. Thus they ignored the religious nature of their predecessors' thought, and made modern philosophical conceptions the judge and jury of the true and false. But we don't easily recognize this, thinking that is how our predecessors should be read.

As Allen himself suggests, however, the apparent dilemma of having either to jettison Christian claims or to hold them in a premodern way may no longer obtain. There have been crucial and far-reaching changes in the way the late twentieth century looks at knowledge. On the one hand, postmodernism (or perhaps more accurately, postpositivism) has been effectively challenging the quest for universal foundations. On the other hand, especially in theology, so-called postliberalism has challenged the previously assumed need to provide universal applications of a position. Bolstered by an appreciation of the narrative nature of human experience and its roots in history and tradition, Christian theology's need to employ an authoritative tradition is now no longer regarded as an embarrassment. This has resulted in several important works that have sought to reconfigure our appreciation of vital areas in theology, such as doctrine. George Lindbeck's *The Nature of Doctrine*[4] is a prime example of trying to locate Christian claims within the practice and tradition of the Christian community. Moreover, the very ability to recognize, as Louth and Buckley have, that there is a dissociation of sensibility, that we have not been telling the story right, is witness to a new understanding of the spirit in which theology ought to be written.

Yet, in musings on Lindbeck and much of the postliberal literature, numerous theologians have complained that what we are witnessing is largely a matter of *pretheological reflection,* a getting ready to do theology. It has yet to be done, however.

The point is an important one. Clearing the decks is necessary, and trying to locate Christian claims within Christian practices is vital. Yet the nature of theology still will not come clear, and theology itself will not get done, until theology can place itself firmly within those practices and think within them. For this reason theology certainly will not be Christian theology until it is seen as a part, somehow, of Christian spirituality.

Each of the contributors to this volume believes that this theology, which is a matter of Christian theology, needs to be written. It is not just a matter of adding religious experience to theological thought or of making religious experience the "data" of reflection. It is a matter of getting us to see that spirituality, that the Christian practice of knowing God, is vital to the understanding of theology itself.

But there is another reason as well. We do live in an era in which there is a deep spiritual hunger, in which people have been given spiritual stones instead of bread for a long time. As the starving rush upon anything that might satisfy their hunger, they often will grab much that is destructive and not nourishing. In this sense, theology not only needs to be seen as related to spirituality for theology's sake; it also needs to be related to spirituality for spirituality's sake. We live in an age where too many people, including ones who should know better, regard religion as *just* a set of practices. These practices are no longer thinking, worshiping, and so on, in God's service. They have become their own ends.

These are concerns that need much thought and effort. In this volume, we want not only to address these concerns, we want at the same time to honor the work of Diogenes Allen, a colleague who has understood these things for a long time and who has said much that makes us think more clearly about them.

Diogenes Allen throughout his career has maintained an often distinctive and, within the field of the philosophy of religion, important position among those making any headway in discussing the relation of spirituality and theology. For, on the one hand, he has been a philosopher of religion of his own century. Questions of the *truth* of the Christian religion have always been central to his project, and woe to those who took him to be a thinker who was simply trying to find subjective room within a world already settled by positivism! On the other hand, he has consistently explored the spirituality of Christianity. He has led as many retreats as he has read papers to academic societies. The combination is unusual, for philosophers and their questions of truth have tended to be notoriously uninteresting to those on spiritual quests, and spiritual quests have been regarded often as sentimental detours by philosophers looking for truth. It is important to understand about Allen's work, though, that if he has done both these things, they have never been separate enterprises for him. That he has made them hang together is precisely why he is such an example for talking about spirituality and theology.

To say that he has made them hang together may perhaps be misleading. Rather, he has been insistent in saying that they belong together at their very root. And just how this is so can be seen from his earliest work.

Dissertations are often works that are best regarded as initial forays into scholarship; they are the first attempts to establish oneself in the conversation of scholars, but generally their ideas need seasoning from the conversation itself, for they often show both a brashness and a naïveté about the sorts of questions at stake. Allen's doctoral dissertation, which was to be published as *The Reasonableness of Faith,* however, was not exactly like that. It was original *and* very canny in its understanding of what the conversation was about and what it claimed it ought to be about. The style and voice, to be sure, were to undergo change, but the idea that drove it was still potent and has been spoken over several years.

In certain ways the style of *The Reasonableness of Faith* was representative of Anglo-American philosophy of religion in the 1950s and 1960s, as well it ought to have been—that was its pedigree. After graduating from the University of Kentucky and with a brief interlude as a graduate student at Princeton University, Allen began studies as a Rhodes Scholar at St. John's College, Oxford, in the 1950s. This was the heyday of analysis in philosophy, and ordinary-language philosophy ruled, with the specter of a positivist-like Wittgenstein (but something seemed suspicious about him) lurking somewhere in the background. It was no easy time for philosophically minded Christians. Allen, who was at the lecture himself, tells of the shock that R. B. Braithwaite created in Oxford when he delivered the talk "An Empiricist's View of the Nature of Religious Belief." That *any* quarter was given to religious belief, that it had any function in life, was not normally something admitted by philosophers.

The climate had changed little when Allen returned to Oxford in the 1960s. He had done much: taken a divinity degree at Yale, served a New Hampshire parish, and gone through a doctoral program at Yale, working with Julian Hartt and Paul Holmer. The return, the use of a remaining year on his Rhodes scholarship, was to finish his dissertation. It was then that he worked with one of the few people at Oxford who was both a man of profound faith and a mind of exquisite philosophic strength and subtlety, Austin Farrer. (Indeed, Allen later remarked that Oxford had produced only one great theologian since Newman, and that was Farrer.) Farrer was an important influence on Allen; as is clear from Farrer's own explicit statement, though, the student also caused a revolution in his teacher's thinking.

Now, within that world of thought in Oxford what was striking about *The Reasonableness of Faith* was its position, stated clearly in the introduction, that it presented a "case for the reasonableness of adherence to God, to belief in him and worship of him by enlarging our notion of 'reasonableness' or 'rationality'" (xiii). To say more: Allen claimed that there were distinctive religious needs, which, if met in faith, showed that faith was a reasonable thing. He also continued, with keen insight, that we need to recognize that the rationales one might give for Christianity are not the same thing as the Christian faith itself—a mistake philosophers regularly seem to make. The point was that Christianity did not ultimately stand or fall on the success of its rationales and defenses but on the actual life of faith.

Allen honestly meant both that there was an argument for the reasonableness of Christianity and that the grounds for Christian faith needed to be distinguished from that argument, and that each needed to be understood on its own. The difference from a position like, say, Braithwaite's is that for Allen Christianity is not simply a sort of subjective gestalt, wrapping together in a narrative package the otherwise indisputable facts of empirical life. Rather, as far as Allen is concerned, there are facts about the world that Christianity alone reveals. These facts, however, cannot be established or even appreciated without taking into consideration the "need for explanations that refer to a deity" (20). But in that respect what Christianity is interested in is not so much a matter of trying to provide a "best account of the world" that competes with metaphysics—it may or may not do so; Christianity is about meeting specific religious needs, and its reasonableness should be judged in how it meets them. The upshot of this position is that an intelligent person can find faith a reasonable thing to have, but also that it is important that intelligent people actually take some time to discern what religious grounds really are.

Discerning those grounds has been much of Allen's own task over the years. This can be seen particularly in a series of books he did in the 1970s and 1980s: *Finding Our Father* (1974); *Between Two Worlds* (1977); *The Traces of God in a Frequently Hostile World* (1981); and *Three Outsiders: Pascal, Kierkegaard, and Simone Weil* (1983). In each of them he sought to examine more closely the internal movements of faith itself. In each of these works, the effort was not a matter of trying to justify Christianity in an unbeliever's court, but of trying to understand Christianity as a Christian. At least two things seem to be going on in Allen's thinking in these books. One was the sort of authors he himself was reading and using to articulate his own thinking. Less and less were they the sort of authors one finds frequently quoted in the *American Philosophical Quarterly* (two of the chapters of *Reasonableness* had originally appeared there), and more and more they included unfashionable thinkers such as Plato and Leibniz, as well as "outsiders" such as Kierkegaard, Pascal, and especially Simone Weil.[5] The poetry of George Herbert was also a crucial source of inspiration. This was not just a preference for a position they all held in common; each of these thinkers was important precisely because he or she actually knew how to think in spiritual categories. They each knew something about the soul and, in Plato's terms, "the tendance of the soul."

They were important to Allen also for a related reason. Allen always recognized in his own work, and he emphasized this as a teacher, the need to think with others, to find a great thinker to think with. These sources provided that for him. But, of course, as thinkers what they do have in common is that they themselves thought that way, despite their own originality. These were thinkers who read each other and thought each other's questions—within the obvious historical limits, of course. (The theological upshot of some of this is seen in essays by Burrell, Henderson, and Springsted in this book.) They formed a tradition, a deliberate handing on of questions. And as such they have also helped one think through what it means to engage a tradition and to respect its questions. (This is a theme that runs throughout many of the essays of the present volume.)

Such a use of a tradition in turn is not separable from the way one does his or her thinking. This shows itself in the way Allen has sought to approach certain kinds of problems. At the same time that Allen was making use of these thinkers, he began to approach numerous traditional problems in the philosophy of religion and philosophical theology in a distinctive way. That way can be best illustrated by reference to a certain kind of use Allen made of a thinker like Weil. Weil points out that in one of her crucial experiences of Christ, a veil was lifted from her mind about the problem of suffering. She says that she discovered that the "supernatural greatness of Christianity lies in the fact that it does not seek a supernatural remedy for suffering but a supernatural use for it."[6] Like Weil, Allen, in looking at suffering in *The Traces of God,* began to look at it as a problem *within* Christian life and less as a problem to be solved before Christian life could be considered. The intellectual problem has not disappeared; its weight is put within a balance, however.

Something of what was going on in those books might be illustrated by a comment Allen frequently made to students. He noted (borrowing from a source I do not any longer recall) that much of American preaching was based on a revival tent model—it always sought to convert the hearer. The problem for most people, though, he said, was how to get from A to B in the spiritual life. Much of his work has been discerning both A and B and what it takes to get from one to the other. It has been an effort to understand what it means to think Christianly, an effort that has culminated most recently in his *Spiritual Theology.* This is not just another attempt to help the alienated soul chart its way to friendlier climes, but a work that recognizes the distinctive nature of theological knowledge, which is to advance in genuine knowledge. But it does it in its own way, often at odds with the spirit of the age.

> Traditionally, attentiveness in contemplation and meditation has been one of the ways that Christians increase their knowledge of God. Around the time of Descartes in the seventeenth century, however, meditative and contemplative attention (a path to knowledge in the philosophy of Plato and Aristotle) gradually disappeared. Instead, knowledge became an instrument for controlling nature in order to produce the effects we want. . . .
> In meditation and contemplation Christians seek to grow in knowledge and love of God by increasing their understanding of what it is they believe and love. . . . Our understanding of these mysteries is limited. But divine truths can be thought about, and some understanding achieved, when they are attended to lovingly. (104–5)

It would be a mistake, however, to gather from the trajectory of Allen's thought just traced that he has since *Reasonableness* been confirming what tough-minded philosophers have always suspected about engagements with spirituality. It would also be to misunderstand what contributions Allen has made to understanding problems of faith and reason and to his philosophical commitment. He has always argued that though Christianity stood or fell on its own grounds, it did not, nevertheless, live an isolated existence; and that the philosophical tradition *is* crucial to understanding Christianity and a key to its self-understanding. Nowhere is this so well seen as in the considerable efforts that went into writing *Philosophy for Understanding Theology,* a book designed actually to teach philosophy, philosophy without which the Christian thinker's past is inaccessible to him or her.

It is also important to understand that all of Allen's spiritual work has been part of a larger project, one that like *Reasonableness* was committed to the defense of Christianity as *true.* What sort of project that is can be seen in a claim Allen made in his inaugural lecture of October 6, 1976, as professor of philosophy at Princeton Theological Seminary.[7] He stated: "I have come to believe that for Christian faith to be thoroughly justified in Western society at the present time three things must be done: (1) the *possibility* of God must be shown in a scientific universe; (2) the human *need* for God must be articulated; and (3) a person must be touched to some degree by God's holy and gracious presence."[8] These three things have in an important sense been the unifying factors in Allen's work. They constitute the elements of his argument in *Christian Belief in a Postmodern World* (1989). Indeed, the lecture in which they were announced was a sort of protoargument of that book.

Christian Belief in a Postmodern World was conceived and written as Allen's apology for the Christian faith, a defense of its truth. As any student of doctrine can well attest, many of the apologies for Christianity over the course of Christian philosophical writing have been anything but apologetic. They have been aggressive and have found the best defense to consist in a sharp offense. A truly wonderful feature of Allen's apology was that it refrained from taking this approach. In part, it was a matter of remembering warnings made years before about not confusing arguments about Christian claims with Christianity. But more positively, it was a matter of actually using spirituality to enlighten the intelligence. I remember Dick once noting in a conversation that throughout his education science had always been held out as the judge, jury, and standard of truth and that theology had always had to contend with science, rarely very well. Consequently, to say something about science was always important to him as it is to any twentieth-century philosopher. *Christian Belief,* therefore, deals with science head-on. It deals with it, though, from a perspective where science is no longer that sole judge and jury. But that is not what makes Christianity true. Rather, as Allen argues, science actually has a theologically important role, for once it is no longer taken to provide an ultimate explanation[9] it can in its own incompleteness point to the possibility of God. It can become, in a phrase he has resurrected, "the book of nature," and hence a *witness* to the creator. That by itself does not establish Christianity's truth. But in a world where we do seek ultimate purposes, and even seem to have a deep need to touch them somehow, the Christian experience of God's grace is sufficient reason for the truth of Christianity. It is not because science is wrong that Christianity is right; it is because, Allen claims, science is right, because for creatures seeking purpose, science's sort of rightness can be a witness to God, that Christianity is true. In this sense it also needs to be recognized that Christian spirituality, while it completes natural experience, never takes place apart from it. Faith does not avoid reason.

It is here that we can understand something of the unity of Diogenes Allen's diverse interests in science and theology, in spirituality, and in the problem of evil, and his interest in and work on figures such as Leibniz, Weil, Farrer, Kierkegaard, Plato, Pascal, Herbert, and even Maximus the Confessor. Each of these figures was a philosopher by his or her commitment to understand the needs of the human soul, including his or her own. Each sought the good that would alone satisfy those needs, yet each sought that good in such a way that the best of scientific thought would clarify and articulate one's relationship to God, without determining it.

It is the last part of Allen's argument, the experience of God's grace and its relation to the knowledge of God, that will form the focus of the following essays on spirituality and theology. We intend to focus particularly on the relationship between Christian practice and theory, especially as it concerns issues of the relation of spirituality and theological knowledge, and theology and philosophy. We are also especially concerned with how spirituality is a part of theology itself. Whereas much of the current literature that deals with Christianity is concerned with the relation between, say, Christian virtues and Christian thinking, we would like to highlight the idea of *theology,* not simply as a reflection of Christian spirituality, but as something that needs to be thought of as a spiritual practice itself.

In Part One, "Spirituality and the Nature of Christian Theology," we seek to discuss how theological knowledge may be understood when spirituality is close to its heart. *Stanley Hauerwas* opens with "Christians in the Hands of Flaccid Secularists: Theology and 'Moral Inquiry' in the Modern University," in which he charts, through his own field of Christian ethics, how theology has been pushed out of the modern university (and thus out of the catalog of worthwhile public knowledge). In doing so, he underscores what difference God and the knowledge of God really does make to moral knowledge, and how Christian moral knowledge must be rooted in the ongoing Christian story. *David Burrell* in "Friends in Conversation: The Language and Practice of Faith" shows how theological knowledge needs to be understood on a pattern of the knowledge gained in personal relations. He also highlights how, in the ancient world, philosophical and theological knowledge understood in such a way was deliberately construed as a spiritual practice. *Brian Hebblethwaite* in "The Believer's Reasons" raises a classic argument about the place of reason and natural theology in theological knowledge. In doing so, he continues an ongoing debate in which he has engaged with Allen about the relation of faith and reason in theology, and provides the other side of the story about the nature of theological thinking. His essay, taken along with those immediately preceding and following it, sets in sharp relief the sorts of tensions that Allen's work has continually dealt with, namely, those of inward spirituality and faith, outward rationality, and truth. *Eric Springsted* in "Theology and

Spirituality; or, Why Theology Is Not Critical Reflection on Religious Experience" continues the discussion by seeking to describe the nature of faith and how, as Burrell had described matters, it is primarily a matter of interaction. As such, he then shows theology as an actual activity of faith, and not a matter of critical distance from it—a way of embracing the whole person and the world. *Edward Henderson* in "How to Be a Christian Philosopher in the Postmodern World," continues the discussion of faith and reason by comparing Christian faith and Platonic Socratism. And, continuing and advancing themes sounded by previous contributors, he shows how they have analogous structures, thus showing that at least for many of the ancients there was not really a question of faith or reason. *Jeffrey Eaton* in "The Primacy of Spirit," by an investigation of the thought of George Berkeley shows what is at stake in the assumptions of the materialism that has dominated so much of modern philosophy. In doing so, he sketches through Berkeley what a philosophy and religion that takes spirit seriously might include.

In Part Two, "Spirituality within Christian Theology," we turn to examine various aspects of Christian spirituality as they affect the way theology is done, both in form and content. *Gerhard Sauter* in "Hope—the Spiritual Dimension of Theological Anthropology," beginning with an insight from Charles Péguy's *The Portal of the Mystery of Hope,* develops an understanding of hope, not as a therapy for disillusionment or as a theologicopolitical project, but as a basic disposition toward life and the future of life, sustained by faith in Christ. Evagrius of Pontus once said: "To be a theologian is to pray truly and to pray truly is to be a theologian." *Daniel Migliore* in "Freedom to Pray: Karl Barth's Theology of Prayer," gives a detailed analysis of Karl Barth's understanding of prayer. He thereby shows the crucial degree to which Barth, a figure so central to twentieth-century Protestant theology, had developed his theology out of the spiritual practice of prayer, and the extent to which he thought theology in the end was directed to that practice. *Elena Malits* in "Teaching Theology by Exploring the Ordinary" addresses herself to the question of spirituality in teaching religion. She takes up, in a discussion of her own efforts in teaching religion to undergraduates, many of the issues—friendship, the integrity of the other, the role of faith in thinking—that have formed the basis of theoretical discussions earlier in this volume, and shows how they are actually engaged as students come to learn and think more deeply about the nature of faith in the world. *Daniel Hardy* concludes this volume with "Spirituality and Its Embodiment in Church Life." In an age when spirituality has become more and more a disastrous hyperindividualistic matter, based perhaps on a misreading of Protestant claims for the conscience, and when such spirituality actually and responsibly grips embodied life less and less, Hardy offers a fitting and important reminder of the nature of the church within Christian spirituality and theology.

A final note needs to be added about what is, unfortunately, not in this volume. Throughout his writings Diogenes Allen has made important contributions to Christian theology concerning the relation of suffering, spirituality, and the knowledge of God. When plans were first laid for this book, George Hall of St. Mary's College, University of St. Andrews (Scotland), had proposed to do an essay on the topic "Knowing the Love of God in Suffering and Affliction." In it Hall proposed to deal with a question Robert and Marilyn Adams had raised about an article of Allen on "Natural Evil and the Love of God." They questioned, Hall noted, "the dependence of [Allen's] position on the 'victim's response,' with the implication that this does not make belief that God is incommensurably good and loving a reasonable belief to the afflicted but spiritually immature." Through an investigation of themes in Weil that touched on theology and tragedy, Hall hoped to respond to the Adamses' question, by thinking about what "knowing" might be in such contexts, about how "knowing is not a single thing, or better, how much depends on the job 'knowing' is doing in several contexts." When he proposed that essay, Professor Hall knew he was terminally ill, but thought he might have enough time to finish it. He did not. We note this, not because of what might have been, but because there is no finer tribute to the quality of a friend's thought than to think on it and find it true when death and suffering faced is a daily reality. Let then the silence of the omission stand as a potent closing statement to the efforts printed here.

NOTES

1. Diogenes Allen, *Christian Belief in a Postmodern World* (Louisville, Ky.: Westminster/John Knox, 1989), 7.
2. Andrew Louth, *Discerning the Mystery: An Essay on the Nature of Theology* (Oxford: Oxford University Press, 1983).
3. Michael Buckley, *The Origins of Modern Atheism* (New Haven, Conn.: Yale University Press, 1987).
4. George Lindbeck, *The Nature of Doctrine* (Philadelphia: Westminster Press, 1984).
5. I well remember Dick Allen's early interest in Weil. Somewhere around 1975 he was beginning to read her because he was using Iris Murdoch (a thinker central in *Between Two Worlds*) in some of his work, and Murdoch had drunk deeply from Weil's well; knowing I was interested in Plato, he suggested I read her, since she had some interesting things to say about Plato. Weil in a very short time became a central focus for both of us, and the chief topic of conversation and collaborative work for now over twenty years.
6. Simone Weil, *Gravity and Grace* (London: Routledge & Kegan Paul, 1952), 73.
7. Allen had come to Princeton in 1967 after having taught at York University in Toronto. Soon after being appointed professor of philosophy, he was given the chair he currently holds as the Stuart Professor of Philosophy at Princeton Theological Seminary.
8. "Leibniz's Relevance for Today's Christianity," *Princeton Seminary Bulletin*, n.s., 1, no. 1, 1977: 13.
9. Much of the argument at this point was taken from Allen's extensive work on Leibniz and is found in his *Mechanical Explanations and the Ultimate Origin of the Universe according to Leibniz* (1983).

PART I

SPIRITUALITY AND THE NATURE OF CHRISTIAN THEOLOGY

1

CHRISTIANS IN THE HANDS OF FLACCID SECULARISTS

Theology and "Moral Inquiry" in the Modern University

STANLEY HAUERWAS

On Being a Theologian
and Ethicist with Two Stories

I am a Christian theologian who teaches ethics. I could alternatively say I am a Christian ethicist, with the hope that most people would concentrate on the noun and not the qualifier, but that probably wouldn't help matters much. In fact, many people have become and still do become Christian ethicists because they do not like theology. They think justice is something worth thinking about or even advocating or doing, but they do not like, or they see little point in thinking about, matters as obscure and seemingly as irrelevant as the Trinity. Such a deliberately nonconfessional view of ethics, moreover, appears more acceptable in the modern university, where it is generally thought to be a "good thing" to study ethics, but it is not a good thing to be a theologian or to do theology. These days, theology just doesn't sound like a discipline appropriate to the university.

Yet I prefer to be a theologian. Or better, I simply cannot think of myself as anything but a theologian despite the fact that a theologian is not a good thing to be if you also want to be a respected academic. Yet being a theologian has become a habit for me that I cannot and do not wish to break. I am also an ethicist, but I do not make much of that claim. After all, "ethicist" is such an ugly word. Of course, there are also intellectual reasons why I do not desire to claim the title "ethicist." Quite simply, ethics too often names what many take to be the useful remains of past Christian practices and beliefs. Such a view of ethics serves liberal social orders well, but it distorts the character of Christian convictions. Accordingly, I have tried—through my teaching and my writing—to show that "ethics" cannot and should not be abstracted from "theology."

Yet even given such an understanding of theology and ethics, it would be reasonable to assume that I might have some useful insights to offer about theology's contributions to the recent call for a renewal of moral inquiry in the contemporary university. After all, moral inquiry surely must be at the heart of what anyone does who teaches Christian ethics. That, however, is not the case. To answer why that is not the case involves a complex history of an equally complex interrelation of theology and the modern university, something I cannot fully develop here. But I can offer one or two cursory remarks.

At least part of that history is suggested by the phrase "moral inquiry." Of course, one should not read too much into a phrase; but then again grammar is not innocent. The use of the phrase "moral inquiry" without any further qualification can misleadingly suggest that moral inquiry exists in and of itself and that it is, moreover, a "good thing." I do not believe that moral inquiry qua moral inquiry or its close kin, critical intelligence, exists, or even if they do exist—which they do not—that they are good things. Yet it is just such grandiose abstractions that are produced and reproduced by the knowledges that constitute the legitimating discourses of the modern university. Moreover, the presumption that the goal of the university is to sponsor such an unqualified account of moral inquiry is at least part of the reason why theology is no longer considered a legitimate university discipline.

First, I will share two stories to set the stage for the other stories I have to tell. One day, out of the blue, I received a call of the sort for which academics live. It was from a senior editor of one of America's most prominent middlebrow magazines. He had just read my recent book *After Christendom? How the Church Is to Behave If Freedom, Justice, and a Christian Nation Are Bad Ideas,* and he said he liked it.[1] Not only did he like it, he thought it was time I wrote for his magazine. I could not believe it. No American theologian since Reinhold Niebuhr had written for such magazines. I thought I was about to become famous.

I recovered from my excitement just enough to ask how he had ever heard of me. It seems that he had gone to one of the very good small schools in the East. In an introductory course in modern theology he had read one of my books, was intrigued, and, even though he was not religious, he had made it a point to read my books ever since. Of course I was flattered and gratified. I had finally been discovered—and by the secular world, no less. Indeed, he was interested in me because I was so unapologetically Christian.

How could I resist the invitation to write for his magazine under those conditions? I told him, however, I did not want to write an article that made me appear as a good Christian for the secularist—namely, the kind that criticizes Christianity in a way that only reinforces secular prejudices. Some Catholics have made careers for themselves by doing precisely that. Because they cannot say enough bad about the church, they are considered "good Catholics" by the *New York Times.* While I have plenty of criticisms of my own regarding the church, particularly liberal Protestantism, I was not about to write an article that was just another bashing of Christianity, even liberal Christianity. So I asked the editor to give me some time to think through the kind of article I might write, and he readily agreed.

A few weeks later I called him to try out my initial idea. I said, "I think I have a terrific title—'Christians in the Hands of Flaccid Secularists.'" There was a long silence on the other end of the phone. I waited. Finally, "That's interesting." I said, "You do not get it, do you?" "Get what?" "That the title is a play on Jonathan Edwards's famous sermon, 'Sinners in the Hands of an Angry God.'" "I'm afraid I didn't read much nineteenth-century stuff." At that point, I knew that this was not going to work. I told the editor, "I do not know how to write even half-serious theology for people who no longer have sufficient knowledge to tell which God it is that they no longer believe in."

That is the problem with modern atheism: it is just so uninteresting. Of course, we can hardly blame atheists for that, since Christians have for some time been offering atheists less and less to disbelieve. Believers and atheists too often come across as equally flaccid. The problem is, how do you teach theology in universities to students who have been taught to think, like this bright young editor, that, in the name of being educated, all positions are "interesting." Theology for such people cannot help but be more "information."

Now the second story. In response to appointments in the English and literature departments at Duke, some of the Duke faculty had founded a chapter of the National Association of Scholars. They were concerned with what they understood to be the lack of scholarly objectivity among their ranks, not to mention the moral nihilism they alleged was intrinsic to this new breed of scholar. Matters got rather heated, with the usual mix of personality conflict becoming confused with intellectual issues. The provost of the university thought it wise for some of us involved in the dispute to spend a day in a retreat getting to know one another. I should say that I was identified as one of the supporters, if not a representative, of the nihilistic barbarians the NAS meant to challenge.[2]

The day started with the provost's suggesting that we go around the table introducing ourselves and saying a bit about our field and our peculiar interests. As is usually the case, this proved to be extremely interesting, as one cannot help but be fascinated with the work of highly intelligent people—for example, the botanist who spends her life trying to understand why markings on butterfly wings differ. She may be a member of the NAS, but what finally matters is her work. It happened that I was one of the very last of the group of about fifteen to speak. I thought to myself, How can I explain to someone who studies butterfly wings that I spend most of my time thinking about God? Butterfly wings not only seem more interesting, but you also seem to know what you are doing when you are studying butterfly wings. I suspect, however, that this sense of "knowing what you are doing" is found more among those who are outside such kinds of study than among those who are actually engaged in the activity.

I thought all I could do was be honest. So I began by remarking that it was not clear that I should be among this group of academics, because I am not an intellectual. I am a theologian. Theology names an office of a community called the church and is in service to that community. So as one who occupies that office I am not free to think about anything I want to think about. Rather I am charged, for example, with the task of thinking about the Trinity, and why Christians think their lives make no sense if God is not triune. I observed it is, therefore, clear whom I serve, but I would like to know whom each of my colleagues around the table serves.

That question, I believe, is the hardest question facing those of us who find ourselves in the university. Moreover, our inability to answer that question is the reason we are equally uncomfortable with the question of the moral significance of what we do. We know that what we do is shot through with moral presuppositions that cannot help but shape ourselves and those we teach, but to acknowledge that invites conflicts between competing moralities, conflicts we fear are not subject to resolution. The recent modern university managed to avoid such conflicts by maintaining, in one form or another, the ideology of "knowledge for knowledge's sake." But intellectual developments and changing demographics have shown us that this ideology is no longer a workable "solution." We continue, however, to take shelter in modernist notions of "objectivity" in order to avoid questions of whom we serve or what the university is meant to do.[3]

That is why the one question you cannot ask around the modern university is, "Whom do we serve?" or "What is the university for?" The easy answer, of course, is that the university has many purposes and serves many constituencies. So the university is simply one further example of American pluralist politics, which is assumed to need no justification. You can probably get away with that answer as long as you have enough resources to spread the wealth. But as resources become scarce, we begin to see that "pluralism" hides the fact that some are more equal than others. Pluralist ideology tries to hide their inequalities because they lack moral and intellectual justification, given the presumptions of liberalism.

I should like to think that theologians are particularly well positioned to join our colleagues in the university to think through these matters. I do not assume, of course, that even if we were able to "think them through," we would have resolved the fundamental challenge facing the university in this culture. For the decisive problem is the gulf between what we do in the modern university and why people support us in those activities.[4] To set aside some people who do nothing with their lives but think about the Trinity requires, first, that you have to have a people who live lives that would be unintelligible if God is not the Father, Son, and Holy Spirit. Such a people must think their lives *hinge* on Trinity. A tension always exists between such a people and those they set aside to be theologians. But our current problem is not that kind of tension. Rather, our problem is we no longer have the practices that would make such a tension intelligible.[5] The reasons why that is the case are complex, but I now want at least to try to suggest how theology lost its servant status and hence became unintelligible.

How Theology Managed to Become a "Curiosity" in the University

In his article "On the Intellectual Marginality of American Theology," Van Harvey observes that many American intellectuals regard theology as something "akin to astrology."[6] Even worse, Harvey observes that theology is thought to be not only obscurantist but divisive, because it constitutes a threat to the common discourse on which our democracy rests. Yet he notes that even secularists might think theology something worth having around, if only to remind us of the contribution that Christian theology has made in the past, not to mention giving us a more sophisticated presentation of those who persist in being Christian. Without theology, Christians will say what they believe only crudely and dogmatically, and thus be even less likely to make any significant contributions to the public discussion.[7]

The burden of Harvey's argument, then, is that the marginality of theology in the modern university is largely the fault of theologians. By their willingness to underwrite every new theological movement, Protestant theologians virtually destroyed theology as an intellectually respectable discipline. As a result, theology has no recognizable center that would enable one to discern the good from the bad. Theologians, like most Christians in a democratic culture, have an inordinate fear of being distinctive, because otherwise people may think that we really do believe something is at stake in our being Christian. So theologians, in a vain attempt for acceptance, try as much as possible to make theology look like history, or sociology, or psychology, or some other acceptable university discipline. This seldom works, since theology then often imitates those disciplines in their weakest forms.

Harvey, I think, rightly suggests that the shovels theologians used to dig their own graves can be located in the "professionalization" of divinity schools and the changing definition of the theologian's role. Drawing on Stephen Toulmin's account of a discipline as the intellectual side of a profession, as well as Burton Bledstein's *The Culture of Professionalism*—a book that maps the growth of, as well as the professionalization of, the university in the late nineteenth century—Harvey observes, "Given this picture of the professionalization of the university in America and the scientific ethos that came to dominate it, a hypothesis regarding the causes of the marginality of theology immediately suggests itself: because the university became the institutional matrix for intellectual life in America, and because the ethos of the university was scientific and hostile to everything that did not lend itself to rational adjudication, theology was necessarily pushed to the margins of intellectual life. Because the universities provided the basis of cognitive authority and served the function of containing divisiveness, theology, resting as it does on religious faith and giving rise to controversy, was simply excluded from the university" (181).[8]

The only problem with this hypothesis, according to Harvey, is that it fails to account for the fact that since the early nineteenth century most of the theologians in this country have been located in divinity schools.[9] As a result, the above description of how theology became marginal fails to take into account the way in which developments in theological disciplines themselves played an important role in theology's loss of credibility. In particular, the sickness of theology can be attributed to theology's becoming almost totally oriented to the training of people for the ministry and the specializations that were assumed to be appropriate to that task. Such specialization resulted in theology's losing its claim to be a knowledge that should matter outside seminary cultures.

In the late nineteenth century seminaries, under the influence of Schleiermacher, divided their curriculum into four main parts: biblical studies, church history, dogmatics or Christian doctrine, and practical theology (183).[10] Such divisions only reinforced the assumption that theology was a subject matter, like law and medicine, for professional training. Theology was no longer considered a subject having to do with the clarification of the faith of the ordinary believer and, as a result, could no longer be considered essential for, in the sense of being integral to, our culture or our politics.

Yet the "retreat" to the seminary by no means meant that theology was made safe but irrelevant. Rather, theology passed through a great intellectual crisis precipitated, according to Harvey, by two autonomous but closely interrelated movements: "the rise of biblical criticism, especially of the New Testament, and the criticism of speculative metaphysics and theology proposed by Kant" (186). In the immortal words of Ernst Troeltsch, "Give the historical method an inch and it will take a mile. From a strictly orthodox standpoint, therefore, it seems to bear a certain similarity to the devil."[11]

That was not, however, the way the matter was first seen. Rather, many thought history was the way theology was to regain intellectual and moral force, not only in the university but in America as a whole. No one better exemplified this attitude than Walter Rauschenbusch, the great representative of the Protestant social gospel, in an essay called "The Influence of Historical Studies on Theology."[12] Rauschenbusch begins his article by observing that the dominance of historical studies in the theological curriculum is only very recent. In the Middle Ages systematic theology dominated, but since the Reformation theology became the study of the Bible.[13] History entered with exegesis, yet, according to Rauschenbusch, it would be a mistake to limit the significance of history to the study of the Bible. For history has an essential place in all theological sciences, since it "irrigates and fertilizes all other departments." Rauschenbusch observes that just as a biblical book gets its significance "only in connection with its historical environment, so any interpretation will be more penetrating and fruitful the more the interpreter knows of contemporary history."

Of course, Rauschenbusch's use of the phrase "contemporary history" is ambiguous. It can mean either the history that we are currently experiencing or the way we now do history. Rauschenbusch probably conflated both meanings, since he believed that the development of "scientific history" was an advance peculiar to our living in a "modern time." He asserts that "human life is continuous, and a subsequent period of history is always the most valuable interpreter of an earlier period." That is why history is a moral science for Rauschenbusch, since it allows us to recover the "real" intent of the prophets and Jesus without the qualifications of later developments. Lyrically he exclaims, "When we have been in contact with the ethical legalism and the sacramental superstitions of the Fathers, we feel the glorious freedom and the pure spirituality of Paul like a mighty rushing wind in a forest of pines. When we have walked among the dogmatic abstractions of the Nicene age, the Synoptic Gospels welcome us back to Galilee with a new charm, and we feel that their daylight simplicity is far more majestic and divine than the calcium light of the creeds."[14]

According to Rauschenbusch, the sense of continuity and development characteristic of historical studies is essential for all theological sciences. Indeed, "It is interesting to imagine how the course of Christian history would have been changed if the leaders of the early church had only had a modern training in history."[15] In effect, that was the great insight of the Reformers, as they appealed to original historical sources against the falsifications and legends produced by the church. The scientific study of history is the necessary means for training the scientific temper and critical faculty of theologians. Ancient and medieval civilizations had no "real" natural science or training in historical criticism, and consequently theology was dogmatic and credulous. Fortunately, we are obviously not so limited, benefiting as we do from the development of modern history over the last century. For, as Rauschenbusch reminds us, "modern history is only about a hundred years old; its mission is only begun."[16]

I have taken the time to summarize Rauschenbusch's article because it remains so relevant. Most people in theology or the academic study of religion would find Rauschenbusch's progressivist assumptions embarrassing, but they continue to assume accounts of the importance of history not unlike his. These are habits that constitute the working assumptions of theologians, not easily left behind. Just to the extent that theology can become history, it has a chance of being a respectable discipline within the university. To question the importance of history for theology would be equivalent to questioning Rauschenbusch's presumption that Protestantism is superior to Catholicism. Of course, most religious thinkers or academics who think about religion no longer have any good reason to believe in the superiority of Protestantism, so history is simply privileged as a challenge to what they take to be a Catholic understanding of truth. History was—and for many still is—the way Protestants displaced Catholicism while no longer believing what the Reformers believed.

Yet Troeltsch was right that history could not be put to such service without changing the very subject matter of theology. According to Troeltsch, history requires three essential aspects: "the habituation on principle to historical criticism; the importance of analogy; and the mutual interrelation of all historical developments."[17] The first of these requires that all judgments in the realm of history are at best judgments of probability. "It is obvious that the application of historical criticism to religious tradition must result in a profound change in one's inward attitude to it and in one's understanding of it."[18] Analogous occurrences are the key to historical criticism, since analogical comparisons require the presumption that history is generally both consistent and repeatable. Troeltsch rightly saw no reason to exclude Jesus or Jesus' resurrection from this principle.

Accordingly, all you have left is to try to make Christianity intelligible within the confines of the historical developments we now call Western civilization. No longer can or does the theologian try to make a case for God, since the metaphysics necessary for such a venture is allegedly defunct and any claims about revelation cannot be considered, given the epistemological constraints that form the modern university. So all that is left for theology is to become "a phenomenology of the collective consciousness of a determinative religious community."[19] Theologians, particularly as New Testament scholars and church historians, can no longer study the resurrection as if Jesus might have actually been raised, but now they study the beliefs and behaviors of people who believed in the resurrection.[20]

It is my hope that this analysis of the marginalization of theology in the modern university illuminates why theologians are hesitant about drawing any moral implications from their work. This is particularly true of those who find themselves in university departments of religious studies. Such departments are often comprised of people who are willing to study a religion on the condition either that it is dead or that they can teach it in such a way as to kill it.[21] The last thing they would want to acknowledge is that they might actually practice what they teach, because such an acknowledgment might suggest that they are less than "objective." Of course, that is why theology is not seen as an appropriate discipline in most departments of religion. To be sure, such departments may think it important to study the practice and faith of such figures as Thomas Aquinas, Maimonides, al-Farabi, or Karl Barth, but they would not think it appropriate to hire such people to teach in a department of religious studies.[22]

Yet, ironically, many of these departments continue to think it important to teach "ethics." That they do so is partly the result of a tradition begun by Walter Rauschenbusch and carried on by Reinhold and H. Richard Niebuhr, Paul Ramsey, James Gustafson, and a host of others. Rauschenbusch, of course, wrote unembarrassedly of Christianizing the social order,[23] but such a sentiment would be thought outrageous by most currently working in the "field" of Christian ethics. Under the influence of Reinhold Niebuhr, Christian ethicists began to talk more of building social ethics on the basis of love and justice. Matters more strictly theological could be left in the background.

James Gustafson has observed that many people who are now writing in the area generally known as "applied ethics," for example, medical ethics, business ethics, and environmental ethics, are often people with theological training.[24] Yet he notes that whether theology has anything to contribute to these areas is less than clear. For a few, such as Paul Ramsey, the theological authorization for the ethical principles theologians use is explicit, but "for others, writing as 'ethicists,' the relation of their moral discourse to any specific theological principles, or even to a definable religious outlook, is opaque. Indeed, in response to a query from a friend (who is a distinguished philosopher) about how the term 'ethicist' has come about, I responded in a pejorative way, 'An ethicist is a former theologian who does not have the professional credentials of a moral philosopher.'"[25]

In fact, many who were once Christian ethicists now describe themselves as "religious ethicists," though it is by no means clear to what the adjective "religious" refers. My own view is that the term "religious" works primarily as a distinguishing disciplinary marker for those who work within the university, that is, those who do "religious ethics" may be able to get a job in a religious studies department, but they certainly will not find a place within a philosophy department.[26] "Religious" also is necessary as a generic term, since many of the issues addressed in these areas involve the development of policy that makes any particularistic identifications a matter of embarrassment. If Christian ethicists are to be players within the constraints of a liberal social order for the formulation of public policy, then the "Christian" qualifier must be suppressed.

The term "Christian ethics," for a discipline one would assume to be committed to moral inquiry, turns out to be quite deceptive. Just to the extent that most people in the field are willing to make normative recommendations, they do so not as Christian theologians, but as "ethicists." As a result, courses in Christian ethics, if they are taught at all, increasingly appear like philosophy courses helping students to distinguish between metaethics and normative ethics for the purpose of deciding whether they should be primarily utilitarians or deontologists. So ethics becomes a further clarification of the students' "values," under the assumption that the clearer they are about their values the better chance they have to be morally good—an assumption that cannot stand much philosophical interrogation. Of course, if all other justification for teaching ethics fails, the "ethicists" can always claim to teach the history of Christian ethics. In doing so, they can introduce students to important subjects such as just-war theory or past understandings of the Christian's relation to the state. The clever students, if they are so inclined, might use such courses as aids in forming their own moral judgments, but that is the student's own business and should not be the object of the course. So ends the story of how teaching theology in the modern university has come to an end.

The Difference God Makes

Given the character of the modern university, the subsequent nature and "place" of theology and/or religious studies, the kind of students that come to the university, and the practices that produce those students, I think there is nothing we can do that is more morally important than to be what we were trained to be—theologians. Our task is very simple: to show the difference that God makes about matters that matter.[27] Fortunately, this is not a self-generative project, for as a Christian theologian I am not required to be creative. Theologians are to be faithful, believing as we do that our faith has been handed on to us by our mothers and fathers through the ages. So my first task as a theologian is to direct my students to those witnesses whose lives shine more brightly than mine ever could.

I am aware that such an understanding of "moral inquiry" will seem quite offensive to many who want to recommend a return to "moral inquiry" in the university. When I taught at the University of Notre Dame, one of my best friends was a biologist who was Jewish. His family was Reform and fairly observant. Walking across campus one day, I observed that it must be about time for his oldest son's bar mitzvah. He said he was not going to have a bar mitzvah, preferring to let his son "make up his own mind" when he was older. I exploded, asking how in the hell could he want to let his son make up his own mind in the face of the thousands of Jewish martyrs who died at the hands of Christians' persecution. I said at least raise your son as an atheist, as that would suggest you have some convictions. He had his son's bar mitzvah.

In like manner, I cannot conceive of what it would mean to teach theology as if God did not matter. Of course, there are pedagogical issues that should not be avoided. I teach primarily in a divinity school that is part of a university. Undergraduates take my divinity school courses, but I do not change my courses to accommodate their presence. I assume that most of them are Christians, though one Jewish student, as a result of one of my courses, decided to become a rabbi. If I were to teach an undergraduate course, I would not be less "theological," but I would not teach the course the same way I teach a course for those preparing for the ministry. Indeed, part of the course would involve them in trying to understand why teaching a course in Christian theology is a problematic undertaking in the contemporary university.

Yet pedagogy should not determine what is taught. You cannot teach about God as if God does not matter, any more than you can raise a child as a Jew as if going through bar mitzvah does not matter. What is crucial is that the course be taught with the intellectual seriousness commensurate with its subject. Challenges, such as Troeltsch's understanding of history, must be met. The displacement of religious practice into the realm of the private by the political arrangements of liberalism must be located and critiqued. The liberal production of "ethics" as an autonomous subject must be questioned, and conceptual alternatives suggested.

Providing such alternatives has been the focus of much of my own work. To expose the moral practices intrinsic to theological convictions requires the display of conceptual resources that, at least until very recently, were largely ignored in ethical theory. Much of my work has involved the attempt to recover the importance of the virtues and correlative account of practical rationality, the role of narratives and practices for the display of morally worthy lives, and what kinds of communities are necessary to sustain such lives. Much of this work, I would hope, can be and even should be of interest to many who do not share my theological convictions. Yet for me such work is finally to be judged by whether it serves to help me better understand the God Christians worship and the difference that that worship should have for our lives.

All of this requires hard intellectual work, which I confess, given my own abilities, dwarfs me. Yet I think that not to try, even in the rather foreign territory in which theologians today must work, would be cowardly. Moreover, it is just so much fun to be a theologian, for the simple reason that nothing could be more interesting than God. One of the great advantages for those of us who would teach theology in the current university is that we are finally free. When universities were explicitly if vaguely Christian, theology taught in the candid manner I am advocating could not be free, since theology was to be done in a manner that would underwrite the presumption that the way things are is the way things are supposed to be. But Christians are no longer in power—at least they are not in power as Christians—so we can now take the risk of teaching theology, if we are able, as edification. The problem, given recent intellectual developments, is not that theology is a problematic subject for the university, but that those of us who teach theology do so in such unimaginative ways.[28]

I am not suggesting that the classroom is the place to make Christians. The classroom is a far too coercive context for that. My reservations in this respect do not arise because I believe in academic freedom or even in the right of the students to "make up their own minds." My concerns are theological, since I believe that nonviolence is intrinsic to Christian convictions about Jesus' cross and resurrection. The presentation of those convictions in a coercive manner would therefore belie the character of God, and thus be a theological mistake.

Christian theology, after all, is finally reflection on the stories of God found in the Christian scriptures and developed through the traditions of the church. Christians do not have a "morality" per se, but rather our morality is embedded in the stories that require constant retellings. Telling a story, particularly stories like those Christians tell of God's dealings with them, is a frightening business, since in the tellings the story is frequently retold in a manner that is surprising and challenging to the teller. That is why violence is antithetical to the telling, since the very character of the story requires the Christian to be open to such retellings.

Therefore, when Christian theology is taught in the university that teaching must include a presentation of the extraordinary diversity of the "tellings" that have been part of Christian history. Such a presentation is not simply "historical," but rather the moral enterprise intrinsic to the story itself. For the story requires that the diversity of gifts that have been present throughout Christian history must be set forth in order to appreciate that the nature of the God Christians worship is known only through those diverse witnesses. So, for example, as a Christian committed to nonviolence, I must also tell of those Christians who thought that they were obligated to kill that injustice not be allowed to flourish.

So to teach Christian theology requires that the student be initiated into an ongoing conversation across the centuries to better know how to worship the God of Jesus Christ. Indeed, as Robert Orsi reminds me, ethics is a performance, a conversation, whose form cannot be separated from the material convictions that conversation embodies. The story theology seeks to tell requires an enactment commensurate with its content. So if the student is to be initiated into the practice of nonviolence, how that is done makes all the difference.[29]

But why would any university, a particularly secular university, want the discipline of theology represented in the curriculum? There can, in principle, be no answer to that question, since the question will be a different question in each case, given the differences between universities. Indeed, I take it to be one of the illusions of the current academy that some universal called "the university" exists "out there" and that it is the aim of each university to try, to a greater or lesser extent, to embody it. What I believe can be said, however, is that any university devoid of serious theological discourse will lack a resource that may make some contribution to lessening the moral impoverishment of all our lives, but in particular the lives of our students.[30]

NOTES

1. Stanley Hauerwas, *After Christendom? How the Church Is to Blame If Freedom, Justice, and a Christian Nation Are Bad Ideas* (Nashville: Abingdon Press, 1991).
2. For my critique of the NAS statement of purpose, see my *After Christendom*, 133–52.
3. John Patrick Diggins's account of Henry Adams wonderfully suggests the dilemma before the university. Diggins observes that "although Adams found teaching a challenging vocation, he also felt that the purpose of education was not only to impart the facts of history but to interpret their meanings as well. Like the philosopher Charles S. Peirce, Adams sensed the dilemma of trying to teach when there are no truths to be taught. Thus Adams pondered the responsibilities of being in a position of intellectual authority and having nothing authoritative to say" (John Patrick Diggins, *The Promise of Pragmatism: Modernism and the Crisis of Knowledge and Authority* [Chicago: University of Chicago Press, 1994], 68). In the "Conclusion" of *The Promise of Pragmatism,* Diggins praises Veblen, who long before Pierre Bourdieu and other French postmodernists "exposed higher education as a system of status rivalry and class pretension, 'a study of total depravity.' But in the end Veblen failed and judged himself a failure. The indulgent America he found developing in the 1890s continued its 'invidious distinction' between wealth and work in the 1990s, and higher education has become a cushy residence of bureaucratic administrations and sinecured professors — the leisure of the theory class" (p. 469).

4. The growth and significance of medicine in the modern university, not to mention the allied sciences that allegedly support medicine, is a fascinating example of one place where there seems to be a close correlation between people's desires and the university. This contrasts sharply with the blatant lack of correlation between the practice of theology and the university. No one much cares whether a theologian may or may not be heretical, but people do care whether a physician is qualified. I tell my students that if you want to have some sense of what the politics of medieval Catholicism was like, you need only hang around the major medical centers associated with universities. People no longer believe that their salvation depends on priests, but they sure as hell believe that they do not want to die, and they think, usually quite unrealistically, that medicine can significantly prolong their life, which accounts for the enormous prestige and power of medicine and medical knowledge in the university. However, this prestige and power are just as likely to corrupt a flourishing intellectual life, which was the case in the past for theology, as they are to engender it.

5. The problem for many of us today who would be or want to be theologians is that most Christians, particularly in the mainline Protestant denominations, couldn't care less what we think about the Trinity. In "Christians in the Hands of Flaccid Secularists" I had planned to argue that one of the problems with these who trumpet Christianity as an alternative to secular presuppositions is that the Christianity they trumpet too often has little relation to Christian orthodoxy.

6. Van A. Harvey, "On the Intellectual Marginality of American Theology," in *Religion and Twentieth Century Intellectual Life,* ed. Michael Lacey (Cambridge: Woodrow Wilson International Center for Scholars and Cambridge University Press, 1989), 172. Hereafter page references to Harvey's article will appear in the text.

7. Brian Gerrish observes that "the place of theology in the modern university can be defended only where its abdication as queen of the sciences is presupposed. Granted that Christian theology can no longer provide, as it did in the Middle Ages, the unifying principles of the entire system of human knowledge, can it nonetheless claim a legitimate, if humbler, place in the university? It may be that theology has its own small niche, along with other arts and sciences, in an academy that has become in principle more egalitarian. But it may also be that the ancient crown of theology has been quietly encased in the museum of history" ("Ubi Theologia, Ubi Ecclesia? Schleiermacher, Troeltsch, and the Prospect for an Academic Theology," in *Religious Studies, Theological Studies, and the University Divinity School,* ed. Joseph Mitsuo Kitagawa [Atlanta: Scholars Press, 1992], 71). As will be clear, I take a more aggressive stance than either Harvey or Gerrish on behalf of theology and its role in the modern university. I do so not because I think theology should again try to be "the unifying principle of the entire system of human knowledge." I do not have any idea, given our current state of knowledges, what such an aspiration would mean. Yet I see no reason why theology should be "humbled" in the university in principle, since I refuse to accept the presumption that the material convictions that characterize the work of theology are epistemologically at a disadvantage in principle vis-à-vis other disciplines in the university.

Gerrish observes that "it is easy to see why the citizens of a secular and pluralistic university could still be anxious about the possibility of a divided loyalty. History has taught them that the church, when weary of argument, will reach for a stick" (p. 73). To which I have two responses: (1) Today the "sticks" are certainly in quite different hands, and, (2) since I believe that Christians must be nonviolent, I am committed to waging the war peacefully, but no less conflictually.

8. For a more complex account of the relation between Protestant Christianity and the university, see George Marsden, *The Soul of the American University: From Protestant Establishment to Established Nonbelief* (New York: Oxford University Press, 1994). Marsden's book is an interesting case study of the problem facing theology. He notes that the stance of "methodological atheism" assumed by many Christians when

engaged in their disciplines contributed to the loss of any sense that theological conviction might matter. Yet his book assumes just that stand; see, for example, my review of Marsden: "Missing from the Curriculum: Review of George Marsden's *The Soul of the American University,*" *Commonweal* 121, 16 (September 23, 1994): 19–20. Douglas Sloan has wonderfully documented the inability of the Protestant mainstream to provide a compelling account of Christian convictions as a knowledge capable of attention in the university. Indeed, the very theologians who seemed to revitalize Protestant theology in the second half of this century—Paul Tillich, Reinhold Niebuhr, and H. Richard Niebuhr—in different ways underwrote what Sloan rightly characterizes as a two-realm theory of truth. That theory, Sloan argues, could only end in the further marginalizing of theology from the university. According to Sloan, the two-realm theory juxtaposed the truth of science, that is, objective results obtained by discourses and empirical reason, and truths of faith, religious experience, morality, meaning, and value. The latter are assumed to be grounded in feeling, ethical action, convention, and "common human experience." Yet, as Sloan suggests, the latter knowledges are on the defensive in the modern university—and, I might add, rightly so. Sloan's book is *Faith and Knowledge: Mainline Protestantism and Higher Education* (Louisville, Ky.: Westminster/John Knox Press, 1994).

9. Bruce Kuklick observes, "When theology withdrew from the center of the college to a professional school, at the margin of the academic community, the tiny but growing American university weakened its continuity with the past and the tradition of classical learning. In the ancient universities, theology had been responsible for animating schools of higher learning with a sense of their comprehensive calling. The professionalization of theology in the United States was thus an early and potent symbol of the fragmentation of knowledge and culture" (Bruce Kuklick, *Churchmen and Philosophers: From Jonathan Edwards to John Dewey* [New Haven, Conn.: Yale University Press, 1985], 87).

10. Van Harvey is summarizing Edward Farley's analysis of this development in his *Theologia: The Fragmentation and Unity of Theological Education in America* (Philadelphia: Fortress Press, 1983). Schleiermacher basically followed Kant by arguing that the faculties of medicine, law, and theology were justified within the universities, not because they were sciences but because they were of service to the state. Thus the study of theology was justified because it served the needs of the public, who were understood to have religious needs. Harvey notes that there was a fatal flaw in this argument when brought to the United States, as the same argument that was used to justify theology in Germany could be used to exclude theology from the university in America. Alasdair MacIntyre's account of exclusion of theology from English universities in the name of creating "unconstrained agreements" is another fascinating aspect of this story. See his *Three Rival Versions of Moral Enquiry: Encyclopedia, Genealogy, and Tradition* (Notre Dame, Ind.: University of Notre Dame Press, 1990), 216–36.

11. Ernst Troeltsch, "Historical and Dogmatic Method in Theology," in *Religion in History,* trans. and ed. James Luther Adams and Walter Bense, with an introduction by James Luther Adams (Minneapolis: Fortress Press, 1991), 16. For a helpful account of Troeltsch's attempt to amend Schleiermacher's understanding of the role of theology in the university, see Gerrish, "Ubi Theologia," 75–83.

12. Walter Rauschenbusch, "The Influence of Historical Studies on Theology," *American Journal of Theology* 2 (January 1907): 111–27.

13. Rauschenbusch's suggestion that systematic theology dominated the Middle Ages is an extraordinary misreading. No medieval theologian would have had the slightest idea what systematic theology might be. Aquinas thought his theological work was primarily to be found in his commentaries on scripture. Systematic theology, in other words, was primarily the creature of Protestant scholasticism combined with the presuppositions of German idealistic philosophy.

14. Rauschenbusch, "The Influence of Historical Studies on Theology," 115. As I hope is

obvious, Rauschenbusch used history as a critique of Catholicism with its "magical" assumptions about sacraments and its hierarchical church government.

15. Ibid., 117.
16. Ibid., 126.
17. Troeltsch, "Historical and Dogmatic Method in Theology," 13.
18. Ibid.
19. Harvey, "On the Intellectual Marginality," 189.
20. There are actually some good reasons why this way of working is not necessarily antithetical to a Christian understanding of truth, given that our faith depends on the testimony of reliable witnesses. Of course, that does not mean that Christians believe any less in the miracles that those witnesses report. For a wonderful account of the philosophical status of testimony, see Alasdair MacIntyre, "Hume, Testimony to Miracles, the Order of Nature, and Jansenism," in *Faith, Skepticism and Personal Identity,* ed. J. J. MacIntosh and H. Meynell (Calgary: University of Calgary Press, 1994), 83–99.
    Moreover, if, as John Milbank maintains, there can only be a science of the particular, then history, "written history, which produces exceptions to the supposed universal rule; lived history, which permits us always to enact the different," is theology's ally! See his *Theology and Social History* (Oxford: Basil Blackwell Publisher, 1990), 260.
21. For a more extended set of similar ad hominem comments on the contemporary study of religion, see Stanley Hauerwas, "A Non-Violent Proposal for Christian Participation in the Culture Wars," *Soundings* 75, 4 (Winter 1992): 477–92. For a very helpful account of the current similarities and differences between the free-standing seminary, university diversity, and schools and departments of religious studies in colleges and universities, see Joseph Kitagawa's introduction to *Religious Studies, Theological Studies and the University Divinity School,* ed. Joseph Mitsuo Kitagawa (Atlanta: Scholars Press, 1992), 1–36. Kitagawa observes that the lack of a clear self-understanding of the objective, scope, perspective, and methodology of religious studies leads some to conclude that almost any approach to religion—psychological, sociological, ethical, philosophical, and even "semi-theological"—is "tolerated in religious studies, as long as it avoids such non-academic religious features as faith, piety, and truth-claims" (p. 7). Yet Kitagawa documents that there are "fuzzy edges" between the sites for the study of religion and theology. In particular, scholars at freestanding church-oriented divinity schools often pursue the same intellectual agendas determined by departments of religious studies, with the result that those they train for the ministry are not prepared well for that task. Of course, it is a mistake to assume that theology gains its purpose from training people for the ministry. All the essays in Kitagawa's volume are important for helping us to understand better the role of theology in the current university. Joseph Hough Jr.'s essay, "The Marginalization of Theology in the University," is particularly important. Hough suggests that at least one of the justifications for theology in the university is the contribution that theology can make to the "common discourse" of the university. I would be sympathetic to that justification if I thought that the university had a "common discourse." The association of theology with the task of training people for the ministry is largely an accident of history, not something intrinsic to the service that theology is to render to the church.
22. It would take me too far afield to look at the development of religious studies as an alternative to theology. Suffice it to say that religious studies departments as they developed after 1950 usually assumed the fourfold structure of the Protestant seminary. This was usually found to be unsatisfactory, since appropriate space was not given to Judaism, Islam, and the so-called Eastern religions. So departments felt the need to become more "pluralistic," but too often such pluralism lacked any intellectual rationale. Some tried to make something of "religion," but no definition or phenomenology of religion has been found to pass muster. Nor has there been any agreement about what kind of methodology is most appropriate to the subject matter of most departments, though as I suggested above the primary methodology tends to be historical.

23. Walter Rauschenbusch, *Christianizing the Social Order* (New York: Macmillan Company, 1921).
24. James Gustafson, "Theology Confronts Technology and the Life Sciences," *Commonweal* 105, no. 12 (June 16, 1978): 386. For a wonderful critique of the very idea of "applied ethics," see Alasdair MacIntyre, "Does Applied Ethics Rest on a Mistake?" *The Monist* 67 (1984): 498–513.
25. Gustafson no doubt feels some ambiguity in making this criticism, since, in doing so, he is criticizing many of his own students. That a good number of Gustafson's students are ambivalent about theology's relation to ethics should not be surprising, given the fact that Gustafson has authored a volume entitled *Can Ethics Be Christian?* a title that certainly gives something less than a resounding affirmative answer to the nature of that relation. I should also say that Gustafson is my teacher as well, one to whom I owe everything, including our considerable theological differences.
26. For a devastating critique of the notion of religion, see Talal Asad, *Genealogies of Religion: Discipline and Reasons of Power in Christianity and Islam* (Baltimore: Johns Hopkins University Press, 1993). Asad observes, "The suggestion that religion has a universal function in belief is one indication of how marginal religion has become in modern industrial society as the site for producing disciplined knowledge and personal discipline" (p. 46).
27. No one has done this task more faithfully than Diogenes Allen. I first encountered Diogenes as Paul Holmer's graduate assistant in a course on Kierkegaard. I was impressed by the seriousness he displayed about the importance of theology and, in particular, argument in theology. I have long suspected that I learned some of my most basic intellectual strategies from his *The Reasonableness of Faith* (Washington, D.C.: Corpus Books, 1968). I hope, therefore, this essay at least manifests the spirit of his life and work.
28. I suspect that the best theology being done in universities today is done in subjects that are not seen as theology. That is perhaps the way it should be.
29. I'm indebted to Dr. Robert Orsi of Indiana University for a wonderful commentary on this essay at the colloquium sponsored by the Wilson Center on the Revival of Moral Inquiry in the university for which this paper was prepared. Orsi pointed out to me that the two stories at the beginning of my paper, as well as the story involving my Jewish colleague at Notre Dame, were conversation stoppers. I certainly did not mean for my questions at the meeting I described with my colleagues at Duke to be a conversation stopper, but rather one that advanced the conversation. However, I certainly can see how my reaction to the young editor, as well as my response to my Jewish colleague, could be seen as attempts to stop the conversation. Indeed, I think, on reflection, I did not respond as well as I should have to the young editor. What is important to see, however, is that Orsi's reactions help me understand the power of such narratives and how important it is to tell them well. I am in his debt.
30. I am indebted to Prof. Owen Flanagan, Dr. Jim Fodor, and Mr. Scott Saye for their criticism and help with this chapter.

2

FRIENDS IN CONVERSATION

The Language and Practice of Faith

DAVID B. BURRELL, C.S.C.

Diogenes Allen dates from a period in Oxford University when language reigned. Philosophers even classified themselves as "ordinary language" philosophers, meaning that they resolved to take their cues and even find their operative distinctions embedded in the rich texture of ordinary discourse. The inspiration, of course, was Ludwig Wittgenstein of the *Philosophical Investigations,* while the foil was the dream of an ideal or perfect language, which Wittgenstein himself had earlier essayed in his *Tractatus Logico-philosophicus.* In retrospect, we can see more clearly how the impetus away from an ideal language signaled the end of an adequate separation of theoretical from practical understanding, of philosophy as pure discourse (replete with a technical vocabulary) from the practices required to employ "ordinary language" accurately and fruitfully. For language is ordinarily learned as a way of negotiating our world, with its accuracy tested as it helps us to do that more successfully. Yet the criteria for successfully negotiating a world gain in complexity as our world unfolds, emerging from one focused on *my* satisfaction to *our* well-being, indeed, to the well-being of the universe. What sort of demands does that put on our use of language?

It requires an awareness, I shall suggest, that our speech will never quite be adequate to our quest for understanding; that our analysis of a situation, as we attempt to negotiate it properly, will inevitably leave something unconsidered. This is palpably the case in human affairs, where our initial orienting judgments tend to reduce another person to two dimensions, and so will betray us unless we leave them open to generous revision. That process is tantamount to "getting to know someone," where the knowledge in question requires vigilant efforts to interpret and reinterpret the person's actions. Often this proves fruitless, of course, or there is little incentive to keep up the effort it takes, but when something about that person lures us on farther, as the prospect of authentic friendship begins to open, we are prodded to a more and more careful use of language. This is not simply to avoid offending someone about whom we have come to care, but as a way of enlisting our friend's services to better assess the world we share. For authentic friendship, as Aristotle so clearly noted, opens persons beyond "our relationship" to what he summarily called "the good"; that is, to a proper relationship to the universe itself.

It is this dynamic which has fueled Dick Allen's treatment of "the reasonableness of faith" from the beginning: language is crucial, yet remains a vehicle for understanding, an understanding to which we are mysteriously called in our effort to negotiate a world that becomes ever more fascinating. The effort that quest calls forth will be concentrated on accurate and fruitful expression—for oneself and for others—but what animates that expression always exceeds what we can say. This phenomenon reminds us how discourse is constantly reaching beyond itself, at the service of something else—hence the guiding image of conversation between friends. For conversation embeds discourse in an interpersonal context, while friendship (à la Aristotle) requires that interpersonal contexts be embedded in something larger than the personal if they are to lead us where authentic friendship promises to lead. Here our own experience readily confirms the contention of Aristotle: friendship requires mutual trust to unfold; yet even that mutuality demands more than two persons can muster, for no one is immune to those power games which erode trust, or even a betrayal that destroys it. There must be something, or someone, more in which, or in whom, we may put our trust if the interpersonal friendship is to develop into what it promises. Here is where life pushes us beyond calculation to trust, beyond reason to faith. Yet that step beyond, as we have seen, is precisely what the logic of love demands of us.

Faith must in that sense be reasonable, yet the reasonableness is not a matter of abstraction, nor a fruitless matter of calculating my advantage, but that demanded by conversation among friends. For nothing but faith can provide a context rich enough to offset the inevitable tendency of relationships to serve an *"égoïsme à deux,"* the tendency that Jews identify as the *yetzer ra*, Christians as "original sin," and Muslims as the state of ignorance (*jëhiliyya*). Why so? One could amass authorities here like Michel Foucault, whose relentless reminders of the multiple ways in which discourse serves power have put us acutely on guard against "civility" or "sweet reasonableness." Yet as pervasive as power may be, it cannot be the last word, as the metaphysical lure of friendship never ceases to remind us, and the struggle to keep friendship authentic can confirm in us. It can even become increasingly difficult to speak the truth, as and when we see it, to someone with whom our life is intertwined, as spouses know so well. Yet the demand to do so, and to have our own perspective corrected or enhanced, never ceases. We can never claim to "have the truth," to fully know another, since our articulations of what we think to be the case are always up for revision. Nor is this assertion simply asserted, for its truth emerges from friendship itself, as that relationship proves to be one that we can never cease pursuing if we are to lay claim to it.

Paradoxes like these lace our lives as we grow into them, and require an increasing sensitivity to the language we use and the way we use it. They call for, not necessarily a technical proficiency in specialized discourse, but rather an acquired expertise in knowing how to use properly terms that are common enough yet defy definition—such as "love" or "friendship." It is in the use of such terms that theory and practice intertwine to produce the kind of understanding that is proper to matters of faith and interpersonal relations. The practices in question will, as we have seen, embrace individual persons in relationship, introducing them into a community of interaction—and communities have histories, so what results is tradition. In this organic way, the internal linkage between tradition, community, faith, and practices begins to emerge as we probe the very conditions for a fruitful, nonexploitative relationship, epitomized by a conversation among friends. Some of these practices will inevitably be ritualized, as exchanges of affection are among friends, and the more so as a friend's presence may be wanting—letters or phone calls are always more than exchanges of information. Moreover, practices among friends will take a shape provided by the context that embraces them, so something of the faith that sustains their friendship will be detectable in the grammar of such practices. Here is where prayer and liturgical ritual enter for those whose faith is an explicit one, yet analogues will doubtless be sought and found by persons open to the dynamic of friendship without an explicit religious faith.

The extensive work of Pierre Hadot has come to the attention of the English-speaking world in recent years, releasing one to speak of "spiritual exercises" as an integral part of doing philosophy. Indeed, as Arnold Davidson cites Hadot in an introductory essay to an astute collection of his articles, "the written philosophical work [of Aristotle and of Plotinus], precisely because it is a direct or indirect echo of oral teaching, now appears to us as a set of exercises, intended to make one practice a method, rather than as a doctrinal exposition."[1] In other words, a particular conception of philosophy as discourse has allowed us to overlook the degree of "pragmatic consistency" which the philosophers' endeavors called for. The Socrates of Plato's dialogues has long offered the paradigm example of such an ideal, but the very expository form of Aristotle's prose could easily mislead teachers and students alike to conjecture that a new ideal of philosophical discourse was already being proposed in Aristotle's approach to doing philosophy. It has been Hadot's genius to identify the integral role of practices in late antiquity as well, notably in the work of Plotinus.[2]

Modern readers of Augustine's *Confessions,* for example, could understandably have been puzzled when the young man in search of truth felt constrained to decide between "the Platonists" and "the Christians" (notably in Book 7), for most of us could identify not a few "Christian Platonists." Yet such identifications in our time usually name "philosophical positions" (or in Hadot's terms, "doctrinal expositions"), whereas in Augustine's time one was speaking of communities of discourse with specified exercises of membership, designed to bring out the existential consequences of philosophical thought and conversation. Discourse was decidedly at the service of building persons of a particular sort, whose very way of life would testify to the truth of the discourse.[3] It is that conception of philosophy, I would suggest, which has animated Diogenes Allen's work from the outset. In this sense, Pierre Hadot's historical and exegetical inquiries have served to contextualize a particular picture of "philosophy as discourse," notably written discourse, which proved so congenial to modernity, thus paving the way for the fresh way of seeing called "postmodern."

What was it that led Diogenes Allen in that direction from the 1950s onward? Unable to penetrate my friend's mind, I can only essay an answer to that question by reflecting on the characteristics of my work that have consistently intersected with his, and indeed that led to our friendship early on. In 1975 I published a series of essays on classical and modern philosophers—from Augustine to Jung—entitled *Exercises in Religious Understanding* (Notre Dame, Ind.: University of Notre Dame Press). The goal was less expository than it was an invitation to readers to apprentice themselves to each of these thinkers, employing an accessible text from each, as they grappled with questions as real to us as to them. The writing itself emerged from teaching introductory philosophy using key texts from Augustine, Anselm, Aquinas, and Kierkegaard. (The Jung text, *Memories, Dreams, Reflections,* was a more personal addition at the time, added with the intent of redirecting some popular misreadings of his work.) The inspiration of my teaching and writing had been Bernard Lonergan's reflections on hermeneutics, directing contemporary readers of ancient writers to identify the questions to which these writers' arguments were directed. This disarmingly simple approach allowed readers to connect with texts and authors from the past so as to allow their work to illuminate the way in which contemporary readers would pose these questions, as well as to cast light on current ways of answering them. It is ever the questions that engage us, and one can learn rather quickly to distinguish the terms that are translatable from those which are not.

Directions of this sort serve to remind teachers that the "history of philosophy" can be more philosophy than history, and so direct students beyond the goal of mastering a particular thinker's position on something—or what is far worse, the teacher's "position" on the particular thinker's "position"—to ask themselves how they might learn to negotiate the question itself from the way in which an acknowledged master has attempted to do it. That is what apprenticing amounts to: watching a master do what I want to learn to do myself. There can never be a direct transfer of skill; the primary agent must be the student's own capacities. But that should be the lesson of any course in philosophy: text and teacher are both, at best, "inadequate secondary causes."[4] It may also be true, of course, that such a view of philosophy would come more naturally to someone engaged in philosophical theology, where the articulations will be *ex professo* inadequate. Here we can extend Hadot's thesis to appreciate the transformation worked in doing philosophy from ancient to medieval times, where the exercises associated with conceptual clarification would explicitly be at the service of a mode of understanding that attempts to articulate things quite beyond our human ken. As Aquinas put it, in a formulation anticipating much of Kant, the "object proper to human understanding is the quiddity of material things."[5]

But why should attempts to transcend such connatural objects in order to understand, as best we can, "matters divine" evoke the need for "spiritual exercises" on the part of philosophical inquirers? Here Hadot's focus on Plato can help us, along with the reflections his dialogues elicit about language. When Plato has Socrates give us his intellectual odyssey in the *Phaedo,* detailing the move from "physical inquiry" to ethical questions, the turning point was Anaxagoras and his conviction that it is "intelligence that orders and is the reason for everything"(97c). The examples that he gives for the ordering power of intelligence, which quickly become Plato's "forms," are all couched in quintessentially analogous terms, like "beautiful" or "good." What this means is that we can only learn the proper use of such terms by invoking examples, and the examples we will know how to present are those which correspond with our experience. So philosophers will be urged to live in such a way as to acquire rich paradigms for beauty or goodness, much as we will judge novelists by the accuracy with which their dramatization of character delineates the texture of human feeling. For Plato it is ever the person of Socrates, notably in the more dramatic dialogues, who exemplifies the paradigmatic meaning of key terms in the argument—as with "life" in the *Phaedo*: the life connatural to the principle of life, which cannot end, is best displayed in the manner in which Socrates guides that portentous discussion on the very cusp of his own death.

Otherwise, such terms are merely abstract, as most students deem them to be. But to begin to follow his arguments—even the manifestly inadequate ones—in such a way as to ask what sort of efforts it may take on our part to appreciate the force of their key terms, is to ask how we might live in such a way as to privilege those dimensions of our life which we normally do not. In that respect, the opening paean to "philosophers" and the way of life to which they are called does more than set the tone for the *Phaedo*: it reminds us what we will be asked to undertake in order to understand, to say nothing of assess, the arguments that Socrates will be presenting. I am suggesting that the reason we will be asked to undertake the requisite exercises lies with the very character of the language used to probe such dimensions of existence: it cannot be grasped in its proper semantic mode without realizing that it is inherently analogous. And analogous terms need to be anchored to a primary analogate, so that other uses can be related proportionally to that central use. Otherwise, they will appear and be employed in a merely "abstract" manner, and prove unable to lead us on to an understanding beyond that connatural to us.[6] It is that "leading" function of language, dubbed *manuductio* ("taking by the hand and leading") by Aquinas, which analogous terms exhibit so powerfully when they are properly used. But again, their proper use will require a mode of inquiry and of life that privileges certain paradigm instances over others: "spiritual exercises," if you will.

Another way to approach this question of the language peculiar to inquiries into the goals of human existence is to remind oneself that relating terms like "good" or "wise" to their paradigm cases demands a keen sense of judgment. That indeed is what analogous usage comes to in practice: locating the paradigm use that will govern the discourse in question, and learning how to relate other uses to that one. So, for example, a couple of twenty-five years or more may well wonder whether they really understood what they were doing when they married, or even when they assessed their relationship at earlier intervals of their marriage. Yet to place themselves back in time imaginatively would reveal that while they certainly had no idea of the depths of the words they used at earlier times, they avowed them wholeheartedly nonetheless. From this later vantage point, which has become their new paradigm, they can see how earlier, as well as project how later, avowals might be understood analogously with reference to the current paradigm case. What Hadot calls "spiritual exercises" are designed precisely to evoke in us new ways of seeing, fresh paradigm cases for orienting our use of these multivalent terms. And the ensuing efforts to relate our continuing usage to these new benchmarks will develop that discerning judgment we have seen associated with properly analogous usage.

Discerning readers will detect in these descriptions an attempt to give some bite and substance to common talk about "experience," especially dear to inquiries in religious studies. Yet unless that talk is linked explicitly to linguistic use, it can fail to evoke any specific resonance in listeners. One of the signal achievements of the Oxford philosophy that Diogenes Allen imbibed has been to tie its assertions to the regularities (or vagaries) of language use, so invoking patterns discernible to all of us. Once that strategy is employed to characterize analogous usage, we will be constrained, as we have seen, to identify things other than language itself—such as the judgment required to use it well. Yet those skills too can be detected in use, as any body of worshipers learns to discriminate good preaching from bad, often by following this rule of thumb: do preachers pretend to comprehend what they are speaking about, or do they display that degree of "unknowing" that properly befits any discourse about things divine? Such judgments are part of any discourse associated with a trade, where know-how requires careful attention to our actions and to our speech.[7] So we return to the way in which philosophical theology depends crucially on practical reason, on "know-how," to conduct its inquiries. That is the intellectual skill which is developed by doing, by engaging in "spiritual exercises," as Hadot reminds us.

Yet if we try to identify these exercises descriptively, Plato set the stage by displaying for us a kind and quality of dialogue in which the doing of philosophy is itself a spiritual exercise. The point of the *Meno,* for example, can well be exhibited by reflecting on the course of the dialogue itself, and reminding oneself that however inadequate may be the definition of virtue that the interlocutors attained, the virtue in question has been abundantly exhibited in the no-holds-barred inquiry that knew that it had not been concluded by such a definition. Again and again, the sense of "unknowing" proper to philosophic discourse will be displayed in the manner in which it is carried out. So dialogue, or conversation, itself becomes a key spiritual exercise, training us as we undertake the mode of inquiry proper to philosophy. In that sense, we are all always apprentices, as teachers learn how to learn from their students in their effort to elicit from them the quality of response that assures that genuine teaching is taking place. That takes place, paradoxically enough, when teachers are not pretending to "teach" (in the accepted sense of that term), but are rather engaging others in an inquiry in which they themselves are already engaged, with no clear sense at all of its outcome. That is philosophical teaching at its best, as Plato displays so well in his dialogues and explicitly adverts to in the *Meno*: a form of apprenticeship in which teacher and learner alike are being called forward by the good they are pursuing, and recognize in the course of their conversation that they are indeed being carried closer to their goal.

As some early Christian thinkers perceived, there turn out to be some key similarities between dialogic encounter in response to the good and a set of spiritual exercises attuned to responding to the good news offered to human beings in Jesus.

It was these affinities which allowed Alexandrian thinkers like Clement and Origen to speak of Christian revelation as "revealed philosophy."[8] Yet the "good" in "good news" is so much more specific, so much more able to be identified, than Plato's Good that response to it will call for a more deliberate and concentrated listening. In the risen Lord, the Lord of heaven and earth, the creator of all that is, is speaking to us individually and inviting each rational creature to a personal participation in the very life of God. That is an overwhelming prospect in Plato's own terms, so the listening component will have to increase proportionally. Hence Christian prayer turns out to be more listening for the voice of the Lord than dialogic in character, though the speaker is also expressly an interlocutor: the Hebrew pattern of covenant and the cognate prayer pattern of *beraka* has informed Christian practice from the beginning. Since the initiative is so manifestly the Lord's, however, it behooves us to attend to what the Lord has to say, and to try to tailor our response to the spontaneous and unearned gift of revelation. Such is the pattern of the Hebrew scriptures, canonized in Deuteronomy, which has shaped Christian prayer from the beginning.

So the "spiritual exercises" commended to Christians in their search for illumination from such a "revealed philosophy" will focus on the eucharistic celebration: a prayer suffused with thanksgiving along the lines of the Hebrew *beraka* formula: "Blessed are you, Lord God of the universe, who have . . . " We are initially reminded of a specific action of God on our behalf, and in recalling that, ask yet further blessings as a way of pledging our wholehearted response. Formation in such a mode of prayer is designed to work against our penchant to begin with our own capacities and desires, imploring divine help to fulfill them. So monastic *lectio divina* sits us down first to listen to the Word of God, to savor it, and to hear it as addressed to us personally. This has become the paradigmatic meditation form in Christianity, moving as it does from initially listening to scripture, selecting verses that can act as mantras to focus our attention, to letting those words penetrate our heart. The step from many words to fewer and even to wordlessness becomes natural enough, yet the initiative remains with the Word of God. Such a "vertical" set of spiritual exercises, however, will be complemented by conversation between persons formed in its patterns, conversation allowing them to seek to clarify together the truth revealed in the scriptures and appropriated by each of them personally.

The dual character of the basic Christian Torah, to love God and one's neighbor, demands that a "horizontal" set of exercises complement the "vertical" one, just as the norm for a wholehearted monastic response to the Word became cenobitic or community-oriented. We have a poignant example of such a dialogue in the ninth book of Augustine's *Confessions,* when he recounts his final encounter with his mother, Monica.

> The conversation led us towards the conclusion that the pleasure of the bodily senses, however delightful in the radiant light of this physical world, is seen by comparison with the life of eternity to be not even worth considering. Our minds were lifted up by an ardent affection towards eternal being

itself. Step by step we climbed beyond all corporeal objects and the heaven itself. . . . We ascended even further by internal reflection and dialogue and wonder at your works, and we entered into our own minds. We moved up beyond them so as to attain to the region of inexhaustible abundance where you feed Israel eternally with truth for food. There life is the wisdom by which all creatures come into being. (*Confessions* 9.x [24])

It proves fascinating to compare this dialogic ascent with the account of his own ascent in Book 7:

By the Platonic books I was admonished to return to myself [Plotinus, *Enneads* 4.1.1]. With you as my guide I entered into my innermost citadel . . . and with my soul's eye . . . saw above that same eye of my soul the immutable light higher than my mind. It was superior because it made me, and I was inferior because I was made by it. The person who knows the truth knows it and he who knows it knows eternity. Love knows it. Eternal truth and true love and beloved eternity: you are my God. (7.x [16])

Note how both accounts incorporate the distinctively Jewish and Christian identification of the Good with God as Lord of heaven and earth, creator of all that is, while relying on Platonic accounts of the mind's ascent to that One to give the contours of a rational creature's journey home.

Yet in the initial dialogue of Augustine with his mother, the path of ascending is mutually confirming. At this point in their lives it becomes purely celebratory, of course, as his personal dialectical journey is over. Yet one does not have to imagine him in clarifying dialogue with other fellow travelers; such conversations are recorded in explicit or implicit dialogue form in his subsequent writings. Even in his preaching, we find him dialoguing with his congregation, so ingrained is that form of communication in him. Yet even in this exercise, he dares not assume the role of master, for the master in such dialogues is "the immutable light higher than [our] minds," Christ himself. So conversation too takes on a new cast, "for where two or three are gathered together in my name, I am there among them" (Matt. 18:20). The personal presence of this light "through whom all things came into being" (John 1:3) hardly militates against vigorous dialectical exchange; in fact, it encourages such exchange by confirming Socrates' conviction that persons engaged in pursuing the truth as they have come to know it can help one another to walk farther along that path. Christ's presence confirms this conviction initially by revealing the contours of the path itself, and in practice by helping to free us interlocutors from our endemic tendency to defend our current stance, and so to be open to others' correction. In this way, God's revelation to us in Jesus as the ordering wisdom through whom all things were made should enhance the classical spiritual exercise of dialogic search for truth, provided its new participants are concurrently steeped in the *lectio divina,* which grants them the freedom of serving a master who is their very creator.

Friends then become friends in the One who offers us friendship with God (John 15:15), thus encouraging the kind and quality of exchange that Plato brings to life in the dramatis persona of Socrates. The rules of engagement with the master, Socrates, are not altered but intensified as we are all called to a radical "unknowing" in the face of the offer of divine friendship extended to us, and so stimulated to let go of our endemic desire to protect our own life, reputation, and opinions. Friendship in Jesus does not rest on agreement so much as on an embracing good, which is promised to each so long as we are willing to submit to the rule of learning from the Word of God and test our understanding of that word with one another. So friendship and inquiry coalesce in ways similar to those commended to us in the interaction of Socrates with his followers, and the interaction among friends becomes a prime example of a "spiritual exercise" in this community of inquiry which is that of "revealed philosophy."

NOTES

1. Pierre Hadot, *Philosophy as a Way of Life,* ed. Arnold Davidson (Cambridge, Mass.: Blackwell, 1995), 21, citing Hadot's "La philosophie antique: une éthique ou une pratique?" in Paul Demont, ed., *Problèmes de la morale antique* (Amiens: Faculté des Lettres, Université de Picardie–Jules Verne, 1993), 11.
2. Pierre Hadot, *Plotinus or The Simplicity of Vision,* trans. Michael Chase (Chicago: University of Chicago Press, 1993).
3. Hadot's extensive illustration of this point has recently been published in Paris: Pierre Hadot, *Qu'est-ce que la philosophie antique?* (Paris: Gallimard, 1995). Chapter 10 treats of the Christianity defining itself as philosophy, notably in Alexandria; and chapter 11, of the later medieval conception of philosophy as the handmaid of theology.
4. Aquinas's touted definition of a teacher, here extended to those who teach us by their texts. I have never been able to locate it in his works.
5. Aquinas, *Summa Theologiae* 1.84.7.
6. This view of analogous usage of language was first suggested to me by the early work of Ralph McInerny, work that has happily been recently reprised in his *Aquinas and Analogy* (Washington, D.C.: Catholic University of America Press, 1996).
7. This dimension of analogous usage is particularly well treated by James Ross in his *Portraying Analogy* (Cambridge: Cambridge University Press, 1981), esp. chap. 7: "Analogy and Religious Discourse: Craftbound Discourse."
8. Hadot, *Qu'est-ce que . . .* , chap. 10: "Christianity as Revealed Philosophy."

3

THE BELIEVER'S REASONS

BRIAN HEBBLETHWAITE

Introduction

Theologians and philosophers of religion today are divided over the question of the general accessibility of the believer's reasons. Or, to put the same point another way, they differ over how far faith is a necessary condition for the appreciation of the rationality of Christian belief. This is not simply a dispute over the possibility of natural theology—of rational arguments, that is, apart from any purported special revelation, for the existence and nature of God. It is also a dispute over the accessibility of the rational arguments used in systematic theology, based, as that allegedly is, on special revelation. Might the sympathetic or even the curious unbeliever be able to entertain the content of alleged revelation hypothetically and assess the rationality of a theistic or Christian worldview based on it? Or is the rationality of Christian theology peculiar and internal to the circle of faith and thus inaccessible to outsiders?

Of course, those persuaded of the more general accessibility of the believer's reasons will be liable to favor an element of natural theology and to look positively on alleged arguments for belief in God. But not necessarily so. It is quite possible to insist on the need for revelation before Christian belief can get off the ground, and yet to maintain the general rationality of the Christian religion as something that ought to shine forth and commend itself to any genuinely open mind, at least as a real possibility.

Traditionally, Roman Catholics and Anglicans have tended to favor the theoretical accessibility of the believer's reasons, both in the external (natural theology) sense and in the internal (general intelligibility) sense, while Protestants, both Lutheran and Calvinist, have tended to favor the fideist's view of faith as the precondition of Christianity's intelligibility. It is an intriguing aspect of contemporary Christian theology that some Roman Catholics, notably Hans Küng, have inclined toward the more fideistic view,[1] while some Protestants, notably Wolfhart Pannenberg, in their reaction against Karl Barth, have inclined the other way.[2] Diogenes Allen, the recipient of the present Festschrift, however, remains firmly in the mainstream Protestant tradition of affirming the priority of faith where understanding the believer's reasons is concerned.[3]

For many years, Dick Allen and I have both been enthusiasts for the philosophical theology of Austin Farrer. Part of the interest of Farrer's work is that it can be read either way in the dispute over the accessibility of the believer's reasons.[4] I tend to read Farrer in a more Catholic spirit, discerning elements of both natural theology and belief in the general intelligibility and intellectual power of Christian doctrine.[5] Allen, by contrast, gives a more fideistic interpretation to Farrer's philosophical theology.[6] In this essay I offer some further reflections on the accessibility of the believer's reasons, with the question of how best to interpret Farrer very much in mind.

Negative Apologetic

Let me begin with some remarks about negative apologetic, with the attempt, that is, to defend the faith against caricature or against purported refutation. Negative apologetic does, of course, stem from the community of faith. It is the believer who attempts to defend the faith by pointing out the inadequacies of critics' conceptions of what they are attacking or the poverty of atheistic arguments. No doubt the fair-minded agnostic might make similar comments, as Anthony Kenny does in many of his writings, though one would hardly call such comments apologetic.[7] But the very fact that logical, phenomenological, and moral deficiencies in atheistic arguments *can* be pointed out by believers and agnostics alike shows that negative apologetic from the believer's side is not operating from an otherwise inaccessible perspective or with a logic peculiar and internal to faith.

Consider, for example, the work of today's best-known exponent of negative apologetic, Alvin Plantinga, on the problem of evil.[8] The claim, by atheistic critics such as Antony Flew,[9] that there is a logical contradiction between belief in an all-powerful, wholly good God and admission of the reality and extent of evil is decisively refuted by Plantinga's version of the freewill defense. Or at least that defense, namely, that not even omnipotent benevolence can cause it to be the case that genuinely free creatures always act well, is shown by Plantinga to have a prima facie plausibility that ought to be apparent to any fair-minded reader, from within or from without the community of faith. It can be challenged, as it is by J. L. Mackie,[10] on the grounds of some "compatibilist" theory of free will and determinism; but that theory is highly controversial, and can itself be judged implausible from within or from without the community of faith.

Plantinga is perfectly well aware that his argument is no more than a logical defense against the charge of contradiction.[11] Much more is needed in the way of theodicy if God's ways with the world are really to be justified; but full theodicies, too, are usually put forward with a claim to a *moral* plausibility recognizable beyond the boundaries of faith. When we attempt to indicate a morally sufficient reason why God creates the human world gradually and indirectly from below, setting us in a regularly structured environment, which has at the same time the power to produce us and all the values of human life and also, as a regrettable side effect, the power to do us so much harm, it is no use appealing to a sense of "morally sufficient" that is wholly internal to faith, with no connection with what counts as "moral" generally.

Other examples of negative apologetic would include attempted rebuttals of atheistic claims concerning the incoherence of the concept of an infinite, yet personal, God. It is, of course, no easy task to expound or defend such a concept. Negative apologetic, in this connection, will involve criticism of any argument that rules out infinite, incorporeal, personality by definition. Again, I may refer to Antony Flew as one who essays just such an argument, declaring that, since the only persons we know are highly developed animal organisms, that is what the word "person" means.[12] Against this the apologist will resist such stipulation, pointing out that humans have spoken of spirits and angels and of the mind behind the whole cosmos in personal terms long before empiricists came along with more restricted definitions. The apologist will go on to defend judicious use of analogy where incorporeal personality is concerned, and may allow some criticisms of classical monotheism, in the direction, perhaps, of a renewed trinitarian theology. Such a doctrine of God is defended by Austin Farrer in the concluding chapters of *Faith and Speculation,* where he shows how reasons of consistency and intelligibility require the abandonment of certain, largely Platonic, elements in classical theism.[13]

The boundaries between negative and positive apologetics are clearly being blurred here. The way to rebut caricatures and easy criticism is to spell out the positive doctrine sensitively and clearly. As Farrer says in another place, when writing of the doctrine of the Incarnation, "Look here: the longer I go on trying to tell you about this, the more I become convinced that the job that really wants doing is to expound the formula rather than to justify it; or anyhow that the justification required is identical with exposition."[14]

My point is that such arguments, whether of negative or of positive apologetic, are conducted in the public arena. The rebuttals and the clarifications are intended to open people's eyes to what the tradition of Christian faith really means, whether or not the reader is prepared to assent to the doctrines and make either a tentative or a firm commitment of faith. Maybe all that can be expected in a particular case at a particular time is the acknowledgment, "Well, yes, at least I see what you mean. I grant that your position is intelligible."

Naturally, Farrer hopes for more. His arguments with his imagined critical interlocutors, who are made to put the case against free will in the Gifford Lectures,[15] or against theodicy in *Love Almighty and Ills Unlimited,*[16] or against the intelligibility of theism in the latter part of *Faith and Speculation,* are designed to persuade. But whether they do so or not, they are rational arguments, employing the criteria of general logic and intelligibility. In no way do they appeal to a purely internal logic that presupposes the horizon of faith.

Faith Seeking Understanding

In turning, for the rest of this essay, to the more positive side of the theme of the believer's reasons, let us first consider the Anselmian tag, *fides quaerens intellectum,* as summing up the view that faith come first and understanding later. As is well known, Karl Barth used Anselm's phrase to mark his break with any kind of philosophical underpinning of theology.[17] Henceforth, theology was to be purely church dogmatics, the community of faith producing from within students and teachers reflecting on and articulating the truth content of the Christian tradition in which they already participate. Anselm himself, it is pointed out, comes up with his ontological argument in the course of a prayer addressed to God. The argument was offered to his fellow monks to aid them in their understanding of the One whom they worshiped daily, not as a dialectical device for demolishing the unbeliever.

On the other hand, it does not follow necessarily that the understanding sought by faith is for internal consumption only. Neither Anselm nor his modern followers would be satisfied with arguments and clarifications that remain wholly opaque to outsiders. Granted that Anselm and Anselmians are indeed believers, their philosophical reflections on the meaning and intelligibility—and indeed on the justification—of what they believe are undertaken and offered in the wider context of critical rationality open to all thinking men and women. Consider another example from Anselm. In the preface to *Cur Deus Homo?* Anselm tells us that the first part of this short treatise "contains the objections of infidels, who despise the Christian faith because they deem it contrary to reason; and also the reply of believers; and, in fine, leaving Christ out of view (as if nothing had ever been known of him), it proves, by absolute reasons, the impossibility that any man should be saved without him."[18] We may not think very highly of the arguments put forward in this work, but there is no doubt that they were intended by Anselm to convince the infidel. Why otherwise should a Christian scholar, and archbishop, leave Christ out of view, as if nothing had ever been heard of him?

It follows that the relationship between faith and understanding is misconstrued if faith is held to be the presupposition of any rational understanding of Christian doctrine. Certainly, the Christian faith—the tradition of creedal teaching as an objective phenomenon in the human world—comes first and provides the data for reflection and scrutiny, or at least some elements in the Christian faith provide the starting point for reflection. Even if Anselm suggests ignoring everything we know about Jesus Christ for his particular apologetic purposes, he is still reflecting on the question of God, humankind, and salvation raised by the Christian tradition. Certainly, too, Anselm and his modern followers are men and women of personal faith, seeking to understand what they believe. But it does not follow that only believers can ever hope to understand such matters. For rationality and understanding are general human powers. There are, as Anselm says, absolute reasons that ought, in principle, to convince anybody. Indeed, it is clear, as I say, that Anselm hoped to persuade the infidel of the folly of his ways. Similarly, in his *Summa Contra Gentiles,* Thomas Aquinas prescinds from citing Christian authorities, and attempts to defend the Christian faith by reason alone. But even in the *Summa Theologiae,* where appeal is made to the Bible and the Fathers, the case does not rely on such appeals. In each case the scriptural or patristic citation is explained and defended rationally.

We may think that Anselm and Thomas and their modern followers were and are overoptimistic in their hope that such rational argumentation could convince the infidel, the Gentile, or the agnostic. For there are many cultural and psychological factors reinforcing unbelief and inhibiting understanding. In my own introduction to this essay, I referred, more guardedly, to "the sympathetic or even the curious unbeliever" and to "any genuinely open mind" as potentially capable of at least some understanding of the Christian faith. Moreover, up to now I have been concerned to show that the phrase "*fides quaerens intellectum*" can be taken to refer not only to one's own personal faith seeking understanding but also to any attempt to show the rational intelligibility of the Christian faith as such.

In the opening chapters of *Faith and Speculation,* Austin Farrer is indeed concerned with the believer's reasons in the more personal sense, and in *Saving Belief* he does toy with the idea that one needs at least "initial faith"—a willingness "to experiment in having God"—in order to appreciate the rationality of what the Christian apologist is saying.[19] Not surprisingly, Dick Allen seizes on this passage to substantiate his claim that Farrer is rejecting the possibility of any neutral assessment of the believer's reasons.[20] But one may well ask how far Farrer's "initial faith" or "experimenting in having God" goes beyond the phenomenological open-mindedness and sympathy that I have allowed to be the necessary condition of unbiased scrutiny. (One might refer to Coleridge's "willing suspension of disbelief" at this point.) Moreover, in *Faith and Speculation,* Farrer himself allows that personal experience of God's will and action in one's own life is not the only factor to be considered where the believer's reasons are concerned. There is still a place for the philosophical examination of the assumptions the believer makes.[21]

The phrase "the believer's reasons," like the phrase "*fides quaerens intellectum,*" can be taken in either of two ways. It can refer to the actual factors that weigh with a particular believer in evoking or sustaining his or her belief. These are largely experiential and are, indeed, what Farrer was primarily concerned with in the opening chapter of *Faith and Speculation.* But the phrase can also refer to the rational considerations supportive of Christian belief in general. These are open to more public scrutiny and are the primary concern of the present essay. Farrer himself was *also* concerned with these throughout his working life.

In the next two sections here, I shall examine these two considerations in turn: first the appeal to one's own experience as a believer and to the blessings one has oneself received as a man or woman of faith, and then the appeal to objective factors in the world, open to rational scrutiny by anyone.

Religious Experience

I have myself been taken to task for characterizing experiential verification of religious belief as "private" or "subjective," by contrast with appeals to "public" or "objective" factors open to scrutiny by anyone. For Dick Allen, the privacy of one's own experience is neither here nor there. It requires faith, the opening of the heart to God, to discern God in nature and history just as much as in one's own life.[22] For my colleague Nicholas Lash, religious experience is not "private," "inner," or "subjective" anyway. Indeed the same is true of any experience. A painful experience in a dentist's chair, he writes, is not simply a private mental state, but an aspect of "my interaction, in the public world of flesh and fact and language, with dentists' drills . . . ," and so on.[23] This is surely indefensible. There is indeed a causal relation between the objective fact of the dentist's drill and my own experience of pain. But the pain is mine, for all that, an inner and thus private fact immediately accessible only to me, even if, as Wittgenstein would insist, it cannot be expressed conceptually in a private language. But the question of language is irrelevant. My pain is my own private, inner, mental state, just as my cat's pain is his alone when his tooth is drawn without anesthetic. The cat's yowl may be a public fact, but the cat's pain is his own inner, private experience (Descartes notwithstanding).

Lash's point is not unconnected to his argument, advanced at length elsewhere,[24] against the idea of religious experience as a distinctive, unique sort of inner experience. Rather, we experience the world religiously when we interpret ordinary things in life and in the world in a way made possible by the religious tradition in which we participate. With this thesis I have much sympathy, although there may well be some distinctive, sui generis forms of religious experience as well, as William Alston has urged.[25] But either way, it is I who experience the world (or God) religiously, or not, as the case may be. And if I do, then my doing so involves inner, private attitudes and feelings, including felt benefits, which I can appeal to by way of confirmation of my beliefs, but which I cannot lay on the table and point to as I can to those features of the outer world that are appealed to in the objective arguments.

One's own religious experience, therefore, plays a different role vis-à-vis the justification of religious belief from that played by the objective facts of the world's contingency and unexplained character, its capacity to evolve mind and personality, its manifestation of objective value, the rational power of allegedly revelation-based systematic theology, and the actual fruits of religion in saintly lives and transformed communities—these being the facts to which appeal is made in the public arguments.

I do not agree with Allen, then, that faith is the necessary precondition of any recognition of the potentially religious significance of nature and the human world, including its religious traditions. But even if he were right, it would still be one's own "inner," "private" experience—the "opening of one's heart" to which he refers[26]—that would be unlocking the doors of perception. Indeed, experiential verification would be doing all the work, and "privacy" would reign.

Of course, we should not equate a person's own, and thus private, *faith* with any equally private religious *experience* the person may claim to have enjoyed. Faith, including both conviction and commitment, is indeed one's own if one has it. But its grounds are various: in my view partly public—the arguments and the facts to which one appeals—and partly private—the experiential confirmation about which Farrer writes in the opening chapter of *Faith and Speculation*. Thus one can appeal to one's own experience in attempting to justify one's faith. But such an appeal is unlikely to carry weight with others, unless there are also some supporting arguments appealing to more publicly accessible facts.

Admittedly, the fact that all over the world and throughout recorded history people have claimed to experience the world (and God) religiously is a publicly accessible fact that can take its place in a cumulative argument in support of religious belief. In this sense the appeal to religious experience is part of the public case. Unbelievers have to explain away the widespread fact of claimed religious experience; and such reductionist explanations are open to the criticisms of negative apologetic for their rational, moral, or simply phenomenological implausibility.

Religious experience, then, features in two very different ways where consideration of the believer's reasons is concerned. If we are pondering the factors that most weigh with an individual believer, it is indeed most likely that it will be his or her own religious experience, whether extraordinary or "in ordinary," to which he or she will appeal. Such appeals are hard to evaluate in the public arena, just because of their inner, private, and subjective nature. If, however, we are pondering the considerations that objectively support the beliefs in question, then it is the prevalence of religious experience claims throughout the human world that will be appealed to, among other things. Moreover, in the public arena, the appeal is likely to be made not so much to one's own rather feeble case, but to the striking, often extraordinary accounts given by others—the mystics and the saints, maybe—as well as to the products and fruits of those claimed experiences in their lives.

The Public Arguments

It is not possible to examine here all the public arguments that cumulatively support Christian belief. I shall simply select two: one from the general area of natural theology, namely, design arguments for the existence of God; and one from what is crudely called revealed theology, namely, the logic of Trinitarian belief. Of course, the phrase "revealed theology" is shorthand. No one is supposing that some *theology* or other is revealed. Revealed theology, by contrast with natural theology, simply consists in arguments and reflections based on a particular series of events and a particular tradition alleged to be the vehicles of special revelation, by contrast with arguments and reflections based on general features of the world and of its and our existence. My point in selecting one example from each of these fields is to indicate, *en passant,* that natural theology and revealed theology are equally rational and equally accessible across the borders of belief and unbelief. As Wolfhart Pannenberg insists, all theology must "be discussed without reservations in the context of critical rationality."[27] James Barr, too, in his Gifford Lectures, sets out to explore "the possibility that there is, ultimately, no important difference between natural and revealed theology, after all."[28] However, this is not my chief preoccupation here. My concern is, rather, with design arguments and with the rational plausibility of trinitarian belief as elements in a public case supportive of Christian belief, whether one's interest is primarily in Christian self-understanding or in apologetics or in a more neutral assessment of the rational plausibility of Christian belief.

First, then, let us consider the supportive or persuasive force of design arguments. Design arguments are primarily teleological, in that they point to features of the world order allegedly inexplicable except by postulating purposive design. They are, of course, vulnerable in two ways particularly: to the problem of evil and to alternative, nonteleological, explanations. These objections are very different in kind. The features calling for explanation in terms of design are still not accounted for, when one has pointed to counterinstances—the fact and extent of evil and suffering—suggestive of lack of design. I concede that the believer needs a theodicy, and I have attempted to provide one elsewhere;[29] but the fact remains that the factors suggestive of design and the factors suggestive of lack of design are not equally weighted. For design arguments, at least today, do not appeal to instances within the world order that can just be matched by appeal to instances of suffering and evil. They appeal to features of the world order as a whole that still cry out for teleological explanation, suffering and evil notwithstanding. Consequently, design arguments are much more vulnerable to the other objection, namely, alternative, nonteleological explanations of those features of the world order as a whole.

It is widely held that evolutionary theory provides just such an alternative explanation. According to Richard Dawkins, for example, there is no place for teleology in a Darwinian view of the universe.[30] But, as Keith Ward has pointed out,[31] evolutionary theory only explains the features of highly organized life-forms here on earth, given certain properties and powers in the fundamental particles or energies of the cosmos, and given the fundamental laws and constants of nature— and even then there are gaps in the story, where the emergence of consciousness, mind, rationality, and personality, together with their concomitant values, are concerned. Evolutionary theory, in other words, in no way accounts for the stuff of the world, if one may call it that, being here at all, with such extraordinarily productive properties and powers. It is that fact which furnishes the basis of a design argument. For the capacity of the world stuff to evolve rational, personal, value-bearing individuals and communities is more intelligible if deliberately intended than if "just there."

Such design arguments have been enhanced by the cosmologists' discovery of the so-called "fine-tuning" of the universe in the early stages of cosmic expansion. The very narrow range of the initial conditions, and indeed of later conditions, enabling the capacities of the world stuff to be realized in the ways we know is very striking.[32] The so-called "anthropic principle" has to be explained away by the unbeliever through increasingly extravagant hypotheses concerning many universes, or an infinite series of expansions and contractions of the one universe allowing the necessary conditions to occur sooner or later by chance. There is no conceivable scientific evidence for such hypotheses, which are in any case as implausible as the supposition that, given infinite time, a monkey typing randomly would come up with the works of Shakespeare. But even if fine-tuning and the anthropic principle could be explained away, the basic premise of design arguments—the capacity of the world stuff so to combine over cosmic and biological evolution as to come up with interpersonal life and value—has not been addressed, let alone explained. Here then is one supporting argument that can at the same time offer a buttress to faith and a plank in the apologist's platform.

We turn to the logic of Trinitarian theology. There is in fact a way of arguing for Trinitarian belief irrespective of the actual data of Christian history and the development of doctrine. This would be to proceed, like Anselm in *Cur Deus Homo?* purely by what Anselm called "absolute reasons," *remoto Christo.* This way has recently been revived by Richard Swinburne.[33] Here I ignore this possibility and consider, as the object of our critical reflection, the actual story of Jesus Christ and what came after as allegedly a revelatory sequence of events requiring Trinitarian doctrine to make sense of it. Very briefly, the argument goes like this: Let us suppose that we have already grasped something of the persuasive power of Christian incarnational belief—perhaps, quite simply, along the lines of Kierkegaard's beautiful parable of the king and the humble maiden.[34] Seeing the point, then, of Christian belief in the divinity of Christ, we ask ourselves how we can make sense of Jesus' prayers to the God he called "Father" and of the sense of union, indeed interpenetration, between the Father and the incarnate Son. We do so by supposing that these relational factors reflect internal differentiation, indeed love given and love received, within the infinite, eternal God. And that means two, at least, personal centers or subjects in God. But equally we have to make sense of the experience of early Christians, and indeed of Christians ever since, of indwelling by the outpoured spirit of God and of Christ—the Spirit, that is, welling up from within and taking us, and our feeble intercessions, into the heart of God. A further, internal, God–God relation is revealed at this point. We make sense of this by positing three, not two, centers or subjects in the one, infinite God. Further reflection on these mysteries leads to our seeing the point of the patristic doctrines of *perichoresis* or *circumincessio,* the mutual interpenetration of the Persons of the Trinity.

At this point, the rationality of Christian Trinitarian belief may be further supported by the a priori considerations to which Swinburne gives considerable weight. For is there not a rationally perceptible incoherence in pure, undifferentiated monotheism, if God's nature is supposed to consist in love? For unless we posit love given, love received, and love shared still more in God, we find ourselves thinking of the creation of a world productive of finite persons in relation as a necessity if God is to have an object of his love. That a finite created world is necessary not only flies in the face of the whole Judeo-Christian tradition (and that of Islam as well), but smacks of metaphysical incoherence, given the manifest contingency of the world we know.

Here, then, are two examples, from natural and revealed theology respectively, of the kind of public factors that contribute to a rational cumulative case supportive of the Christian faith. In the final section of this essay I consider how the public and the private appeals hang together.

The Interrelation
of Public and Private Appeals

One of the features of Austin Farrer's philosophical theology that I have long admired is the way in which he holds together the rational arguments for theism, the public appeal to the figures of Christ and the saints, and what I call the private appeal to one's own experience, namely, the way in which, for the believer, the reality of God's will is found, experientially, by one who lets that will take effect in his or her own life. I have often quoted, from one of Farrer's sermons, the passage where he tells his congregation how to disbelieve in God by splitting the evidence up: "Keep the mystery of the world's origin carefully separate from your experience of God and then you can say that the cosmic facts are dumb. . . . Keep the believer's experience of God by itself, and away from the general mystery of nature; then you can say that it is so peculiar, so odd a little fact in this vast indifferent universe, that to attach universal importance to it is too absurd." And he goes on: "Now I'll tell you how to believe. . . . Poor [though our own experience may be] and too thin to bear the weight of evidence . . . , [it does] not stand alone. We see clearly enough that what we have an inkling of, the saints apprehend and Christ simply achieves. Ah, but is not this whole phenomenon of life invaded by the divine a mere freak in the vast material solid of the universe? Nonsense, the universe isn't solid at all . . . it is, as a totality, unexplained, and subject to the appointment of creative will in all its infinite detail."[35]

Of course, the sentence Allen seizes on is the one that suggests that, apart from our experience of God which Allen equates with the opening of the heart that we call faith, "the cosmic facts are dumb." This yields the fideist interpretation of Farrer. It takes faith to discern "the appointment of creative will in all the universe's detail." But I do not think this fideist interpretation is right. Even here, in this sermon, preaching to believers, Farrer is careful to observe that if you keep experience and mystery apart, *you can say* that the cosmic facts are dumb; and his assertion at the end of the quoted passage—"Nonsense, the universe isn't solid at all . . . ; it is, as a totality, unexplained"—is surely not an assertion that relies on faith or experience to make its point. Moreover when we look carefully at the concluding paragraphs of chapter one of *Faith and Speculation,* the chapter in which he has stressed the importance of experiential verification of religious belief in the believer's self-understanding, Farrer remarks that the appeal to experience lets us off nothing, philosophically speaking. For if talk of experience of God entails reference to "creative omnipotence, it has to be shown that the universe of finites allows of being interpreted as his creation." And then he goes on: "Can you argue that the finites *allow* of being read as creations of the Infinite, without arguing they *ask* to be read as such? How can the finites even *allow* of being read as creations of the Infinite, without arguing that they *ask* to be read as such? How can the finites even allow of dependence upon an infinite, unless it is in virtue of an existential insufficiency which requires such a dependence?"[36]

It is clear from this that Farrer had not really moved over into the fideist camp. For him, the believer's self-understanding finds rational support in the cosmological argument, which carries some weight as an argument independently. This, I think, was Farrer's view throughout his writing life, from *Finite and Infinite*[37] to *Faith and Speculation.* Similar points are made regarding design arguments in Farrer's *A Science of God?*[38] and I have sketched my own version of these here. Admittedly, Farrer does add a throwaway line at the end of the first chapter of *Faith and Speculation,* perhaps conceding too much to the fideists: "We may let ourselves off the claim that the force of the proof is evident to the unbelieving mind. We can say, if we like, that the existential insufficiency is imperceptible apart from awareness, and that such an awareness comes through faith." That, of course, is precisely what Dick Allen likes. But again I note the force of the "may" and the "can" in Farrer's remarks. All he is saying, on my view, is that men and women of faith are unlikely to have philosophized their way into faith and that they do not have to philosophize about it. Fair enough. But what interests us as philosophers of religion is the fact to which Farrer reverts at the end of this chapter, namely, that while it is indeed the assumptions of the believing mind that provide the data for our scrutiny, that scrutiny proceeds by arguments whose rational force is, in principle, accessible to all.

NOTES

1. H. Küng, *Does God Exist?* (Garden City, N.Y.: Doubleday & Co., 1980).
2. W. Pannenberg, *Systematic Theology,* vol. 1 (Grand Rapids: Wm. B. Eerdmans Publishing Co., 1991).
3. D. Allen, "Faith and the Recognition of God's Activity," in *Divine Action,* ed. B. Hebblethwaite and E. Henderson (Edinburgh: T. & T. Clark, 1990).
4. See B. Mitchell, "Two Approaches to the Philosophy of Religion," in *For God and Clarity,* ed. J. C. Eaton and A. Loades (Allison Park, Pa.: Pickwick Publications, 1983).
5. B. L. Hebblethwaite, "The Experiential Verification of Religious Belief in the Theology of Austin Farrer," in Eaton and Loades, *For God and Clarity.*
6. Allen, "Faith and the Recognition."
7. See, e.g., A. Kenny, *The God of the Philosophers* (Oxford: Oxford University Press, 1979); and *What Is Faith?* (Oxford: Oxford University Press, 1992).
8. Alvin Plantinga, *God, Freedom and Evil* (Grand Rapids: Wm. B. Eerdmans Publishing Co., 1978).
9. A. Flew, "Theology and Falsification," in A. Flew and A. MacIntyre, eds., *New Essays in Philosophical Theology* (London: Macmillan & Co., 1955).
10. J. L. Mackie, *The Miracle of Theism* (Oxford: Oxford University Press, 1982).
11. A. Plantinga, "Self Profile," in *Alvin Plantinga,* ed. J. E. Tomberlin and P. van Inwagen (Dordrecht: D. Reidel, 1985).
12. A. Flew, *The Presumption of Atheism* (London: Elek/Pemberton, 1976).
13. A. M. Farrer, *Faith and Speculation* (New York: New York University Press, 1967).
14. A. M. Farrer, *Interpretation and Belief* (London: SPCK, 1976), 128.
15. A. M. Farrer, *The Freedom of the Will* (New York: Charles Scribner's Sons, 1958).
16. A. M. Farrer, *Love Almighty and Ills Unlimited* (London: William Collins Sons & Co., 1962).
17. K. Barth, *Anselm: Fides Quaerens Intellectum,* trans. I. W. Robertson (London: SCM Press, 1960).
18. *St. Anselm: Basic Writings,* trans. S. N. Deane (La Salle, Ill.: Open Court, 1961), 177.
19. A. M. Farrer, *Saving Belief* (London: Hodder & Stoughton, 1964), chap. 1.
20. Allen, "Faith and the Recognition."
21. Farrer, *Faith and Speculation,* 12ff.
22. Allen, "Faith and the Recognition."
23. N. L. A. Lash, *Theology on the Way to Emmaus* (London: SCM Press, 1986), 143ff.
24. N. L. A. Lash, *Easter in Ordinary* (Notre Dame, Ind.: University of Notre Dame Press, 1988).

25. W. P. Alston, *Perceiving God* (Ithaca, N.Y.: Cornell University Press, 1991).
26. Allen, "Faith and the Recognition," 206.
27. W. Pannenberg, "History and Meaning in Bernard Lonergan's Approach to Theological Method," in P. Corcoran, ed., *Looking at Lonergan's Method* (Dublin: Talbot Press, 1975), 98.
28. J. Barr, *Biblical Faith and Natural Theology* (Oxford: Oxford University Press, 1993), 126.
29. B. L. Hebblethwaite, "The Problem of Evil," in *Keeping the Faith,* ed. G. Wainwright (Philadelphia: Westminster Press, 1988).
30. R. Dawkins, *The Blind Watchmaker* (New York: W. W. Norton & Co., 1987).
31. J. K. S. Ward, *God, Chance and Necessity* (Oxford: Oxford University Press, 1996).
32. See R. G. Swinburne, *The Existence of God,* 2d ed. (Oxford: Oxford University Press, 1991), appendix B.
33. R. G. Swinburne, *The Christian God* (Oxford: Oxford University Press, 1994).
34. S. Kierkegaard, *Philosophical Fragments,* trans. E. and H. Hong (Princeton, N.J.: Princeton University Press, 1985).
35. A. M. Farrer, "How Can We Be Sure of God?" in idem, *A Celebration of Faith* (London: Hodder & Stoughton, 1970), 106.
36. Farrer, *Faith and Speculation,* 13.
37. A. M. Farrer, *Finite and Infinite* (London: Dacre Press, 1943).
38. A. M. Farrer, *A Science of God?* (London: Bles, 1966).

4

THEOLOGY AND SPIRITUALITY

or, Why Theology Is Not Critical Reflection
on Religious Experience

ERIC O. SPRINGSTED

I had the great good fortune to study with Dick Allen over the course of two academic degrees. Crucial as his classroom and seminar efforts to instruct me were to my education, they were not, however, the most important part of my education. Rather, I learned most from Dick Allen at a lunch table in his dining room, where over the course of four or five years we (along with Jeff Eaton for the first couple of years), without any discernible plan but with increasing mutual enthusiasm and edification, read and discussed together Epictetus, Plato, Aristotle, and finally Simone Weil. I do not think it is possible to overestimate the importance of learning any *Geisteswissenschaft,* theology and philosophy particularly, in the context of friendship, nor, as Aristotle saw, to overestimate the importance of a common pursuit of the knowledge of the Good to forming a friendship.[1]

Theology and philosophy learned in the context of friendship, in the context of an interpersonal activity, can take on a very different character than it might have when it is learned simply in a classroom. It is, for example, something that one learns in good part because of the grace of another's trying to help one understand, and that one learns by trying to help another understand. One learns to take personal responsibility for what one knows. Now, Dick and I learned much from those discussions, including much *about* Epictetus, Plato, Aristotle, and Weil. But I suspect what was most important about those discussions was what we learned about the nature of theology itself (and ancient philosophy), namely, that it does always involve personal grace and responsibility, that it is itself therefore primarily a spiritual enterprise. For theology is something that shapes the thinker; it is *not,* as is platitudinously claimed in contemporary theological circles, "critical reflection upon religious experience."

But what does it mean to say that theology is or ought to be spiritual? Such a claim is not analogous to saying that physics is scientific. For whereas physics is scientific because it is in accord with scientific method, that is, it reflects critically on empirical data, theology is not spiritual because of a spiritual method. Although there are spiritual methods, they do not involve the same sort of theoretical bases that scientific ones do. Rather, theology is spiritual because it involves an improvement, or is tied to an improvement, of the spirit. That theology has something to do with spirituality, therefore, means that we not only think of God, but by thinking of God truly at all we are at the same time involved with him in such a way that our spirits are improved by that involvement, by that thinking. This is what it means to say theology is spiritual, for there is an important connection between the thought and the improvement of the thinker. This makes theology, thinking on God, unique not only because God is unique, but also because the thought is related to a change within the thinker that comes from an active relationship with God. I do not believe that sciences make anything like this claim that one becomes like what one studies.

The Nature of Faith

In order to explain this claim, I want to start at a place that is, undoubtedly, overly familiar to most philosophers of religion, namely, Pascal's "wager argument." It is not the wager or the argument itself that I am particularly concerned with, however, but rather the story that Pascal is telling about faith. In this vein, I would like to start at the end, that is, with the advice that Pascal offers to the man to whom he is speaking (a professional gambler, to be precise), who, despite seeing the rationality of making the wager in question, cannot make it—which is to say, he still refuses to believe in God. Now, Pascal's advice in this situation is that the man follow the example of many before him: "Follow the way by which they began; by acting as if they believed, taking holy water, having masses said, etc."[2]

Ever since Pascal penned this advice, it has been roundly attacked as being everything from making faith into a matter of fraudulent self-suggestion to inviting dishonesty and superstition. The heart of the criticism that has been directed against Pascal was perhaps best put by the American philosopher W. K. Clifford.[3] He illustrated his point by using this example: A shipowner was about to put a ship to sea filled with many emigrants hoping to go to a new land. He had many reasons to doubt the seaworthiness of the ship, however, and that caused him many doubts about whether he should let it sail. In time, however, he was able to overcome these doubts, reasoning that in years past, when it was young, it had weathered many storms, and also reasoning that providence could not fail to protect all these worthy emigrants. Therefore he let it sail, and later collected his insurance money when it went down in mid ocean. This man, Clifford contended, was guilty of the death of all those people, for, he pointed out, the man had no reason to believe on such evidence as was before him. He did not earn his faith in providence by examining providence; he simply stifled his doubts.

Now, one way of describing what the shipowner did is to say that he followed, more or less, Pascal's advice: he trusted and acted before he had sufficient reason to believe that such trust and action were warranted. In short, he had faith before he had formed an adequate belief about that in which he trusted. He had faith before belief.

I put it this way for a simple reason, namely, that what Clifford appeals to is what appears to be mere common sense, not only in things worldly, but also in things religious. That is to say, we assume as a matter of course that belief—belief that God exists, that God is good, that God is capable of doing the things people claim God is capable of — must be established, at least with some probability, before we can put our trust, our faith, in God.

The thought seems obvious. If we didn't first believe that God exists, if we didn't already believe that God is good, we couldn't trust God. This way of going about things also seems to be taken on good authority. For example, St. Thomas Aquinas in his magisterial *Summa Theologiae,* in one of the first questions of that huge book,[4] seeks to establish that the existence of God can be proved, and proves it, before he goes on to describe what God is like, and what life in God, the life of faith, is like.

And yet for all the apparent obviousness of this approach to thinking about faith and belief, I think that it is wrong. I think St. Thomas Aquinas also thought it was wrong. For example, when he asks the question, "Can the existence of God be proved?" the reason he gives for saying that it can is very simply that St. Paul in scripture says that it can. Which is simply to say that it is pretty clear that before Aquinas has established whether the existence of God can be proved or not, he has committed himself to trusting scripture as the word of God, sufficient to provide him a way and the truth. Thus, for Aquinas it is not at all obvious that belief in God must be warranted before we can have faith in God; rather, for him faith precedes belief. For Clifford, the order is reversed.

Now why Aquinas and Clifford differ is important to understand, for their disagreement lies chiefly in their characterization and understanding of the nature of faith and the problem involved in Pascal's advice. Consider the sort of air that talk like that of W. K. Clifford has. It gives a sense that one first stands apart from what might be committed to, apart from what one might have faith in, and from that distance one simply surveys the landscape of possibilities. It is from that vantage point and after such a survey that one can legitimately then decide whether or not to commit oneself. Now, I should point out that this sort of process works fine when trying to determine whether or not a ship should sail. Indeed, as Clifford saw, it is ethically demanded. And it works fine for anything that we can survey and have knowledge about from a distant standpoint. It works fine in cases where engineering decisions have to be made; it works fine when arrangements for travel are undertaken; it works fine when one cooks dinner.

It even works fine when one is trying to determine answers to certain big questions such as whether life has meaning or not, for with those questions, too, one can stand off at a distance and add up the sum total of possibilities before making a decision as to one's commitment level.

But this method doesn't work very well at all with things that we don't have control over, or with things that we can only know by committing ourselves to them, things that we don't know all about ahead of time, things that we have to work with in order to know them. Thus, for example, it doesn't work at all well with people. When we want to get to know people better, we don't ask ahead of time what they are like, for the only way of finding out what they are really like is by dealing with them. And indeed, if they ever thought that we would refuse to deal with them until we had all the evidence in on them, it is likely that we would fail to get to know most things about them, including their telephone numbers. The person who tries to decide whether the institution of marriage is meaningful or not may reach an answer, but is not likely to get a husband or wife, for such a person fails to understand that what counts in marriage is nothing less than a full-fledged commitment to another person.

This method also doesn't work very well with God. For God is not a possibility we can survey; God is not even the sum of possibilities. God is not even the meaning of our lives; God is the creator of them and the Word that upholds every thought we have, including thoughts about God and meaning. And for that very reason we can never stand back and survey the evidence, for whatever evidence there is, and whatever surveying might be done, is nothing more than what God has created and what God is at the very heart of. As the psalmist once sang, "O Lord, thou hast searched me and known me! Thou knowest when I sit down and when I rise up; thou discernest my thoughts from afar. Thou . . . art acquainted with all my ways. Even before a word is on my lips, thou, O Lord, knowest it already" (Ps. 139:1–4).

And because, as the psalmist understood, God is at the very center of our being, creating whatever being we might have, there is no standing apart from God and surveying the possibilities. There is with God, as with human beings, only responding to their presence. For their very existence addresses us and demands a response. What we then come to know of their existence very much depends on how we respond to that address.

Throughout his writings, St. Augustine frequently quotes a passage from Isaiah that he translates in this way: "Unless you have faith, you will not understand." Or as it is sometimes put, from faith comes understanding. When Augustine pulled this quotation from Isaiah out, he did not mean by it that one simply had to accept certain things and that in time one might understand them. That is something you say only to children. What he meant was this: understanding, which is something much deeper and more profound than mere knowledge, or even reason itself, comes only when we respond with ourselves, our hearts and minds and bodies, to that by which we are addressed. It comes only when we respond with our commitment and trust. For Augustine, God's Word, the Word by which all things were created, addresses itself continually to the human heart. Our response to that Word, our faith in that Word, thus is the very beginning of our coming to understand — not understanding simply either the world or ourselves, but understanding at all. For what is understanding but the acceptance and love of all that is created? What is understanding but our commitment to what addresses us? We can know many things and reason about many things without loving them; we can reason about them and know them from great distances. But *understanding* them means accepting and loving them as God created them. It is only when we understand things in this way that we will ever know what we believe about them.

It is at this point that it is worth returning to Pascal's gambler and being reminded of an important reading that Diogenes Allen suggests for why Pascal gave out the advice he did to the gambler. As Allen notes, that advice is the conclusion of a long argument about faith.[5] Now in the beginning of it Pascal suggests, in a way that appeals to where the gambler's treasure is, that faith is a good bet, for, he says, if there is eternity, then by giving up all to believe in it one can reap an infinite reward. On the other hand, if there is no eternity, whatever one might thereby lose by living a life of faith is simply finite. Thus the expected return on this bet outweighs any possible loss one might incur. Now Pascal knew what he was talking about when he formulated the bet this way: after all, he virtually invented probability theory. But as the argument with the gambler goes on, the gambler simply cannot make the wager even though he sees clearly the rational advantages to it. Nowhere does he seem to doubt the rationality of the wager. In this sense, if one would compare him to Clifford's shipowner, he has seen the evidence and knows the risk *is* well worth it; he is *not* guilty of taking a bad risk, like the shipowner, at all. Yet as it turns out—and this is the real point—he can't make the bet, even though reason directs him to do so. Why? His life just won't turn itself that way, at least not by rational argument. Now the larger point Pascal wants to make is this: that reasoning about evidence, that is, reason itself, is not the gambler's problem, nor is it ever the problem with faith. The problem is in the gambler's heart and life, in his commitments. That is why Pascal recommends acting as if he believed; for the gambler's problem is one of action. It is only by responding, it is only by action, that this will ever wash clean. In this sense, Pascal saw as did Augustine and Aquinas that faith, that one's commitment, comes ahead of all else. It is of a different order. It is that which alone allows us to understand; it contributes to the flourishing of our reason.

The Content of Theology

What this telling of Pascal's story shows is something about the nature of faith; it does not yet tell us what the nature of theology or theological reasoning is. And herein lies a problem. As Newman saw in the *Grammar of Assent,* faith is a "real" assent to a particular, unique, and concrete call. Theology, on the other hand, to the degree that it is rational, to the degree it is shared and discussed by other rational beings, is "notional," and deals with universal propositions.

The distinction between "real" and "notional" assent does not, I think, constitute an either/or, and I shall be concerned to show how it does not, in a later section of this essay. At this point, what needs to be shown is simply, given the nature of faith, which is a response of the whole person to a call on his or her life, what that means for the practice of theology as both a rational and a spiritual enterprise. In order to do so, let us consider a position that Austin Farrer took.[6]

Farrer recognized at the outset that it is fairly clear that serious continued thought about God does not come about because we have proposed "God" as a possible hypothesis among others to account for phenomena and have found inescapable evidence that makes us admit the hypothesis, like it or not. Rather, he argued, we hear about God, or perhaps apprehend the idea independently, and then entertain it. It is only after entertaining it in a sort of experimental way that we seek the evidence for it. Simply put, the intelligence, as befits its role in a thoughtful life, imagines what it would be like for there to be a God. This is a kind of faith— "initial faith," he calls it.[7] As it imagines what it would be like, it also comes to think of what sort of evidence would incline us to commit ourselves to the thought. But why should we continue to entertain it, much less commit ourselves whole-heartedly to it? Farrer argues here that at this point evidence is not irrelevant, but also points out that because of this initial faith we are in a subjective condition favorable to the reception of the evidence insofar as the evidence is revealed by our sympathy to receiving it.[8] This sympathy, though, does not replace evidence, but only inclines us to consider it. We thus continue the experiment, he thinks, because of the evidence.

But what is the evidence? Well, let us first look at what the idea of God is that it is supposed to support. God, if he is God as theists present him, is at least creator, sustainer, and perfectly good, and as such the alpha and omega of our lives. This is important, for in experimenting with the idea of God we are not experimenting with the possible existence of an item in the world, but with an entire picture of the world. And, as Farrer adds, this picture carries with it a number of built-in attitudes. For example, to experiment in thinking God is to experiment in thinking oneself God's creature and finding in God the very meaning and purpose of our existence and the existence of all that is. Already we see that theology is not, as Farrer later pointed out, really in the range of the sciences, which view the world with a necessarily limited methodological perspective or from a disinterested distance; rather, it is a surveying of the whole in its relation to the creator. In that case, only certain sorts of evidence are even appropriate for convincing us of God's existence. One sort is that which Farrer sought to explicate in *Finite and Infinite,* namely, that the world is capable of being read as the effect of a first cause, and that it even demands such a reading.

Yet as Farrer went on to explain in his last major work, *Faith and Speculation,* that is not the only evidence; in fact, it is actually only correlative to the evidence by which believers are actually convinced. *That* evidence is far more personal and the sort that comes from living the life of faith; or, in other words, it is experimental evidence. It is the evidence of having sought for God's goodness and having found it in one's life. As Farrer succinctly put it: "The Gospel offers God to me as good, not simply as fact. In embracing the good I am convinced of the fact."[9] Simply put, I am motivated by a good that I desire, which is promised to come from the life of faith; as I pursue that good I find that it is, indeed, forthcoming.

Now there are two good reasons for Farrer's embracing this position. The first is related to his notion of "initial faith." The believer in experimenting with the idea of God is dealing with a question of whether or not to submit his or her will to a creator. What will motivate the believer to do so is less the initial certitude that there exists such a being, than the importance of religious interest, and what we look for to confirm that we have actually got hold of anything real in faith is also going to be religious. Thus the position of *Faith and Speculation* far more closely represents how God is actually thought of by theists.

The second reason has to do with what Farrer by this time had clearly understood, that the metaphysical defense contained in *Finite and Infinite* relied on a metaphor of vision that allowed us to think that an idea's sheer luminosity gives us knowledge.[10] But this he later thought was a mistake. Instead, he now argued, knowledge arises only from interaction with the object of thought. Therefore, there is "no thought about reality about which we can do nothing but think."[11] If, then, there is to be knowledge of God, it must come from interaction with him. The position that the believer finds warrant for continued belief from his or her experience of goodness received thus allows us to discuss faith as an empirical question and therefore as a question of real knowledge. It also allows us to see and discuss faith as believers actually practice it, or think they practice it—that is, as interaction with God.

Now, as Farrer clearly saw, this position does not philosophically justify belief; it only indicates that investigation ought not to be unrelated to the believer's actual reasons. But rather than attempting justification of such belief, we need to note one corollary. On Farrer's empirical demand, the substance of the thought of God is not a bare ideal. Rather, as he says, the only thing that can give substance to our thought of God is "an experience which employs our activity in relation to God, where that activity is something other than thought itself."[12] It is not that we cannot imagine the idea of God otherwise, but rather since the reason for bothering with God is salvation, and bothering with it *is* committing oneself to a personal will, the only way in which we would think of God is in terms of our experience of his action as it has enjoined our action. The content, then, of our thought about God is derived empirically.

This does not mean, though, that we can see where and how God's action has influenced our lives; Farrer insisted the evidence of our experience of God lies in our past, and "our thought of God is the summary of a tale which relates the actions of God."[13] Our evidence for God is the blessings we have received; but unless we crudely assume that those blessings are lottery winnings for which we have prayed, we understand them only after a period; indeed, a change in our understanding may well be the most important sort of evidence that we could have. Augustine's tale of his life and his conversion is clear witness to this.

At this point, though, we have a first important connection of theology to spirituality. If theology has any real content (as opposed to a strictly abstract content), it is derived from the improvement of spirit that believers have claimed is the result of God's action. We also have reason to think that theologians might have a strong interest in linking theology and spirituality in an ongoing enterprise, for if spirituality is at the root of theology and is a concern for salvation, one would hope that continued thought on God would have something to do with salvation.

The Thought of God Is God

But how? Since we have shown that theology ought to be linked to spiritual experience, and that it is in some sense notional, it would appear that theology precisely is "critical reflection on religious experience," whether one's own or somebody else's. Theology may simply be a matter of spending experiential capital, and not investing it. So why is not theology inevitably a stepping back from the idea of God, instead of an engagement with it?

Initially, we may simply observe that the personal engagement of the theological thinker is required at least insofar as it is the case that unless the thinker is in a position to see the evidence of faith as evidence, he or she simply will not have much of an idea of its worth or what to do with it. Personal acquaintance is invaluable. This suggestion, of course, raises the specter of fideism, and I shall want to say something about that below. But at this point, suffice it to note that what is being suggested is little different from Aquinas's procedure in the *Summa Theologiae,* when he argued (I, Q. 1) that revealed propositions, which cannot be demonstrated but are only taken in faith, could serve as first principles in theological reasoning. It is a matter of reason to deduce things from them, a matter of faith to know and to care that they are indeed the first principles. This, of course, makes theology at least a matter of articulating the faith in notional language. But it also doesn't quite leave its religious basis. Borrowing a distinction from Boethius, while this makes theology a matter of *speculativo* (an intellectual discipline) and not *speculatio* (spiritual gazing or contemplation)[14] as it had been in, say, Augustine, it is not entirely divorced from this grounding in the practice in faith.[15]

But the link I want to establish between theology and the spiritual is even stronger than this. What I want to find is a way by which we can conceive continued thought of God as *spiritually fecund.* Here I would like to approach this question by showing how the dynamics of faith are such that they draw thought into the life of faith by showing that because faith is concerned with spiritual fecundity, that is, with multiplication of the good it is committed to, it will seek to multiply that good in thought. The basis of my argument is taken from threads that are interwoven throughout the notebooks of Simone Weil.

Within Weil's writings there are a number of references to what she calls a "proof by perfection."[16] It is, Weil thinks, the only valid proof there is of God. Briefly stated, it runs like this: It is only by desiring something perfect that I am made any better. If what I desire is unreal, it clearly has no power to effect anything. If it is imaginary, that is effective only psychologically; it is no better than its source, the imaginer. If, however, in the course of desiring I am made better, then this something which draws me is real. Although Weil in places where she speaks of this proof does not say what counts as real effect, elsewhere she makes it very clear. Even as Aquinas took Paul's phrase "faith working through love" as defining the form of faith, so in her own way does Weil. Faith is, for her, the ability to sacrifice our personal perspectives and egos for the life of others. Since for her the will is a part of that ego, any such real sacrifice would not be in the will's possibilities of self-realization. If the sacrifice is made anyhow, it must be made out of a source of action that is beyond our wills.

Where Weil understands the certainty of this proof to lie is obviously not in its syllogistic conclusion. In fact, it is not a propositional proof at all—she is giving a phenomenology of how we, in fact, are convinced. Thus the certainty involved is personal and experimental, and it arises only from engaging by desire the object of thought. In this case she is really talking about something like the "grammar" of thinking about God. The key to understanding what Weil intends by this line of thought lies in what she sees as the unfolding of our relation to perfection, a relation, she thinks, that involves the unique fact that the desire of true perfection is always effective. As she strongly puts it: "Whereas the desire for gold is not the same thing as gold, the desire for good is itself good."[17] Let us unpack this thought.

Initially, Weil thinks the idea that God is perfectly good and even reality is basically a definition. It simply stays at that, though, unless we can engage that perfection. But, she thinks, engagement would appear to present us with a dilemma. On the one hand, if God is perfectly good, we cannot make a single step toward grasping that good because doing so inevitably misfires. It misfires because it indicates a desire not for the good itself but for an ersatz good. This is to say, we think that good could be made better if *we* possessed it, which is also to say that it is not perfect but could stand improvement. Yet, on the other hand, if God does not engage us, he is either not perfectly good or does not actually encompass reality. This is to say that a part of the world, namely us, is not encompassed by God.

The solution to this dilemma, which is characteristic of Weil's thought, comes not in our actually moving toward God, but in God moving toward us. Thus the Good grasps us and makes us over; the Good tailors us to it, we do not adjust it to our life. As Weil puts it, God descends to meet our need. We are not left entirely out of this action, for what causes that descent is our desire. However, this is a "deep desire," which is neither a bare wish nor a striving to possess; rather, it involves something she calls "non-active action." It is nonactive insofar as it indicates a matter of passivity on our part to God's action—we do not strive; but it is action insofar as it actually engages our being in the world. Or, using terms she otherwise employs, this desire is found in steadfast attention to God and waiting upon him. Although her language is highly charged, her point is that the desire for goodness is itself a form of goodness. The idea is clear, for such a stance of attention to the good wants the good for itself on no other conditions than those which the good supplies. That in itself is good.

This solution, however, is still no more than a definition that convinces by its luminosity. The key to unlocking the door to concreteness lies in an intermediary term, "faith." Once again, though, we need to consider carefully Weil's own peculiar usage of terms. Weil, as she makes clear in numerous places, does not consider faith as an intellectual adherence to anything;[18] rather, she calls it a "submission of those parts [of the soul] which have no contact with God to the one which has."[19] What this means is simply that faith is a consent of the whole person to God's action. Not all of what we think, feel, and do is directed toward perfection; some of it is simply directed to getting across the street. Where faith enters is when all of our life is ordered to our deep desire for the good. On the one hand, this means that we do nothing to oppose the fulfillment of desire, and on the other it means that our entire being is engaged by the object of desire even though not everything in us is concerned directly with it.

Weil's usage of the term "faith," of course, has its connections with the traditional religious sense of faith as trust. But she develops the idea further by pointing out *why* we trust and how that involves our very being, namely, in order that the good in which we trust might be expanded. Or, more accurately, that trust is precisely what refuses to be anything but what God makes of it; it is a life given over to God's good. She notes that the relevant article of faith is "concerned with fecundity, with the self-multiplying faculty of every desire for good."[20] In this sense, faith is not only a consent of the whole person to God's action, it is a consent motivated by the desire that God's goodness might be shed abroad, in and through us and even despite us. Yet, Weil adds, this is nevertheless faith, because we do not know, prior to our commitment, that the Good is actually fecund and will be effective; it is only by our experience of having been made better by having chosen to live this way that we are convinced of its efficacy. Again there is no direct observation of God's action, for it is seen only in the end result. Ironically, though, once we actually desire it, it is embodied and shed abroad not only because we as embodied agents desire it but because as embodied agents we act on it. It is only a seeming paradox, then, when Weil says that "faith creates the truth to which it adheres."[21] Faith creates that truth in that it is an effect of the fecundity of the good. Faith *is* a good, made by the Good.

Now, what can we conclude for the relation of spirituality and theology given this analysis of the believer's presumed engagement with God? Let us first look at what Weil thought the relation was.

Weil, despite her own deep Platonism, was quite willing to distinguish between the intellect and the spirit and to argue that the direct concern of the intellect was with furthering a universal, but therefore abstract, method and that this forbade it direct access to God. Like Newman, she saw intellect as dealing with the notional, and not the particular or concrete, and God is particular and unique. God and God's Word are not instances of any general thought. Yet, she thought, the intellect in the life of faith can nevertheless operate as a sort of mediator between the spirit and the body. On the one hand, this means that although hard, critical thought is limited to an understanding of the finite world, the world it contemplates and orders the body for action in is a world of purpose and goodness that the spirit has apprehended and presented to it. On the other hand, whenever the intelligence grasps the world as an ordered whole it suggests to the spirit the possibility of a transcendent, creative purpose which the spirit may then grasp. These two operations of the intellect are not exclusive acts, however, but ones that interpenetrate. Thus, at the same time, that thought can be inspired to that inspiration. Or, in our terms, theology as critical thought, even as a second-order discipline if it is indeed always that, can still be the means of intellectually ordering a vision of the spirit and creating a world for faithful action, and also a means by which the spirit can find increased opportunity to wait upon God's action.

Weil's way of putting this involves saying things in a way that is strong drink for the contemporary theologian or philosopher. But this can also be put another way that is more modest. It is this: If, as Weil suggests, the movement of faith is a submission of the whole person, including the intellect, to an active engagement with God, then it must be understood that this movement is motivated by a desire for the eternal generation of the good. Whether or not faith has actually engaged God is only known experimentally. Nevertheless, this means not only as Farrer suggested, that the religious idea of God *begins* in experience, but that it is the inherent motivation of faith itself to coordinate all of one's being, including one's thought, in such a way that the perfection that it originally engaged is shed abroad both in one's own being and in the world at large. It is the coordination of thought and life; it is "faith working through love."

Theology and the Inner Word

I would like to put this yet another way, a way that is far more ancient, and which may well be the seed of its later bloom. In the writings of St. Augustine, the good bishop develops the notion of what he calls an "inner word." What he means by the "inner word" is a word formed in the soul that stands behind the vocally expressed word that issues from the mouth and that falls upon the ear. The importance of that inner word is that it contains our knowledge and appreciation and concern for what we say.

Now the function of the inner word in Augustine's thought is not as an inner explanation for what we say; talking is not a matter of translating from "mentalese" to Latin or English. Rather, Augustine recognized, what we say is not just out there, and it is not neutral. There is a sort of shape or form to what we say that involves us and gives us, the thinkers, away in what is thought and said. This is understandable, since for Augustine what constitutes knowledge in the mind of the thinker is a unity of understanding, memory, and will. What knowledge is, therefore, is not simply a fact, but the mind of the thinker as well. And what is known, insofar as it is known, is in an important sense the shape of the thing itself, consented to and entertained by the mind, shaping the mind in relation to it.

There are, I suppose, huge epistemological issues that can be raised here. But they are not the most important ones at all. What I am concerned to think about is what the personal and moral dimensions of knowing are, given this sort of view of knowledge. Or, even more simply, I am concerned to note that there *are* personal and moral dimensions to knowing and that is what Augustine is after. And to the degree that there are such dimensions, it seems to me that knowing becomes a task not simply of knowing what is the case (after all, Augustine recognizes, the devil himself knows the existence of God, probably even better than most), but of forming a personal inner word that exhibits justice to what is known, and which thereby makes us just. The task of knowing in the fullest sense for Augustine — and I think for Weil and Pascal too — therefore is always a matter of becoming something ourselves, a matter of unifying our understanding, memory, and will. For often, Augustine recognized, the inner word we express is an expression of our own inner fragmentation, and what is known is shaped by selfish self-willing.

In the case of the moral virtues, and in the case of knowing God, to form that inner word is to become that very thing we know, for to know these things is not simply to know something, it is to have a certain shape to what else we know; it is to be a certain way ourselves. Thus Augustine explains: "The word conceived and the word born are the very same when the will finds rest in knowledge itself, as is the case in the love of spiritual things. For instance, he who knows righteousness perfectly, and loves it perfectly, is already righteous."[22] To know God is to know God's word and to love it, and in so doing, it is to make that word our inner word, the very shape of our lives; it gives shape to all the words we speak. To know God as the Selfsame, to know the Selfsame, "that which always exists in the same way; that which is not now one thing and again a different thing,"[23] *is* to be healed of our own fragmentation of spirit.

Now if theology actually believes that it has an object of knowledge and that that object is God, then it seems that something like what Weil and Augustine are pointing to is right. Namely, it appears that the ultimate task of theology is transformation of the thinker, of fitting him or her to the inner life of God. Otherwise, it is nothing more than what is insidiously called "religious studies" in most university curricula, one of the few intellectual disciplines where professors do not have to believe that they have a real subject matter or that they need to be proficient practitioners.

This can be put less contentiously by stating briefly what differences this might make to the intellectual discipline of theology. (The personal difference to the thinker should be obvious by this point.)

For much of modernity, theology, once queen of the sciences, has had to establish itself as a science at all. No longer that which defines "knowledge," its intellectual worth has been measured by scientific methodology. Even in the presently more generous time of postpositivism, a time when theology has been conceded some kind of distinctive subject matter, it has faced attempts to make it in the image of the established natural sciences, even by its friends. Thus, for example, Wolfhart Pannenberg has called for "a general concept of science . . . which would . . . transcend particularity and unite theology and the other sciences."[24] Ian Barbour, in a well-meaning attempt to find some sort of rapprochement between science and religion, has made theology "critical reflection on the life and thought of the religious community . . . [whose] context is always the worshipping community."[25] It is in the way it organizes its knowledge, in its models, that Barbour finds links to science and sees the possibility of fruitful interaction between theological and scientific knowledge.

Now, as I have described matters, there may well be much to be harvested from such suggestions. Insofar as theology is a notional and an intellectual discipline it includes critical thought. Insofar as it is a function of faith it does too, for it seeks the multiplication of the good, in the intellect as much as in anything. This includes critical thought, to the extent that it enables the multiplication of the good through teaching, apologetics, exegesis, and even interreligious dialogue. In this sense faith is not innately unscientific, dogmatic, and credulous. In fact, insofar as it is earnestly attentive to unexpected movements of God's action in multiplying his good, it can positively invite method, freedom of opinion, and critical judgment so that its object may be universal.

Nevertheless, to leave it at that level is to understand things at what will be a secondary level. It may well be to leave intact numerous assumed mischaracterizations of both faith and theology. This includes taking belief to precede faith, and to take faith as *chiefly* an intellectual position opposed to knowledge, which can be discussed strictly notionally. In each of these cases, the sense that faith is also an order of the heart that reason does not know (Pascal), or an inner word, the shape of our minds and knowledge (Augustine), or the ordering of our lives in light of the Good we desire (Weil) is ignored.

In this sense, what *its* real place in intellectual life is may well be ignored, as well as consequently what it has to offer to thought. What that contribution might be can be seen in a point that Weil makes in *The Need for Roots*. In a section dedicated to trying to find ways that human life can be rerooted in the world of necessity, and by its mediation, in the life of God, Weil suggests that the key to much of modern science is understanding its lack of motivation to think on any sort of overarching Good, its failure to think about the relation of the Necessary to the Good. Thus when modern science studies truth by studying the web of necessity of which the universe is composed, as it ought, it has left matters at that: blind, brute necessity. It has not put the surveying intellect and the order it discerns within the world within any larger context; it has not sought to think about how its symbolic world signals an overarching order that is the presence of the Good. And Weil thinks it does, or should, signal such an order. She writes: "The order of the world is the same as the beauty of the world. . . . It is one and the same thing, which with respect to God is eternal Wisdom; with respect to the universe, perfect obedience; with respect to love, beauty; with respect to our intelligence, balance of necessary relations; with respect to our flesh, brutal force."[26] The point applied to theology is this: The primary importance of theology (or philosophy, as Plato, Epictetus, and Augustine called it) is not simply to contribute to the construction of intellectual representations of the world, although it can do that too; it is to submit them and to submit the representing mind, to a higher order. It is to make us recognize that there is no knowledge worth having that does not involve self-knowledge or moral and spiritual questions. It is to force us to recognize another dimension to thought, which in the modern world has been so monodimensional.

That is how Plato, Augustine, Epictetus, Pascal, and Weil approached knowledge. That is what I learned from Dick Allen at a lunch table.

NOTES

1. On this notion and others mentioned in this section, see David Burrell's contribution to this volume.
2. Blaise Pascal, *Pensées and the Provincial Letters,* no. 233, trans. W. F. Trotter and Thomas M'Crie (New York: Random House, 1941), 83.
3. W. K. Clifford, "The Ethics of Belief," from *Lectures and Essays* (1879).
4. Thomas Aquinas, *Summa Theologiae* 1, q.2. a.2.
5. Diogenes Allen, *Three Outsiders* (Cambridge, Mass.: Cowley Publications, 1983), 39–40. Cf. "The Wager Argument is thus used to show a particular kind of person who does not believe that it is his passions, not intellectual reasons, which hinder his belief, and Pascal offers him a way to overcome this particular barrier to belief. So the Wager Argument belongs to the level of the 'flesh,' which is below the level of the mind" (p. 40).
6. A position for which, we might add, he admits he was deeply indebted to Diogenes Allen.
7. Austin Farrer, *Saving Belief* (New York: Morehouse-Barlow Co., 1964), chap. 1.
8. Ibid., 22.
9. Austin Farrer, *Faith and Speculation* (New York: New York University Press, 1964), 10.
10. Jeffrey Eaton, *The Logic of Theism* (Lanham, Md.: University Press of America, 1980), 35.

11. Farrer, *Faith and Speculation,* 22.
12. Ibid., 28.
13. Ibid., 35.
14. This distinction is cited in Edward Farley's consideration of the problem of spirituality in *Theologia* (Philadelphia: Fortress Press, 1983), 39.
15. Cf. G. R. Evans's comment on this change and development in the nature of theology: "The fire and energy with which they worked upon the new academic discipline of theology came from something more than intellectual curiosity, strong though that was in many of them. Theology has an importance for the believer which sets it apart from all other disciplines of mind. The tendency for the academic study of theology to shed the devotional and contemplative concomitants which accompanied exercises in speculative theology within the monastic tradition should not be allowed to blind us to the continuing association of all these elements in the minds of individual scholars" (*Old Arts and New Theology* [Oxford: Oxford University Press, 1980], 215).
16. See S. Weil, *Pensées sans ordre concernant l'amour de dieu,* (Paris: Gallimard, 1962), 136; *Notebooks* (London: Routledge & Kegan Paul, 1956), 434; *First and Last Notebooks* (London: Oxford University Press, 1962), 342.
17. Weil, *First and Last Notebooks,* 316. Note: Weil tends to use "God" and "Good" somewhat interchangeably.
18. E.g., "Last Text," in S. Weil, *Gateway to God,* ed. David Raper (New York: Crossroad, 1982): "When I say 'I believe' I do not mean that I take over for myself what the Church says on these matters, affirming them as one might affirm empirical facts or geometrical theorems, but that through love, I hold on to the perfect, unseizable, truth which these mysteries contain, and that I try to open my soul to it so that its light may penetrate into me" (p. 62).
19. Weil, *First and Last Notebooks,* 132.
20. Ibid., 307.
21. Ibid., 291.
22. Augustine, *De Trinitate,* Book IX, chap. 9.
23. Augustine, *Commentary on the Psalms,* Ps. 121, 3.5.
24. W. Pannenberg, *Theology and the Philosophy of Science* (Philadelphia: Westminster Press, 1976), 19.
25. Ian Barbour, *Religion in an Age of Science* (San Francisco: HarperCollins, 1990), 267.
26. S. Weil, *The Need for Roots* (London: Routledge & Kegan Paul, 1978), 281.

5

HOW TO BE A CHRISTIAN PHILOSOPHER
IN THE POSTMODERN WORLD

EDWARD HENDERSON

> Sing praise to God, who spoke through man
> In diff'ring times and manners,
> For those great seers who've led the van,
> Truth writ upon their banners;
> For those who once blazed out the way,
> For those who still lead on today,
> To God be thanks and glory.
>
> . . . .
>
> For Socrates who, phrase by phrase,
> Talked men to truth, unshrinking,
> And left for Plato's mighty grace
> To mold our ways of thinking;
> For all who wrestled, sane and free,
> To win the unseen reality,
> To God be thanks and glory.

So wrote Percy Dearmer in a hymn naming Plato and Socrates with prophets and church poets and musicians.[1] The hymn allowed worshipers to praise God for the long tradition of Christian philosophy, a tradition that began in the earliest years of the church as philosophically educated converts sought ways to understand their new faith.

Now, in these last years of the twentieth century, we find ourselves swept by a powerful philosophical current to the conclusion that all human understanding is situated: we cannot, by means of a metaphysically neutral and universal rationality, escape the limits and conditions set by language, culture, and history so as to attain sure and final knowledge of the way things are. The Cartesian project of absolutely grounded and indubitable knowledge is dead. Can we still praise God for Socrates and Plato? How can one be a Christian philosopher in this postmodern world?

One answer: Deny that the truth of faith and the reality of God transcend the language or story in which they are affirmed. This answer assumes "strong postmodernism," the position that if we are to talk of truth, we must take it as a function of the language game we play, the conceptual framework by which we think, the form of life by which we live, or the story in which we live. The primary narrative, the grammar of the language game, or the defining concepts of the framework are neither true nor false: they are the means of believing, not the objects of belief; they are posited and used, not inquired about and known. Those who live by the Christian story, therefore, may speak of truth and falsity according to the story and within the life it structures; but if they speak of the truth of the story itself, they can rightly mean only that it is the story they choose to live by. Any rational inquiry that seeks to establish the foundations for the story must fail. If there is any reality "behind" the story, it is not an unsituated truth about an unsituatedly real God; it is some noncognitive motive—for example, will to power (Nietzsche being currently a major inspirational source for strong postmodernism). There is no rational access to any truth or reality outside the story unless it belongs to some other story. "It's turtles all the way down!"

The problem with strong postmodernism is that it is an inescapable part of faith that the God faith believes is a God whose reality transcends the story by which God is known and loved. If believers accept strong postmodernism, they must simply assert their story with its reference to the unsituatedly real God. There are two ways of doing this: the relativistic way and the fideistic way. Relativism would mean acknowledging that all stories are on equal footing. Fideism, on the other hand, would rule out reflective considerations and questions about the story and simply assert that the Christian story alone gives true knowledge of the reality beyond all situations. For Christians who believe that the reflective, questioning mind is one of God's good creatures, it does not seem right to take the fideistic approach. And, inasmuch as Christians believe the God they worship cannot be reduced to a function in a story and set on all fours with all other stories, the relativistic approach is also unsatisfactory. Consequently, strong postmodernism does not seem the most promising way to be a Christian philosopher in the postmodern world.

Diogenes Allen[2] takes neither the fideistic approach nor the relativistic approach, but shows instead that the perennial Augustinian way of believing in order to understand remains suitable for a world that insists on the situatedness of all human understanding. The Augustinian believer practices philosophy as a discipline within faith, as part of a cooperation with God in God's work of transforming the believer into a person who loves God with all his being and his neighbor as himself. The believer whose heart is thus open trusts God as one who brings it about that there is a way things are, independently of the situated ways humans understand them. Such a reflective philosophical believer also trusts that the God of truth assists in improving understanding, making it more truthful about the way things are and about the God who makes them so.

How can such an exercise of faith be a practice of philosophy? We can see how if we understand faith according to the biblical story, and philosophy according to the tradition of Platonic Socratism. For Christian faith and Platonic Socratism have analogous structures. Faith insists both on the situatedness of all human understanding and on the reality of a God who transcends all situations and makes things as they are. Platonic Socratism similarly insists on the situatedness of human understanding and affirms a reality that transcends all situations and makes things as they are. Note well! Christian faith and Socratic philosophy claim *situated* understanding of *unsituated* reality. That is not the same as *unsituated* understanding of unsituated reality. That they do not claim.

The analogy between Christian faith and Socratic philosophy can be seen further in their non-Cartesian character. The Cartesian project distorted both faith and philosophy. It distorted faith because its identification of rationality with certainty led to the conviction that faith was reasonable only if philosophy could establish for it an absolutely grounded foundation in an indubitably certain rational knowledge of God's existence and nature. Yet traditional faith itself required no such unsituated knowledge as a necessary foundation. On the contrary, it insisted (and insists) on the situatedness of all human knowledge, including the knowledge of God.

The Cartesian project analogously distorted the Socratic method of examining opinions. Descartes's method of doubt in his *Meditations* was to throw out every opinion that could not be established with presumed unsituated certainty. But Platonic Socratism does not proceed by getting rid of uncertain beliefs; it takes them as the places where transcendent truth appears (*doxa* = opinion = appearance) or shows up, then uses them to improve understanding in a way that always includes "Socratic ignorance" and thus always recognizes the situatedness of understanding.

To understand how philosophy can be practiced as a discipline of faith, we need to look in more detail at the structure of both faith and Socratic philosophy. We shall interpret faith in the light of certain biblical stories, the stories of Creation and Fall and the stories of Jesus, always taking it not as a mode of cognition only, but as a comprehensive way of life. Similarly, we shall interpret Socratic philosophy in the light of Plato's presentation of Socrates in *Apology, Republic, Meno, Symposium,* and related dialogues, arguing that it is also a comprehensive way of life and not only a mode of cognition.

The analyses will show how Christian faith and Socratic philosophy are analogous. Each begins with the acceptance of human limits (situatedness) and proceeds by loving trust in and dependence on a transcendent reality, in relation to which practitioners are willing to suffer the loss of conditional goods for the sake of being transformed, and in hope of membership in a community of agapic relationships. Diogenes Allen's influence on these analyses will be so patent as to need no explanation.

Faith in Biblical Perspective

The Stories
of Creation and Fall

The stories placed at the beginning of the Hebrew scriptures present the structure life must have if it is to be lived as faith in the God who is creator of all that is, and they provide a dramatic theological background for the remainder of the Pentateuch, indeed, for the whole of the Hebrew Bible and Christian New Testament. The Priestly story of creation and the Yahwistic stories about Adam and Eve present human beings as inescapably situated in the middle of a world. Although the stories give humans a privileged position with ruling functions, bearing the image of God and drawing life from the breath of God, they do not give them final knowledge or control over the world in which they are brought by God to be. Whatever else may be true of human beings, this one fact is critical: human life is life in the confusing middle of things, finite, limited, dependent, *situated* between God and not being.

The story of Adam and Eve's disobedience is the story of their response to the condition of human situatedness. Temptation, fall, sin: these have to do with the way God's human images, human persons, live in their situatedness. The fall to the temptation discloses the wrong way to be situated in the middle. The right way is implied as the way that Adam and Eve abandoned. Tradition calls the wrong way the way of sin; the right way, the way of faith.

According to the story, Adam and Eve find themselves in a good world, a garden. The creator has intended good for them in making the world the kind of world it is. In it their needs are met. They enjoy intimacy with YHWH. They also enjoy intimacy with each other and an ideal relation with the other creatures in their world. They are above the other creatures, not only by having a ruling position among them, but by being, as the Priestly story has it, in God's image or, as the Yahwist has it, by receiving their life from the breath of God.

It is, nevertheless, clear that they are limited and confused. Their privilege in the garden does not mean that they need only to wait passively while all they need will be handed them. They are to exercise their peculiar, God-imaging abilities so as to care for the garden, its creatures, and themselves. Yet it is clear from the story's command that they do not have the knowledge of good and evil, a knowledge that might seem necessary to fulfilling their God-assigned roles. Even life in the garden was not without the difficulties of deciding what to do and how to do it. Being creatures situated in the middle carries with it responsibility and the need for wisdom to guide its exercise. Being images of God makes Adam and Eve different from other creatures. They can imagine various possibilities and attempt to effect various outcomes. It is the awareness of those possibilities that makes their responsible roles possible and wisdom about good and evil desirable!

The serpent is an image of the way such imagining of possibilities unfolds. As the craftiest thing God has made, the serpent represents something within human creatures, that very distinctiveness that makes them images of God and breathers of divine breath, able to know they are situated between God and not-being and that there are other possibilities than those already enjoyed. At the same time, the serpent, also being other than Adam or Eve, represents the way ideas and imaginings seem to come from outside their minds and the way envisionments of possibilities tend to lead where there has been no expectation they would. In such imaginings, God's images deceive themselves. The questions and suggested answers of the serpent are such self-deception.

The serpent proposes a radical possibility: Adam and Eve might escape their perplexing situation in the middle and acquire for themselves the knowledge that makes God the creator and places God beyond the confining limits of the created world. For the knowledge envisioned is the knowledge of good and evil—precisely the knowledge a creator would have to have in order to create a world and call it good. Adam and Eve, being in the middle, would have opinions about good and evil, but not knowledge. To their situated imaginations it might well seem that such knowledge ought already to have been given by the creator, that it is owed them by the one who made them responsible. Furthermore, such knowledge is attractive, desirable for its own sake.

The temptation is, essentially, to seize the knowledge of good and evil and thereby become divine, to become the creator in God's place, to stop being creatures and to become creators. That such a change could be possible is an illusion and a deception. It is also the heart of sin.

The sin of Adam and Eve consists in their rejecting the good intended by God's creating. Rather than accepting God's good, they attempt to change the *kind* of world God has created into a fundamentally different kind of world—"kind" of world, we say, because the stories do not say God determines every event and action, leaving no room for human discretion, judgment, evaluation, and decision, room, that is, for considered actions that would make important differences in the garden. God does not command Adam and Eve to sit passively while all their needs and the needs of their fellow creatures are automatically met and all relationships kept automatically in harmony. They are commanded instead to exercise dominion, to till and keep the garden, to do the things that need to be done in order to realize the good God intends for them and the rest of creation.

The story represents only a certain kind of action as the sinful denial of God's good and as the attempt to re-create the world in a fundamentally different way. Sinful action is that action in which created and situated human agents attempt to change their status as situated creatures to being themselves creators, by seizing that knowledge of good and evil and exercising the creator's role.

Another side of the stories of Creation and Fall is that they define the life of faith, the opposite of sin. A lived relationship of faith in the God of their creation is the life Adam and Eve ought to have chosen. It is the life that accepts the world as a good that God has created and themselves as creatures situated in the middle of it. Thus the stories present two opposed ways to be human: the faithful way and the unfaithful way. The unfaithful proceeds by setting up some human understanding of good and evil as the equal of God's: absolute, final, transcendent, able to be applied to the re-creation of the world according to the standards claimed as transcendently true. To attempt or to claim such knowledge is to attempt to escape from human situatedness and to be God. The faithful way, on the other hand, must be a way that recognizes and lives by obedient dependence on God, accepting as good the world God creates and intends, and, as part of that good, one's own condition of situated middleness. Although the stories of Creation and Fall say little to describe that way of faith, the rest of the Hebrew and Christian scriptures are about little else than God's calls to faith, God's people's failures at it, and God's responses to those failures. We are justified in reading the lessons of those stories into the stories of Creation and Fall.

Letting ourselves be guided by the other stories of faith, we can say that the life of faith in the story of Adam and Eve has an interpersonal form. So long as they are faithful, God walks and talks with Adam and Even in the garden. God also communicates to them the divine desire that they not eat the fruit of the tree of the knowledge of good and evil. When they do, God calls them up short and acts to counter the effects of their disobedience. So long as they keep faith, Adam and Eve live by recognizing God as God, showing love to God as the source of good by desiring what God desires, obeying God's commands, trusting that doing so will ultimately lead to good, and enjoying God's presence.

Beyond the stories of Creation and Fall, the Bible presents, reiterates, extends, and deepens these same themes in story after story. Among these the great story of the exodus, with its wilderness sojourn and the giving of the Law, is most important as presenting the way of faith. Here are the themes of recognizing God as God and the source of good, of God's knowledge of good and evil and God's desire for the good expressed as commandments, of the struggle to understand and to desire what God desires, to obey what God commands, and to trust that doing so will lead to the real good God desires, no matter what suffering must be endured as a result. More important still is the specification of God's desire summed up in the Shema and in what Christians know as the great commandment: "Hear, O Israel, the Lord your God is one God; and you shall love the Lord your God with all your heart, with all your mind, and with all your strength; and your neighbor as yourself!" It is surely not contrary to the theology of the biblical redactors to read this specification of divine knowledge and desire back into the stories of Creation and Fall.

In these stories, set by the redactors at the beginning of the Hebrew Bible, is the heart of that way of understanding and being that is the form of life called "faith." On this account, faith is not primarily the acceptance of beliefs as true on the ground that they have been revealed by some supernatural act of God operating outside of and coercively overriding human rationality. Nor is it the acceptance of beliefs as true because they have been certified by the external authority of unsituated reasons. It is a way of living in the world that involves both an understanding of the human condition and a commitment to live in it by means of a personally structured dependence on and engagement with the God who transcends the world and is the Good by which it exists. It is a form of life that attempts to embrace the good God intends and trusts that doing so will in fact result in the realization of God's real good for the faithful.

Jesus, Exemplar of Faith

It may strike some as odd to take Jesus as the exemplar of faith, for many understand him docetically, as the Christ who simply is the God in whom persons are supposed to place their faith. As God, having the knowledge of good and evil, he would not be faith's exemplary practitioner. He would know and live by ultimate and unsituated knowledge in the divine certainty of its unsituated truth. But docetism is not orthodoxy. The Jesus of orthodox faith is a Jesus whose humanity is real, the Son of God whose incarnation is into the situated existence in which all humans find themselves. This Jesus is the man who lived the life of faith perfectly. Consequently, we must say that the New Testament presents Jesus as perfecting the life of faith.

Begin with the assumption of the real humanity of Jesus of Nazareth. He is a man born into a particular time and place, situated in a particular historical, cultural, and linguistic context. His mind was formed in the setting of first-century Judaism, under the tutelage of his family and the village rabbi, under the pressures and conflicts brought on by the Roman presence, and in awareness of a variety of Jewish understandings of their history and hopes for their future.[3] Under the kenotic assumption, we need not suppose that Jesus' mind was somehow an unlimited and perfect knowledge of all things as they are and ought to be. He could not have explained Gödel's proof, presented a comparative analysis of social and political organization since the appearance of the human species, settled the question of whether the universe oscillates between big bangs and big crunches, or told who would win the Heisman Trophy in 1996. What he knew was the Hebrew scriptures, the customs, practices, and values of the Judaism of his time. As Austin Farrer put it, what Jesus knew was not *that* he was the incarnation of the eternal Son of the Father. What he knew was *how* to be the Son of God and Messiah in the world in which he was situated.[4] Even that was an understanding he had to achieve in the effort to love God with all his heart and his neighbors as himself.

The Christian scriptures present Jesus as fulfilling Jewish hopes, yet doing it in so unexpected a way that even his family, closest followers, and most intimate friends did not understand until after the resurrection—and, indeed, we cannot even say that later Christian sages, or ourselves today, have fully comprehended. Jesus is a new and more faithful Moses, come to deliver God's people from bondage. He is the anointed heir of David, the coming King, the Suffering Servant, the Son of Man, Messiah—all images from the Hebrew scriptures in terms of which a Jew who sought to be faithful and obedient would be expected to think. They are images that define the particularity and peculiarity of the situation in which Jesus had his being. Jesus, it may be and has been argued,[5] did understand himself through them. But his life adapted and redefined them.

The decisive element in Jesus' peculiar fulfillment of these roles and their hopes is that he saw how to live them in perfect faithfulness. The Gospel representations of Jesus show him as the perfectly faithful man and expand the presentation of the life of faith beyond the Genesis stories.

The stories of Jesus' baptism and temptations in the wilderness can be read in relation to the story of Adam and Eve. At baptism Jesus receives the breath of God, just as Adam did. This confirms his belief that he, like Adam, is a beloved Son of God. But Jesus is perplexed about what that means and about how to live up to that identity. As Adam and Eve were perplexed, so was Jesus. As Adam and Eve were in intimate relation with the Father, Jesus went into the wilderness to be with the Father. And, as in the Genesis story, the Tempter comes. The temptations present possibilities for ways of being God's beloved Son, ways that if chosen would essentially reject the world God has created and try to replace it with a different kind of world, based on different ideas about good and evil. The temptation to turn stones to bread is to try to be in the world as one not subject to the need for food and drink, perhaps even to transform the world into one in which all the needs that make people dependent are satisfied and the dependence removed. The idea was a delusion. It called for the rejection of Jesus' own place as a creature situated in the world and for the rejection of God's knowledge of good and evil. It also called for an effort to re-create the world according to the idea that the real good is a world in which there is no neediness or dependence.

The temptation to throw himself unharmed from the Temple was the temptation to use religion as a manipulation both of God and of his neighbors. It would be an abuse of intimacy with the Father because it would be an attempt to make people follow without having to be transformed into lovers of God and neighbor and without having to suffer the loss of conditional goods. It would hide from them the nature of God's desire and the essence of faith. It would be a re-creation of the world in the belief that the real good is a world in which humans overcome all passivity to its limits and conditions. Such a world would not be a real world but a fantasy, a dream in which, through religion, the world would be made perfectly malleable to human desire. That is not the world God has created.

The last temptation was to choose coercive power as the ultimate good by which the world should be ordered. Such a means of gaining the allegiance of people, even if the purpose were to do them good, would make it impossible to realize the real good for which God has created, the good of loving communion among God and God's human creatures. For love and coercion are ultimately incompatible. To love is to desire the good of the beloved and so to rejoice in its fulfillment and to sorrow in its loss. This loving form of life can only come from within. It cannot be externally coerced. The way of power, however necessary it may be as a conditional good, is not an ultimate good, such that re-creating the world by it could fulfill God's loving desire for the good of his creatures. Jesus saw that and rejected the temptation as an unfaithful way.

All the temptations, then, are based on human ideas about what is ultimately good and evil and what kind of world would make the realization of ultimate good possible. Jesus' victory over the temptations was the enactment of belief and trust that the real good God intends is the good of living in loving communion with the Father and with one's neighbors. The temptations asked him to substitute false goods for God's good — and then to claim the place of God by re-creating the world according to the false goods.

The temptation stories frame the presentation of Jesus' life as a faithful life, as a life lived by an understanding of how to be the faithful Son of God within the situation into which he was born. But the circumstances of his time and place threw up difficult challenges, in which the sinful possibilities were continuously present. It is the way Jesus responded to these challenges that reveals more completely what he understood to be required by God's desire and therefore by faith. As he proceeded to his ministry of bringing the kingdom, he lived by the form of personal communion in intimacy with the God he called Father, and he acted in the Father's name. He accepted his role as instrumental. It was his Father who would establish the kingdom. His claim to knowledge was limited to seeing how to be faithful to the Father in the light of what he saw as the heart of the Law and the Prophets: to love God with all his heart and his neighbor as himself. He taught the Father's desire and offered hope for its fulfillment. When he healed and fed he sought always to point beyond present events to their meaning in the life of faith, and thereby to bring others to a change of heart and mind, so that they too would see things from the standpoint of faith and embrace the divine desire as their own. He realized that his way of faith put him at odds with all those who were convinced their own sense of good and evil was unsituated truth. It became increasingly obvious that the kingdom, the life of faith in and loving communion with the Father and neighbors, was going to be rejected. It would be rejected by the people because they did not understand what it would be to love God and neighbor—even his own disciples could not grasp and accept its requirements. It would be rejected by the religious because they could not shake the sense that religion was an instrument in their hands. And it would be rejected by those who held political position because they could not give up the conviction that power was the good by which they would be saved.

Every encounter with the religious and with the politically established was a fresh temptation. The most important temptation he faced was presented by one of his own disciples, Peter, when he tried to talk Jesus out of giving himself up to the powers in Jerusalem, or, in a different setting, out of washing his feet. But the absolute core of the faith Jesus lived was seeing and being committed in trust to the fact that God had given a good world and that the only way to receive the good intended in it was to sacrifice everything else absolutely and unconditionally to the divine desire, the desire expressed in the commandment to love God and neighbor. Jesus withstood every temptation to abandon that faith. Rejection, suffering, death, he believed, could not stand in the way of that good. The Father can be trusted, no matter how impossible it may be for creatures to see how the victory is going to be won.

The handing over of Jesus, his trial, his crucifixion and burial constitute the ultimate victory over temptation and the way of sin, the ultimate victory of faith. Note that in the story of Jesus' arrest and trial, Jesus actually hands himself over in a complete surrender of power over his own life.[6] This act of faith was a fresh rejection in a new circumstance of the possibility that he might re-create the world according to some vision of his own rather than live by the commandment he had received. Jesus trusted that the Father's intended good would come only through his obedience to the great commandment and the refusal of any alternative, even though the Father's own knowledge of good and evil had brought about the very world in which the sinfulness that would put him to death was the ordinary way of life.

The resurrection negated neither the humanity nor the faithfulness of Jesus. Nowhere in the Gospel records did Jesus claim to have accomplished it himself. It was done for him. Neither did he claim to know when or exactly how the final fulfillment of the kingdom of faith would be accomplished. That, he said, is only for the Father to know. All Jesus claimed to know was that in his faithful life, the life that led inescapably through the crucifixion, the Father has brought the kingdom. In Jesus the purpose of creation was realized. His hope and faith were that it would become a kingdom of many members, all living by the Father's desire.

From this interpretation of the stories of Jesus we can distill the essential elements of his life of faith.

1. Jesus accepted the human condition of inescapable situatedness within a world.
2. Jesus understood that he should not try to escape his situatedness so as to create a different kind of world by means of his own putative knowledge of good and evil.
3. Jesus believed that the creator God, the God of Israel and of himself, is a God who intends good for his creatures. Good is, so to speak, built into the fabric of God's creation.
4. Jesus recognized in the great commandment the expression of God's own desire for creatures, the articulation in human terms of that knowledge of good and evil by which God has created.
5. Jesus let himself be completely formed by the divine desire, let himself be made who he is by an unconditional commitment to God and God's good as the only good that transcends all conditions.
6. Jesus trusted that unswerving obedience to the divine command would lead to the good God intends for his creatures.
7. Jesus was therefore willing to suffer through the loss of any or all conditional goods that might result from his trusting obedience to God.
8. Jesus lived this commitment in the form of interpersonal communion with and personal dependence on God as his Father, trusting that the Father would provide whatever help would be needed to fulfill the commitment.
9. Jesus saw that the good God intends can be completely realized only in a community in which all are formed by the divine desire, in which all truly love God and their neighbors as themselves. He therefore saw that his life of faith pointed toward a community of perfected love and that his work included initiating and hoping for such a community.

Turning now from Jerusalem to Athens, we shall see that Socratic philosophy, although different from it, exhibits something very like the elements of faith, making it possible for philosophy to be practiced as a discipline within faith.

Platonic Socratism

In the immense divide between Jerusalem and Athens, certain familiar differences between Jewish and Greek intellectual situatedness stand out. Jewish monotheism and Greek polytheism have among their most important differences different senses of history, of the presence of the divine in the life of the nation, and of the connection between God and national and individual purpose. Second, there is the Jewish understanding that persons are embodied whole entities as opposed to the Greek division of the person into the metaphysically distinct soul and body. A third, and for our purposes most important, difference is that between the primary use of narrative understanding, on the one side, and the use of discursive philosophical questioning and reasoning, on the other. This amounts to the difference between understanding by reference to what particular human and divine agents do, on the one side, and understanding by reference to universal structures and principles, which are supposed to pervade the created order and be discernible in principle to all inquiring and reasoning minds, on the other.

In addition to these cultural and conceptual differences, there are the great differences between Jesus and Socrates themselves—as characters in their respective stories. Kierkegaard was right to stress the difference between Socrates as the midwife and Jesus as the incarnate Son of God. Christians affirm that momentous difference and the particular differences it makes. Can we imagine Socrates riding messianically into Athens on a donkey, saying, "Take my yoke upon you," or, gathered with his friends on the day of his execution, saying, "This is my body; this is my blood"? The two belong to very different worlds and are very different persons.

Diogenes Allen, in *Quest: The Search for Meaning through Christ*,[7] emphasizes that the Gospels present Jesus as concerned with saving persons whole, not with helping them understand universal principles. They present Jesus as one who actually has the power to effect saving transformations, turning people inside out, making them new persons, and incorporating them into the divine life through their relation with him. Thus he changes Zacchaeus through a few words of kindness and casts out "seven demons" from Mary Magdalene. Despite the completeness (*seven* demons) of her corruption, she is not beyond Jesus' transforming power. In fact, Jesus' ministry has just such transformations at its heart. Not so Socrates! He could awaken people to their ignorance, assist them in understanding themselves, possibly even move them toward more just lives by helping them improve their opinions about the universal principles of friendship, justice, *eros*, courage, beauty, and the like. But, as shown in the case of his close friendship with Alcibiades, he could not transform the heart. Indeed, he seems to have thought the heart does not need to be transformed, that all the transformation that is needed will follow on the attainment of knowledge, that to know the good is to do the good.

Furthermore, Socrates dedicated his life to helping the citizens of Athens, those who at least had the possibility of being among the *kala kagatha*, the beautiful and the good. He did not spend his time with the poor, the sick, the ugly, the outcast. He was not concerned with slaves, nor with women and children, but with those able to exercise political leadership within the city. Jesus, on the other hand, declared that he came to save sinners, and paid loving attention to all manner of them, including women, children, tax-collecting collusionists, and lepers.

Finally, Socrates tried to help others discover truths to live by, but he understood himself only as a midwife who helps others deliver what is already present within them. Jesus presented himself as the living presence of the Truth God is. He did not primarily teach universal truths for the understanding; he embodied the truth of the Father's love and will. His life, crucifixion, and resurrection *were* (and are) the message. He gave himself, not universal principles. In receiving Jesus, one did not (and does not) so much improve one's mind as enter into the life of God as a community of love. That is, Jesus lived, within the circumstances and limits of the world, the eternal love, obedience, trust, and hope that constitute the life of eternal God, the life shared among the persons of the Trinity. To receive Jesus in faith was (and is) to let oneself be incorporated into that life. Experiencing this, Christians have affirmed Jesus as God incarnate, Savior of the world. Despite his exemplary courage, his concern for the welfare of Athens, and his willingness to die rather than renounce his divine calling, and despite his being Plato's primary example of the just life, Socrates does not come close to being the Truth that is eternal *agapē* in our midst. Nevertheless, the life of Socratic philosophy is a comprehensive form of life that shares essential structural features with the life of faith Jesus exemplified.

We need not worry with the question of the historical Socrates,[8] for the Socrates who defines the philosophical life is the dramatic character Plato gives us in his dialogues, particularly the middle and later ones. *Apology, Crito, Meno, Phaedo, Gorgias, Republic, Symposium,* and *Timaeus* are especially important. Taken together they present Socrates as a philosophical hero, as a person whose method of testing opinions was part of a wise, courageous, self-controlled, just life. The dialogues provide the arguments for this way of life and give us Socrates as the one who preeminently exemplifies it. Therefore, all this essay's references to Socrates are to Plato's character.

Socratic Philosophy

Socratic philosophy is Socratic life, and that is the life of becoming and being just. It is not, as professional "philosophers" typically take it to be, simply the cognitive method of testing opinions and constructing ways of understanding. Socratic method as a cognitive process is an essential part of Socratic philosophy, but it is not the whole thing. We see this when we pay attention to the drama of Socrates and not only to the arguments. Always Plato sets the arguments about opinions and the positive construction of hypotheses within the context of Socrates' life. The discussions interpret Socrates' life, and Socrates' life interprets the discussions. Thus, it is clear in *Republic* that Socrates is the example of the just life lived in an unjust world, being wholly just but being believed to be unjust, suffering the punishment of the criminal yet standing forth in spite of it as stronger, happier, and more beautiful because of the intrinsically good individual he has made himself through the love of the Good and the Beautiful.

Socratic philosophy, therefore, as the just life, is the art of ruling over oneself, over the circumstances of one's life and one's relationships with other persons in order to produce oneself as a real good,[9] both a good for the community to use in its own activity of being just and a good for and within oneself. As an art, justice is practiced on the basis of knowledge — about what one's real good is and about how to get that good out of oneself and one's circumstances.

This Socratic life, as much more than cognitive method as it is, nevertheless defines the form philosophical cognition must take when incorporated into Christian faith. And it does so because it is a way of knowing that belongs within a form of life that parallels faith. Like faith, Socratic philosophical life recognizes the inescapable situatedness of human knowing, affirms a reality that transcends all situations, and proceeds through loving trust in that transcendent reality, cultivating agapic community, and suffering the loss of conditional goods for the sake of the one good that ultimately matters, namely, being an intrinsically good individual, a truly beautiful reality in the world.

The Socratic method of examining opinions operates within the confused and confusing conditions of community life. Persons seeking happiness find themselves confronted by a host of problems. What is courage? friendship? justice? Socrates' activity begins in the middle of that confusion by bringing the problems to consciousness in the form of questions and eliciting answers from the various kinds of characters that make up the city's population.

The answers they give are opinions, *doxai*, beliefs, convictions. Their bearers initially hold them as straightforwardly true. In most cases, too, the opinions proposed as answers come from beyond the persons who give them. They come, for example, from one's father, or from a poet, such as Simonides or Homer, perhaps from a Sophist, or even, they sometimes say, from the gods.

Socrates' aim in the method is to test whether an opinion proposed is for its holder knowledge, mere opinion, or something in between. Note that opinions are not in themselves bad things. They are not the causes of ignorant or unjust life, at least not simply and directly. For opinions, as the word *doxa* suggests, are *appearances*. But appearances are appearings *of* something, places where some reality shows up or is manifest. We could say that if we want to become wise, opinions are our first friends. We simply must begin with them; without them we could never get started. For Socrates there is no question of sweeping the ground clear of all opinions and beginning, as Descartes attempted to do, from the ground zero of absolutely certain knowledge, building certainty upon certainty. Rather, the pursuit of knowledge must keep the opinions present and work with them, converting them into improved understanding.[10]

That Socrates knows and accepts this means that he knows and accepts that we human beings are *situated in the middle of confusion,* between the divine knowledge of the way things are and ought to be, on one side, and no understanding at all, on the other. That is what opinions are, the appearances of reality within the situatedness of human existence.

Socrates' first objective in the practice of his method is to determine whether the one with the opinion understands what it means and what its status is. Does he think it is knowledge, lifting him out of the limits of situated being and making him a god, giving him thereby authority to order life on its terms? If so, can the holder give the reasons that justify thinking that that way of understanding is absolute truth?

Of course, we find that the opinion holder usually begins by thinking he has divine knowledge but that he cannot give the necessary reasons that will show the understanding to be true. That being so, Socrates' next objective is to bring the opinion holder to recognize that the opinion is not knowledge and that he is not a god. If that can be accomplished, then the opinion holder will be brought to the first and most important kind of wisdom, to Socratic ignorance, to knowing he does not possess an unsituated knowledge of the way things are.

The attainment of Socratic wisdom is the explicit recognition of situatedness. As Jesus accepts his situatedness within the world and does not attempt to live as though he were the creator, so Socrates accepts his situatedness and does not claim to know. Nor does he stop with the recognition of situatedness. He continues to practice the method after the initial discovery of ignorance, going on in the conviction that once the ignorance of opinions is recognized, the opinions can be improved and their holder made wiser. It is important that wisdom be thus supported, for wisdom is the basis of the just life. Therefore, as Jesus seeks to lead those among whom he is situated into faithfulness within their creatureliness, so Socrates seeks to assist those among whom he is situated into an improved understanding that incorporates their recognition of ignorance and makes them more just.

Plato's Socrates did not think it possible to escape altogether the condition of human situatedness and so attain final, comprehensive, and unsituated knowledge of the way things are and the way they ought to be. Of course, it is not uncommon to read Plato the other way, as thinking unsituated knowledge is possible. But if we take him that way we set the life of Socratic philosophy at odds with the life of faith. To make Socratic philosophy a model for Christian philosophy in the postmodern world, we have to read the dialogues as presenting a Socrates who regarded ignorance as an ineradicable ingredient of all human understanding and our ability always to recognize its presence as a necessary part of wisdom.

Consider the Divided Line and Cave images. They can be taken consistently with the idea that Socrates' method is a method for living between divine absolute knowledge and no understanding at all. The *Meno, Republic, Phaedo,* and *Timaeus* can all be read this way. Charles Bigger, Edward Ballard,[11] and Iris Murdoch[12] have stressed it. In the *Meno,* to take one instance, Socrates responds in two parts to Meno's argument that it is impossible to learn. One part is the myth of recollection, the other the experiment with Meno's slave. When finished, Socrates offers an important perspective, saying in effect (at 86 b, c) that "I do not know whether this story [that learning is recollection] is true or not, but I am sure that it will make us better if we believe it is possible to improve our understanding than if we allow ourselves to be stymied by the idea that learning is impossible."

The point is that Plato does not present the theory of recollection as an instance of divine or unsituated knowledge, an unambiguous and absolute grasp of reality as it is in itself. It is a device for creatures who must live in the confusion that goes with being situated in time and place. To them it says, "You will do better if you become aware of your ignorance and believe your opinions can be improved and learning can go forward. But if you think the opinions you have are all you can have, you are condemned to make no improvement, to draw no closer in your situatedness to the unsituated truth about unsituated reality."

The same point applies to the images of the Good, the Divided Line, and the Cave. They are constructions by a Socrates who knows and accepts that he is a person situated between divine, unsituated knowledge about unsituated reality, on the one hand, and no understanding at all, on the other. The image of the Good is an essential part of these pictures, and Socrates is quite clear that the image is but a likeness, not unsituated knowledge by an unsituated mind. The great images of *Republic*, so often taken to express an utterly optimistic rationalism, are, in the words of *Timaeus*, "likely stories" (28d, 30c). In addition, there is the explicit claim in *Theaetetus* that knowledge is "true belief with an account" (*Theaetetus*, 206d–210b).[13]

Further, even if Plato thinks in *Republic* that knowledge can ultimately escape the situatedness of human understanding, Socrates does not claim to have done so. The realization of that kind of knowledge is at least postponed to another life, to a different condition of being in which the limits of human situatedness are different. Furthermore there is recognition that even in the life to come, knowledge would not be simply and immediately given; it would have to be achieved through the dialectical process.

The stories and images, therefore, have the effect of telling us, not that we ought to think we can in our present lives have absolute and unsituated knowledge, but that we ought always to recognize our ignorance, the situatedness of our understanding, yet never stop trying to improve our opinions. The images of the Good, the Divided Line, and the Cave have practical force. They mean that although we are not divine and cannot in this life have divinely unsituated knowledge, it is *not* a useless matter to seek improved understanding. Opinions are not all equally true or equally false. Sophistic relativism need not prevent us from pursuing and practicing justice through wisdom.

In the practice of Socratic method, therefore, the belief in the Good is not the belief that we human knowers can escape our situatedness; it is rather the recognition that we must always submit our opinions to judgment by the light of the Good, so that our ignorance can be exposed, our understanding improved, and our lives integrated.

Socratic method, however, not only accepts the inescapable location of understanding within the limits of place, time, and language; it also operates through the affirmation of a reality that transcends all situations: "the Good Itself" in *Republic* or "Beauty Itself" in *Symposium*. To practice the method is to believe opinions can be improved so that they express more truly the reality that appears in them. But why should we believe that unsituated reality, the way things are, appears in beliefs? Why not be skeptical of the very idea of improving beliefs? Why not adopt the completely skeptical assumption that all ideas and beliefs are simply devices for increasing power or the effects and functions of some psychological dynamic? Such a skeptical path is always open. It is the position, in fact, championed by today's strong postmodernists, and it means that any "improvement" in opinions is not an improvement in understanding the way things are but an improvement toward some noncognitive end. If we are to practice the Socratic art of being just, we cannot make that skeptical assumption. Instead, we must assume or affirm that there is unsituated truth about the way things are and an unsituated reality that establishes that truth and makes it possible for us to know it in our situated ways.

That affirmation—of the Good Itself and the truth it establishes—is a form of

trust or faith. It is not the indifferent recognition of fact. Wherever there is a So-
cratically just life, its practitioner commits in trust, not only affirms facts. One puts
one's improvement, so to speak, into the hands of the Good and depends on it actually to make the improvement possible. That there is such unsituated reality is
not known by unsituated, indubitable proof. One must venture it, trust that it is,
and depend on it. To practice the art of philosophy as the art of life is to engage
actively in such trusting endeavor.

Trusting dependence on the unsituated Good means loving it. Plato makes a
point in *Symposium* (177e) of having Socrates say, in spite of his famous insistence
on ignorance, that *eros* is the one thing about which he can claim to know. It makes
perfect sense that Socrates should claim that knowledge, because *eros* is the desire
for that which one does not have. That makes knowledge of *eros* consistent with
Socratic ignorance. Knowing wisdom is always lacking, one feels the need to improve one's understanding. The practitioner of Socratic philosophical life needs
and knows he needs the wisdom that enables him to be just. It is the Good Itself
that makes that wisdom possible. Hence, the philosophical life lacks and needs the
Good, and therefore loves it and longs to have the relationship with it that will
engender wisdom and the other virtues that are part of a just or good life.

Socratic philosophical life also means the willingness to suffer in the pursuit of
the unconditional good that justice is. This is a central theme of *Republic,* where,
in Book II, Glaucon wants to know whether justice is intrinsically good, so that
one should choose and pursue it even if it should result in one's being wrongly
punished as a criminal. Plato quite clearly and intentionally presents Socrates as
the example who proves the point. Yes, leading the philosophical life in pursuit of
justice may lead to such suffering, but the result is happiness and strength—even
in death. To be just is the one good above all goods, the one thing the philosophical life can guarantee. But it means suffering. One must be willing, as Socrates
was, to suffer the loss of all conditional goods in order to realize the one unconditional good, one's transformation into and life as a whole and just individual.

The last parallel between faith and philosophy is that the life of Socratic philosophy requires an agapic attitude toward those others with whom one is situated
in the world. It has been frequently claimed that neither Plato nor other Greek
philosophers had an idea of love as *agapē,* and it is true that Plato never defined
the concept. Nevertheless, implicit within the account of the philosophical life of
justice is an orientation toward others that is very near to agape, the desire for the
good of the other.

Republic I supports the claim of implicit agape in two ways. First, there is the
argument that it cannot be part of justice to harm one's enemies. Second, there is
the treatment of justice on the model of various practical arts. That justice excludes
doing damage to anyone's good as a person does not by itself mean justice requires
a positive desire for the other's good, but it does point in that direction. The idea
that justice is an art provides the more positive emphasis, for arts, such as medicine and financial management, say, are defined and evaluated by the good they
produce for some client other than the practitioner. This point is clearly included
when justice finally receives its definition in *Republic* IV. It is the art of produc-

ing oneself as an integrated whole, such that one is both an intrinsic good to oneself and a good for the community. Here again, Socrates is Plato's example. Socrates' life is a response to a divine command. He is not only to be virtuous for the intrinsic good it brings to himself; he is to give himself without reserve to assisting his fellow Athenians to attain their good as well, suffering whatever losses of conditional goods might result. He must give himself so completely to his neighbors' improvement that he may not stop even to save himself from execution.

Nevertheless, Socratic philosophy does not have the same scope in its love for others as has Jesus' life of faith. The difference between Socratic justice and Christian love is the difference between what Kierkegaard called the ethical and the religious ways of life.[14] Socrates represents the ethical life. He does not see the poor, the hungry, the sick, the powerless as equal to citizens of standing and to himself in the active love of God nor exhibit a compassionate, feeling concern for them. However, the life he exemplifies and teaches does require its practitioners to produce good for those who are clients of their art of justice, for those, therefore, with whom they find themselves situated in the city. And the recognition that justice excludes harming enemies implies that even the good of enemies is to be done. This near-agapic attitude may not go as far in loving others as Jesus' life of faith, but it approaches and is compatible with it.

In sum, the features of the Socratic philosophical life are as follows:

1. Socrates accepted the inescapable situatedness of human life.
2. Socrates understood that he should not think his or others' understandings could in this life escape or overcome the perspectival limitations of being in the world; therefore, he should not try to escape his situatedness so as to realize divine unsituated knowledge and make himself a god.
3. Socrates believed in and was committed to the unsituated Good as an unsituated reality that brings into being the way things are and ought to be and that makes it possible for situated persons situatedly to know and be formed by unsituated truth. Though he recognized that he could not know the Good Itself as it is in itself, he insisted that it must be believed to make it possible for human lives to become intrinsically good things in the world.
4. Socrates sought to be completely formed by the Good, to be made a just individual by unconditional commitment to it and to the requirements of human justice it establishes.
5. Socrates trusted that unswerving devotion to the Good in the practice of his method and in the art of justice would lead to good, for himself and for the others among whom he lived, even if the resulting life brought suffering and apparent defeat.
6. Socrates was willing to suffer the loss of conditional goods for the sake of the unconditional good he believed must come from commitment to Good.

7. Socrates saw that justice is essentially oriented toward the community in which one is situated. As an artist, the just person must produce a good for those who are clients of the art. The greatest good the artist can produce is assistance to others in becoming just. Therefore, the life of philosophy for Socrates meant working toward a community of reciprocally just members.

Bringing Athens to Jerusalem

There is one overshadowing difference between Jesus' life of faith and Socrates' life of philosophy: the difference between an unsituated reality who is a personal agent, who creates and redeems the world, and an unsituated reality that is a nonpersonal principle or cause. Because of this difference, faith has the form of an interpersonal relation with God; philosophy does not. Philosophy does not, that is, unless it is incorporated into faith, into the setting of life as interpersonal cooperation with God. And there is the main point of this essay: Socratic philosophy can be incorporated into and practiced as a discipline of faith in the God of Abraham, Isaac, and Jacob.

It does not have to be! In the past century, most philosophers have practiced the Socratic life without seeing it in the context of devotion to a personal God. Nietzsche regarded Christianity (Judaism too) as "Platonism for the masses," less philosophically respectable because it anthropomorphized nonpersonal principles. And one of today's most vigorous proponents of the Good, Iris Murdoch, cannot believe the personal agency of the Good. It is more reasonable, she thinks, to uphold it as presented in Plato's *Republic,* a nonpersonal principle and practical standard.[15]

On the other hand, Christian believers not only can incorporate Socratic philosophy by identifying the Good as God, they can argue that it is more reasonable to do so than not. Diogenes Allen presents two of the traditional arguments for the existence of God in forms that are especially suitable for making such a claim in the postmodern context. The order of the world, especially the values of the physical constants, "point to the possibility," not simply of some "cause," but specifically of intentional agency as their cause.[16] Likewise the existence of the world.[17] The arguments are not proposed as unsituated knowledge all reasonable persons must accept, but as pointing to the possibility that divine personal agency is responsible for the existence of the world in which morally responsible persons capable of living by faith in God can exist.

The affirmation of the personal God is not the automatic recognition of unquestionable fact by a value-neutral rationality. That Cartesian/Enlightenment idea of unsituated rationality is out. Rather, the person situated within a context of need for meaningful existence and seeing the possibility of a creator-redeemer God who offers unconditional good while demanding unconditional commitment affirms God by taking up the life of faith. Such affirmation comes from that "open-heartedness" that defines both faith and philosophy; namely, the trust that there is unsituated reality and the willing recognition of demands placed and good offered.

Affirming God is more reasonable than affirming only the nonpersonal principle of Good, because affirming God is the most devoted response one can make to the Good. To see the Good as actively and intentionally demanding unconditional devotion and offering unconditional good is to honor, love, and commit to the Good in the strongest possible way. It is not that Christianity is Platonism for the masses, but that Christian faith is the fulfillment and intensification of Platonic Socratism. Stopping short of responding to the Good as to the God who creates, knows, cares, and redeems betrays limits to the heart's openness to unsituated good. For the Socratic philosopher who does not affirm God, it is as though he chooses against faith in order not to give himself as completely to the Good as appropriate and possible if the Good is God, as though the philosopher wishes to avoid recognizing a person whose desire and will always take precedence over one's own. As Milton's Lucifer declares, "I will not serve!"

Furthermore, it is reasonable for the open heart to affirm the Good as God because God is a higher good, who makes greater demands and offers greater good than the Good Itself. God is a higher good because God, as one whose agency always promotes the real good of creatures, commands not only the ethical life of doing the good defined by one's roles, but the life of seeing and caring for all persons as ones who are equal before God, as ones loved unconditionally by God. These others whom one is commanded to love unconditionally include the most vicious and hideous of enemies, the Hitlers, the Stalins, the Karadzics of the world. The command to see and care about them as ones whom God loves as much as oneself is the most extreme command possible. If the Good is but a nonpersonal principle, one can have no obligation so to see and care for them—it is enough to act toward them as one's role and the law stipulate; one cannot be obligated also to care for them feelingly, so that one mourns their failure to be who God wills them to be and rejoices in their improvement. But if one's heart is fully open to the Good, one will affirm the higher command and with it the agent God who, by virtue of being a personal agent, can make so extreme a demand and stand before us as so high a Good.

The good God offers is a greater good than the Good as nonpersonal principle because the God who is personal offers the perfection of personal existence as incorporation into the agapic life of God, not only the integration of oneself into a just individual. Lest the hope of such perfection be dismissed as wishful thinking, it must be said that it is not simply a self-centered desire to enjoy being just or, perhaps, to enjoy immortality. It is the hope of being transformed into one who centers on and rejoices in the good for others, into one who truly does love God with all one's being and one's neighbor as oneself. Consequently, it is a hope that involves intentional cooperation with a grace that comes actively from God to effect one's transformation. It is a hope that defines life as a response to the most extreme possible demand.

It is reasonable, therefore, to incorporate the Socratic form of philosophical life into the life of faith in the God who loves and acts. Doing so, the examination of beliefs in the effort to improve them becomes part of a life of personal encounter and response. The pursuit of understanding becomes a prayerful trust in and dependence on God and an effort to cooperate with God's grace in transforming mind, heart, and life.

This way of being a Christian philosopher defines two basic ways of committing what we might call "cognitive sin." One is the obvious one of claiming unsituated knowledge of the way things are and ought to be. In this light, the Cartesian quest for certainty is a sinful illusion. Perhaps its most blatant expression is the grand system building that seeks to answer all questions and eradicate all mystery. Kierkegaard certainly thought so. Or perhaps it is even more blatant and destructive in the form of Comtean positivism, the belief that, through the positive form of understanding, humankind can overcome all superstition and ignorance and get down to the work of remaking the world into one that utterly eradicates the physical, moral, social, economic, political, and even spiritual problems that beset human life. Marxism offers still another version of the same conviction. And there are many other expressions of the cognitive sin of claiming unsituated knowledge of good and evil. Totalitarian political projects exemplify it. And one can sin in this way not only by the explicit claim that one's self or one's party has the final truth by which to re-create the world. One can even disclaim in words the finality and absoluteness of one's understanding, while in actions regarding it as absolute and oneself as divine. Christian philosophy requires constant vigilance to guard against such lapses—and repentance when one becomes aware of their occurrence.

Perhaps especially important for theology is the claim to have received by divine revelation an absolute, certain, unsituated knowledge of God. It is an unfaithful claim. This does not mean there can be no use of the idea of revelation, but it does mean that so-called revealed doctrine must be regarded in the light of human situatedness and brought under the Socratic interrogation that requires the recognition of the ignorance in belief. It is contrary to the life of faith to hold that particular doctrines are beyond criticism and improvement, that they are absolute knowledge given miraculously by God and known absolutely by us. That does not mean Christians cannot insist on essential doctrines and distinguish orthodox from heterodox understanding. But it means that the doctrines established as essential must not be taken as the equivalent of God's own knowledge; they must not be regarded as fully understood, needing no examination for the sake of improved understanding. The bare and static reiteration of verbal formulas will not do. Orthodoxy must be dynamic; it must involve ongoing examination and fresh appropriation of belief. There is, of course, nothing new about this point. Throughout the history of the church it has been asserted, showing that Christians have traditionally recognized the inescapable fact of human situatedness.

The second form of cognitive sin is more subtle than the first. It is to deny that there is anything to cognition other than a multiplicity of understandings that arise at different times and in different circumstances, and that have their historical growth and decay, not because they are perspectives on the way things truly are and ought to be, but because of factors that have nothing to do with truth. Strong postmodernism, the position that there is no truth and no reality outside the story or language game one follows, is the currently most prevalent expression of this more subtle form of cognitive sin.

At first glance, however, it might not seem to exemplify the biblical understanding of sin. It seems to be the opposite of claiming divine or unsituated knowledge. But faith requires *both* the recognition that human understanding is situated *and* the affirmation that there is an unsituated truth about the way things are and ought to be. Faith means living by trusting and obedient dependence on God, and that means examining, criticizing, and improving understanding because one trusts that there is God's truth and God's good to be known.

The relativism implicit in strong postmodernism's denial that there is unsituated truth about unsituated God (rather than *situated* knowledge of unsituated truth about unsituated God) amounts to the denial of human situatedness and ignorance. It becomes in practice an elevation of oneself to God's place. For if we deny the reality of a way things are and a way they ought to be, we lose the possibility of coming to an improved understanding that comes closer to truth. We also lose the motive for critical examination and the appreciation of the limits of understanding. Human desire, will, and understanding then take on the divine role of creating. Relativism, which appears to be the opposite of absolutism, thus ends up producing the same totalizing outcome, an outcome that from the standpoint of Christian philosophy is sin.

Conclusion

If we are truly to live the recognition that human understanding is always structured by presuppositions of language, history, and story, we must hold that recognition in tension with the recognition that God is unsituated reality transcending human situatedness and graciously bringing into being unsituated truth about the way things unsituatedly are. We must always say that our understanding, even the understanding that asserts this very claim, is situated and subject to improvement. But we can only say that if we also recognize that there is unsituated God and unsituated truth by reference to which our understandings are limited and able to be improved.

There is nothing new here; it is an ancient wisdom. We are finite but subject to the desire to be infinite. We know a little but desire to know everything. We can do some things but desire to be the very makers of heaven and earth. To be Christian philosophers, we must faithfully accept the good God offers in creating us as finite persons with finite understanding. St. Augustine called it "faith seeking understanding."

Socratic philosophy and faithful life are not, however, simply the same thing! The Socratic philosopher does not have to incorporate devotion to the Good and the Beautiful into a life of obedient trust in the divine Persons Christians believe God to be. He does not have to practice philosophy, that is, in the interpersonal form that is an essential character of faith. On the other hand, the person who does live by that interpersonal form, taking the Good Itself to be, belong to, or derive from a transcendent divine being who is Creator and Redeemer and at least personal, can practice Socratic philosophy without fear that such rational examination and construction will pervert the faith that exercises it. He will trust that God has ordered creation so that there is a "way things are." And he will trust that the God of Truth, who loves us, desires for us the good of improved understanding. He will accept his situatedness as a good God intends; and he will, therefore, know better than to think himself able to arrive at a complete and certain knowledge that will make him God. He will also know better than to think that within his situatedness all opinions are equally true or false, that is, that the rationality God gives us is no more than a means to attaining power over the world and others or a cause of ignorance and confusion, leaving us forever unable to know the good God is and intends. He will practice the pursuit of understanding in a stance of worshipful humility and as a service to be performed for God and neighbor. In fact, such love of wisdom within the relation of faith becomes part of that love of God and neighbor. The faithful, prayerful, interpersonal way of being devoted to the Good gives heart to mind and opens understanding to the grace God gives. Intentionally, by prayer, to trust in God and in God's action in faith's seeking of understanding is the most respectful possible use of one's situated mind and the most obedient possible relation to the Good. The practice of Socratic philosophy within the faithful relation to God elevates philosophy to its highest possible expression. We could do worse than follow Diogenes Allen in thus believing in order to understand.

NOTES

1. Percy Dearmer, hymn 299, sts. 1 and 3, *The Hymnal of the Protestant Episcopal Church in the United States of America* (New York: The Church Hymnal Corporation, 1940).
2. Although Diogenes Allen was never formally my teacher, his friendship and his books have been enormously important in forming my mind and also my teaching. I have regularly used his books in my classes at the Louisiana State University. His influence so pervades this essay that it would be impossible for me completely to separate his thought from my own. I take full responsibility, however, for whatever misuse I may have made and whatever confusion I may have generated in appropriating his thought.
3. Research into the historical conditions in which Jesus lived is ongoing at a furious pace. This account depends on no detailed historical claims, but it is especially indebted to the work of N. T. Wright in the following three books: *Who Was Jesus?* (London: SPCK; Grand Rapids: Wm. B. Eerdmans Publishing Co., 1992); *The New Testament and the People of God*, vol. 1 of *Christian Origins and the Question of God* (London: SPCK; Minneapolis: Fortress Press, 1992); *Jesus and the Victory of God*, vol. 2 of *Christian Origins and the Question of God* (London: SPCK; Minneapolis: Fortress Press, 1996).
4. Austin Farrer, "Very God and Very Man," in *Interpretation and Belief,* ed. Charles C. Conti (London: SPCK, 1976), 135–36.
5. N. T. Wright, *Jesus and the Victory of God.* See especially part 3.
6. William H. Vanstone has written a remarkable study of the Gospel accounts of Jesus' being "handed over" to the authorities; see *The Stature of Waiting* (London: Darton, Longman & Todd, 1982). I am indebted to my friend and colleague David Baily Harned, who brought this work to my attention as he was researching his forthcoming book *Patience: How We Wait upon the World* (Cambridge, Mass.: Cowley Publications, 1997).

7. Diogenes Allen, *Quest: The Search for Meaning through Christ* (New York: Walker & Co., 1990), xvi–xix.

8. Mary Sirridge, my colleague at the Louisiana State University, distinguishes between Plato's dramatic character and the historical Socrates by referring to the former as "Plocrates." It is a clever way to prevent confusion. However, it should be unnecessary to resort to it here. Let it be understood that "Socrates" always refers in this essay only to Plato's character.

9. It is often said that Plato taught a rejection of the world and the effort to escape it. However, neither *Republic* nor *Symposium* supports that interpretation (*Phaedo* is another matter). The image in *Republic* I of justice as an art that produces a good is related to the discussion of *eros* in *Symposium*. Diotima does not teach Socrates that the love of the Beautiful itself is a mystical escape from the world, nor even that the world is something from which one should seek escape. She teaches (at 212a) that one who loves Beauty, who has intercourse with it (the imagery, after all, is explicitly sexual), will thereby engender beautiful realities *in the world*. Jowett translates: "Remember how in that communion only, beholding beauty with the eye of the mind, he will be enabled to bring forth, not images of beauty, but realities" (*The Dialogues of Plato*, trans. B. Jowett [New York: Random House, 1937], 335). Nehamas and Woodruff render the passage similarly: "'Or haven't you remembered,' she said, 'that in that life alone, when he looks at Beauty in the only way that Beauty can be seen—only then will it become possible for him to give birth not to images of virtue (because he's in touch with no images), but to true virtue (because he's in touch with the true Beauty).'" The just man of *Republic* is an artist who looks to the Good and to the Beautiful and brings forth a good and beautiful reality; namely, himself as a just and virtuous person.

10. For example, *Republic*'s study of justice does not eliminate the opinions of Book I (except for the opinion that we owe our enemies harm); it clarifies and improves them. Thus, Thrasymachus's opinion that justice is the advantage of the stronger turns out not to be wrong but to be a misunderstanding by Thrasymachus. Thrasymachus thinks that life is a competition for a limited quantity of good or happiness, so that the more others have the less there will be for oneself. On that assumption, whoever is stronger and is thereby a ruler can secure his own good only by overcoming the good of others. Practical arts, such as shipbuilding, medicine, and money management, on the other hand, are defined by the production of some good for those others who are their clients or users. Therefore, if justice is an art, it cannot aim at such an overcoming of others; it must intend to do them good. Justice cannot be the interest of the stronger, in the way Thrasymachus understands that. However, by the time Socrates and his friends have completed the discussion of justice, we see that, while it cannot be the whole definition of what justice is, part of the truth about justice is that it is the interest of the stronger. For artists of justice are, as artists, in the position of ruling or being stronger with respect to those in relation to whom they practice the art. Truly to be *artists*, they must produce some good for those who are the clients of their art. But in doing so, at the same time they produce good for themselves, namely, the internal and intrinsic good of being just and beautiful individuals, possessing the virtues of wisdom, courage, self-control, and justice.

11. Charles Bigger in his classes on Plato at the Louisiana State University (1964–1994); Edward Ballard in his classes at Tulane University (from the 1950s through the 1980s).

12. Iris Murdoch, *Metaphysics as a Guide to Morals* (London: Penguin Books, 1992), 402–3.

13. It is common to see the position in *Republic* as different from that of *Theaetetus* and *Timaeus*. Be that as it may, we can preserve Plato's teaching on justice and on the Good—and certainly on Socratic method—in terms of the idea that knowledge is not absolute and unsituated, but is belief improved by an account and held in awareness that even in improved belief one remains ignorant.

14. See Diogenes Allen's *Three Outsiders* (Cambridge, Mass.: Cowley Publications, 1983) for his excellent treatment of Kierkegaard's *Works of Love* in relation to the distinction between aesthetic, ethical, and religious life.

15. Murdoch, *Metaphysics,* chap. 15, "Martin Buber and God."

16. Diogenes Allen, *Christian Belief in a Postmodern World: The Full Wealth of Conviction* (Louisville, Ky.: Westminster/John Knox Press, 1989), chap. 3.

17. Ibid., chap. 4.

6

THE PRIMACY OF SPIRIT

"Truth is the cry of all, but the game of the few."
George Berkeley, **Siris**

JEFFREY C. EATON

What If Materialism?

Recent studies in the philosophy of mind afford a good place to start thinking about the problems and prospects of spiritual philosophy, a philosophy that is at once inspired and reasoned. In the book *Consciousness Explained,* Daniel Dennett says, "The prevailing wisdom, variously experienced and argued for, is *materialism:* there is only one sort of stuff, namely matter—the physical stuff of physics, chemistry, and physiology—and the mind is somehow nothing but a physical phenomenon."[1] Above all, Dennett proposes to banish dualism from his thinking about consciousness. Dualism, he says, is "fundamentally unscientific" as an approach to the problem of consciousness, or to anything else for that matter. This is what it means to accept the prevailing wisdom of materialism. It's a bold claim, but one for which modern people in the West are well prepared, having inherited the legacy of materialist metaphysics that characterized the new science popularized in the Enlightenment.

If the prevailing wisdom of materialism is wise, there is plainly no hope for a spiritual philosophy, or for any theology that is more than the idealization of something in the physical world, say, the process of moral deliberation and action, or that is not study of the artifacts of theological traditions to understand their part in the making and unmaking of culture. If the prevailing wisdom is wise, meaningful talk about God is effectively ruled out of court, a state of affairs George Berkeley (1685–1753) foresaw even as the great cultural engine of the Enlightenment was roaring to life. He issued a warning in his *Philosophical Commentaries:* "Matter once allow'd. I defy any man to prove that God is not matter."[2]

As it happens, Dennett's tour de force can by grace and common sense be fended off. After hundreds of pages of all sorts of interesting and provocative cleverness from the laboratories of cognitive scientists, as well as consideration of certain investigations into the philosophy of mind, Dennett, or Dennett's brain, reveals that the title of his book may be a bit ambitious—that his explanation of consciousness is incomplete, even far from complete, and that his achievement has actually been to shift metaphors for consciousness from those that are suggestive of the qualities of the Cartesian Theater to the cybernetic metaphors that are cele-brated in theories of artificial intelligence. He shamelessly admits that his "expla-nation" of consciousness leaves out the causal nexus between unconscious events, neurophysiological processes in the brain, which he takes to be explanatory, and consciousness, which he proposes to explain. That is to say, his explanation leaves out the very mystery in favor of the abstract ideas of matter and materialist causa-tion. In short, he explains consciousness away.

John Searle is more circumspect in his treatment of the subject of consciousness. But, modern philosopher that he is, he recoils from the idea of immaterial souls or mental substances. He seems also to be a materialist, but of a more finespun variety than Dennett. He says, "What I want to insist on, ceaselessly, is that one can accept the obvious facts of physics—for example, that the world is made up entirely of phys-ical particles in fields of force—without at the same time denying the obvious facts about our own experiences—for example, that we are all conscious and that our con-scious states have quite specific *irreducible* phenomenological properties."[3] But he is not, he insists, a dualist (or a monist either). He would like to move beyond these cat-egorical rigidities.

Searle nicely captures the modern dilemma when he writes of the terror that motivates materialism. It is the fear of subjectivity. Subjectivity is a surd in the modern picture of the world, one that seems to fly in the face of modern science as it has come to be understood.[4] He prefers to think of consciousness as a "causally emergent property of systems," emergent from the electrochemistry of brains but irreducible without remainder to the physical structure of brains. That remainder, according to Searle, is not so great as to allow consciousness to be able to cause things that cannot be explained by the physical structure of the brain. When Searle says consciousness is irreducible to brain function, he means that it is ontologically irreducible, ontological reduction being the idea that one thing is really nothing but another thing. Nor is this irreducibility dependent on the devel-opment of cognitive science. It simply cannot be accomplished because subjective experience is an existing feature in the world which is left out of the description of neuron firings proposed to explain it. However, Searle thinks this irreducibil-ity has no deep metaphysical consequences for the scientific understanding of the physical world. "Pretheoretically, consciousness, like solidity, is a surface feature of certain physical systems. But unlike solidity, consciousness cannot be redefined in terms of an underlying microstructure, and the surface features then treated as mere effects of real consciousness, without losing the point of having the concept of consciousness in the first place."[5] In short, we define consciousness differently than we define physical properties like solidity, heat, color, and so on, and this is what accounts for its irreducibility.

But what if the irreducibility of consciousness were taken not as an *exception* to the general reducibility of phenomena in nature in terms of underlying physical reality, and viewed instead as a clue to the irreducibility of natural phenomena in general? What if we took this remarkable fact about consciousness as intimating immaterialism instead of being an odd exception to a thoroughgoing materialist description of things? What if Berkeley?

What If Immaterialism?

Berkeley's contributions to Western intellectual history are numerous and important. Mathematicians are in his debt for his challenge to the idea of the fixed infinitesimal (*Analyst*), and physicists for his bold anticipations of Mach's ideas concerning the relativity of motion (*De Motu*), having demolished Newton's understanding of motion as absolute. In philosophy he continues to be appreciated for his challenge to the notion of abstract ideas and for his contention that the meaning of words is to be found in their context (*Principles*). These are among the acknowledged contributions of Berkeley. But none of these is more than a byproduct of his philosophy of immaterialism, which was largely ignored in his own time, dismissed for many reasons, but not least of all because it was considered to be an outrage to common sense. It is still so considered.

The point of departure for Berkeley's philosophy was the problem of perception, which he assumed was the essence of the problem of matter. According to Berkeley, there are two types of knowable objects, spirits and ideas. By "ideas" he means sense perceptions: the objects of sense are bundles of ideas. The word "idea" is a source of confusion in determining what Berkeley was talking about if we fail to understand that he is using the word as he received it from Locke to indicate an immediate object of sense. This was the reigning terminology of Berkeley's day, and once we appreciate this, we can see that first and foremost Berkeley means what we would call sense data when he uses this term. Sensible ideas are what we see and feel, and just that. Collections of ideas are what we commonly call "things." My desk is this brown, hard surface that I see and feel, walnut wood of a certain height and width and length. All of this is immediately perceivable by someone whose physical senses are intact. The wood of the desk also possesses a certain molecular structure, which is available to perception with the help of a microscope, and it has an atomic structure which a more powerful microscope can reveal to perception, and there are descriptions for all these perceptions that are made possible by various scientific conventions. But regardless of how deeply one penetrates into the structure of this desk, one will never arrive at its matter if what is meant by matter is an insensible substrate independent of a perceiving mind. Berkeley believed and argued that this way of viewing things is a return to common sense, whereby our knowledge of objects is the consequence of perception of the perceived and the perceivable, and that scientific knowledge is a derivative of this common sense, not the reverse.

Sensible ideas are known by spirits, by which Berkeley means minds, the essential property of which is activity. Spirits understand and will perceive and imagine. They are vital centers of experience, and by virtue of their activity are utterly distinct from their objects, which are sensible ideas, the existence of which depends on their being perceived. The two realms of existence, sensible ideas and spirits, are not to be confused or conflated, and to this end Berkeley says, "*Spirits* and *ideas* are things so wholly different that when we say *they exist, they are known,* or the like, these words must not be thought to signify anything common to both natures."[6] As matter is not to be found among the objects of sense, neither is it to be found in the perceiving subject.

With the delineation of active spirits and the ideas that are the objects of the activity of spirits, we have the elements of Berkeley's New Principle, which, after nearly three hundred years, is still startling and fresh: *esse est percipi.* Unthinking things have no existence apart from their being perceived, which is not to say that sensible objects are produced by the mind, but that they are objects of the mind's activity. His point is that all things are mind-related. According to the New Principle, if something is perceived, it exists. Existence is not a state independent of perception which things possess, not a condition that is independent of the *activity* of perception. Berkeley states the New Principle dramatically and categorically, but it needs extension, for on the face of it, it is not clear how the New Principle applies to spirits. Berkeley extends the New Principle in his *Philosophical Commentaries,* where he says, "Existence is *percipi* or *percipere* or *velle:* i.e., *agere.*"[7] Ideas and spirits exist by virtue of their being related in the act of perceiving: ideas are perceived, spirits perceive as well as being perceived. The dramatic statement of the New Principle is for the purpose of driving home the point that there is no such thing as absolute existence, existence unperceived, existence out of all relation to spiritual activity as is presupposed in the theory of matter.

The belief in matter, stuff independent of mind, is for Berkeley the chief rival of belief in God. The New Principle begs the questions for which, according to Berkeley, only God will suffice as the answer, namely: What becomes of the perceivable when unperceived by human spirits? and, What is the cause of change in nature if there are no material causes? The theological application of the New Principle is clearly stated in the *Principles:*

> All the choir of heaven and the furniture of the earth, in a word all those bodies which compose the mighty frame of the world, have not any subsistence without a mind, that their being is to be perceived or known; that consequently so long as they are not actually perceived by me, or do not exist in my mind or that of any other created spirit, they must either have no existence at all, or else subsist in the mind of some external spirit; it being perfectly unintelligible and involving all the absurdity of abstraction, to attribute to any single part of them an existence independent of a spirit. To be convinced of which the reader need only reflect and try to separate in his own thoughts the being of a sensible thing from its being perceived.[8]

The New Principle, in claiming the mind-dependence of all things, gives absolute primacy to spirits and ultimately to the eternal spirit, which is God. The sensible ideas that are perceived by human spirits have their cause and substance in the eternal Spirit, God. Sensible ideas are given to us in the ordered system of nature, a divine sensible language through which God is revealed in the natural world.

Therapeutic Philosophy

In drawing the distinction between ideas and spirits, Berkeley emphasized the passivity of ideas relative to the activity of spirits in order to clarify the mind-dependence of all existents. And in doing this he overstated the case. Sensible objects can be construed as activity patterns without backing away from Berkeley's New Principle. It is as activity patterns that sensible objects manifest themselves to sense, and it is activity patterns that constitute the substance of the sensible. This alternative understanding of sensible ideas allows for the operation of active secondary causes without resorting to the postulate of a self-subsistent, imperceivable stuff or activity. Austin Farrer helps to rehabilitate Berkeley on this score when he writes, "The creature is in its creaturely action, self-sufficient: but because a creature, insufficient to itself throughout, and sustained by its Creator both in existence and in action."[9] This is a correction that we might assume Berkeley would receive with gratitude. A new physics such as Farrer had at his disposal would enable Berkeley to envision a conception of his New Principle that is less static than it is in its original formulation, though no less oppositional. Farrer suggests *esse est operari,* but this principle, as importantly and usefully different as it is from Berkeley's original, nevertheless shares the essential Berkeleyan insight into the dependence of all things on the activity of spirits. The two principles reflect the different physical theories that were the backdrop of the respective understandings of causation. However much aspects of Berkeley's thought may have anticipated aspects of relativity theory, he was working in the milieu of classical physics, and it is to that physics that his metaphysics was related. Farrer, of course, looks to post-Einstein physics for his theory of causation. Both see the prototype of causation as a *causa causans,* an agent, but Berkeley, at least in his early years, will not see this prototype extended or blurred by allowances of secondary causation. For him, all operations in nature are an immediate effect of God's will. For Farrer, the will of God is sufficiently mediated to allow the effects of nature to be active in themselves, a condition Farrer describes in his proposal of the paradox of double agency. Had Berkeley allowed for secondary causes, the character of his argument would not have changed. This allowance takes nothing away from the sovereignty of divine causality in nature or the primacy of spirit. And it seems his position on natural causes did soften in his later works, but he would not give ground on the question of an autonomous material principle in nature. There is, to be sure, something artificial in his early understanding of causation, and yet, our only insight into the nature of causation is our own agency. Natural causes are not perceptible except as effects, having no discernible principle of action, however precisely observed and described. In this sense it is perhaps not as scandalous as it appears to call the movement of sensible things passivity, as Berkeley does. He is simply saying that sensible things cannot do what they do on their own. Only spirits can act; spirits are centers of active experience, regarding which it is not possible to frame an idea of their activity. Agency is known in its exercise as volition.

In article 29 of the *Principles* Berkeley offers his causal argument for the existence of God. He says: "But whatever power I have over my own thoughts, I find the ideas actually perceived by sense have not a like dependence on my will. When in broad daylight I open my eyes, it is not in my power to choose whether I shall see or no, or to determine what particular objects shall present themselves to my view; and so likewise as to the hearing and other senses; the ideas imprinted on them are not creatures of my will. There is therefore *some other* will or spirit that produces them."[10] The passivity of sensible objects, which is to say, their inability to account for themselves, is an argument for immaterialism, even as it is an argument for God. The ideas of God are the things of nature, and the study of nature is the study of the mind of God, in whom all things live and move and have their being.

Misinterpretations of Berkeley are legion, but the most influential misuse of Berkeley's work belongs to Hume, who understood Berkeley better than most. Hume extended Berkeley's criticism of pseudometaphysics in the name of common sense to a denial of metaphysics and the relegation of philosophy to the methodization of common life and convention. In so doing, Hume capitulated to expediency in a way that would come to characterize the analytic tradition of philosophy. Berkeley's intentions were to restore respect for common sense but not to reduce philosophy to the commonplace. He sought to raise his readers' sights to sublimities of truth and goodness, intimations of the infinite, not to reduce them to the parsing of the mundane. Hume took Berkeley's criticism of the received metaphysics in the direction of a Pyrrhonic skepticism, the consequence of which was the subduing of both discontent and aspiration, the planing down of metaphysical hierarchies, and the quantifying of the qualitative. Berkeley wanted to correct metaphysical absurdities, which Hume concluded meant the elimination of metaphysics. Berkeley was offering a therapy for the condition from which Hume would suffer as surely, if more brilliantly, than the "minute philosophers" whom Berkeley devastated in *Alciphron*.

Hume sharpened insight into certain logical muddles, but his mitigated skepticism reduced reason to ratiocination. In lesser hands, reason was reduced still farther to pedantry for the sake of justifying the values of the modern world. But Berkeley was of a different inclination. He viewed the therapeutic function of philosophy in a way that would better fit Marcuse's description of philosophy's goal in *One Dimensional Man* than that of Hume's mitigated skepticism:

> Philosophy approaches this goal [its therapeutic function] to the degree to which it frees thought from its enslavement to the established universe of discourse and behavior, elucidates the negativity of the Establishment (its positive aspects are abundantly publicized anyway) and projects its alternatives. To be sure, philosophy contradicts and projects in thought only. It is ideology, and this ideologized character is the very fate of philosophy which no scientism and positivism can overcome. Still, its ideological effort may be truly therapeutic—to show reality as that which really it is, and to show that which this reality prevents from being.[11]

Berkeley called the modern world into question. No wonder he was labeled a skeptic! His goal, however, was throughout his life what he said it was in his epigrammatic description of his *Principles:* to rid the new science of its false principles and to root out the causes of skepticism, atheism, and irreligion. He sought to restore common sense to philosophy, to root out the mystification of abstract ideas so that authentic mysteries of God and the human soul might come to light, so that the sheer givenness of things might again be thrown into relief. Berkeley's criticism of matter exposed the futility of the idea that undergirds the modern world, and, in the bargain, unveiled the spiritual reality that was smothered and prevented from flourishing because of the currency of this idea. Berkeley understood that, left to stand, this idea would result in a spiritually desiccated world in which all things, including human beings, are accorded only instrumental value, where predatory dominion over nature replaces sociability with the natural environment, and where the rhythm of work and leisure are replaced with obsessive labor and acquisitiveness. Contained in the idea of matter is the end of history, recently pronounced, this end being the implacable and supreme forces of market economics as final determinant of social reality. Thus, the spiritual is subordinated to technical means for which there is no end whatsoever.

Whatever else was Berkeley's philosophy of immaterialism, it was a response and challenge to that reductionism which would sap the world of its mystery, which, of course, would be perfectly acceptable if the world were devoid of mystery. His appeal to common sense was an appeal to the mystery that is everywhere present in our common experiences, insofar as common experience defies reduction and final formulation. It was a call to rediscover the mystery of the familiar and to reorient inquiry to apprehension, which lifts the mind to appreciate the unfathomable, away from the idea of comprehension, which reduces the world to abstraction. In *Alciphron* Berkeley writes, "But a minute philosopher shall, in virtue of wrong suppositions, confound things most evidently distinct: body, for instance, with spirit; motion with volition; certainty with necessity. . . . To me it seems that if we begin from things particular and concrete, and thence proceed to general notions and conclusions, there will be no difficulty in this matter. But if we begin with generalities and lay our foundation in abstract ideas, we shall find ourselves entangled and lost in a labyrinth of our own making."[12] Berkeley's intent was to restore philosophy to right suppositions, and specifically to the primacy of spirit, something that had been obscured by those he called "minute philosophers."

The Spiritual Philosopher

Thinking about what postmodern religion might look like, Don Cupitt has gone back to Berkeley and cited his reversal of metaphysical materialism. But Berkeley's God is too real for Cupitt, who believes the times call for a departure from all forms of Platonic realism that would hold out for objective truth within the manifest world. There are no essences, according to Cupitt, a contention that has become a mantra among postmodernists. With postmodern aplomb he declares, "*There is only this.* This is contingent flow of verbal signifiers in which I am caught up, and which is outsideless, must be Being-itself, absolute Reality."[13] In a world after metaphysics, a world after God, the task of religion is to make life meaningful and worthwhile. God is the poetry to do this, the art of poiesis. Words are constitutive of experience, and religious words constitute religious experience. The job of responsible people today, according to Cupitt, is to change from a realist vocabulary to an antirealist vocabulary, because antirealism is common sense today.

Now, Cupitt's theological proposal, if it can be called that, is rooted in a naturalist metaphysics. Religions are cultural constructions with no final claim on the truth. Religious beliefs are words about words, talk about language and the way language orders the world. We dwell in language; as human beings, we are comprised of language. God is the symbol of where words come from and of the flux of language itself, which is our life-world. To do justice to this God, we need, Cupitt says, "a new kind of religion for this new world, an objectless, abstract practice of life as expressive religious art."[14] This is a religion which synthesizes the classical worldview of God as infinite creator and the modern worldview that emerged out of the Enlightenment and which mathematized the creation and made humankind the measure of God.

If this is an apt representation of the postmodern vision applied to the subject of religion, I would say that the postmodern is not an antithesis to the modern at all, but merely a cadence in the persistent theme of modernity. Admittedly, this cadence seems to be a departure from scientism and positivism, seems to be a turning from the most distinctive expressions of modernity. But its antirealist antimetaphysics is nevertheless thoroughly and unjustifiably materialist, and in this sense modern. Postmodernists like Cupitt have understandable scruples regarding the prejudice and dogmatisms that are paraded as truth, and not least of all paraded in the name of Christ. But from the fact that we cannot pronounce finally on the question of truth, from the fact that "truth" is often a political bludgeon to enforce the pseudometaphysics of the ruling elites, whether in science or society, from the fact that we cannot claim for ourselves a God's-eye view of things, it does not follow that we know nothing truly or that there is nothing to be truly known. The exposure of the pretensions of modernity does not entail intellectual nihilism. Undifferentiating iconoclasm does not follow from the fact that the metaphysics of modernity is unfounded. The pendulum swings, but absurdity remains, the imposture of modernist enthusiasm is traded for the imposture of postmodernist skepticism.[15]

The object of Cupitt's religion is "the God of language," the symbol for the universe of language in which, he says, we live and move and have our being.[16] Epistemically, perhaps, but what is the whence of these language users and the referents of their language? What is the ontological status of the sensible universe in which we live and move and have our being? Why is that question ruled out of court? Is it because the real has been ruled out of court?

The world for Berkeley is also language, but a divine, sensible language. The divine Spirit is displayed for the apprehension of all in the constituents of the natural universe. The special sciences lend precision to the general apprehension, which is available to common sense, and the workings of nature allow of endless exploration. There is no bottom to such investigations. An idea of sense is something real, according to Berkeley. Something not an idea of sense is an image. Ideas of sense are produced by God, ideas of the imagination are produced by finite spirits. The ideas of sense form a continuous uniform pattern, which discloses the will of God as the Author of nature. We may formulate the particular ideas of sense into regularities which we take to be the laws of nature. These regulations are corrigible, insofar as we misread effects for causes or take sequence for agency. Or we can go wrong by misinterpreting contingencies as necessities. The check against wayward speculation is common sense. Genuine metaphysics arises, according to Berkeley, out of common sense, which is nothing less than communion with the Spirit who is the Author of nature. Genuine metaphysics criticizes received opinion, even as it enlivens common sense by drawing out its metaphysical implications. Aberrant metaphysics enshrines the abstract idea of matter, an affront to common sense, which inevitably leads to the obscuring or abandonment of the reality of the sensible world presented in the divine sensible language. Philosophy is, in this telling, a spiritual discipline for the purification of common sense. Common sense is not prereflective or unscientific, but is, rather, the very possibility of arriving at philosophic understanding.

Cupitt's metaphysical relativism (antiessentialism) is typical of the postmodern reaction to the breakdown of modernism. It is also the dialectal flowering of the skepticism that Berkeley attempted to stave off with his philosophy of immaterialism. Like logical positivism and the incommensurability thesis, Cupitt's postmodernist relativism is self-refuting. After all, if everything is relative, then the relative is also relative. But many postmodernists seem able to live with this aporia, so great is their zeal to deny the real for the sake of the really real nonreal.

Hillary Putnam has suggested that this view is reductionistic in the same way as is the modern scientism postmodernists are so anxious to decry. "That rationality is defined by an ideal computer program is a scientistic theory inspired by the exact sciences; that it is simply defined by the local cultural norms is a scientistic theory inspired by anthropology. . . . Both sorts of scientism are attempts to evade the issue of giving a sane and human description of the scope of reason."[17] But more than this, they are both a source of atheism and irreligion insofar as they exclude the spiritual, either on the presumption of a substance we know not what or by denying substance because we know not what. The presumption and the denial alike are rooted in a monistic naturalism, materialism, which is simply inadequate to our experience as conscious agents who are among the constituents of nature of which we are not the cause. The philosophy of immaterialism is the affirmation of God as Spirit, intimately present in the sensible ideas that comprise our experience, an affirmation, as we have seen, that is implicit in Berkeley's exposure of the absurd as represented in the doctrine of matter, a doctrine on which the modern world is founded.

I have called up the shade of Berkeley to commend his much misunderstood and generally overlooked philosophy of immaterialism as a practical response to the misplaced values of modernity and as an alternative to postmodernist zealotry. I say a "practical" response, not because his work lacks theoretical rigor, but because his manner of approach to the problems he addressed, whether in optics or mathematics or economics or philosophy, was essentially pragmatic. Pierce and James both recognized Berkeley as a precursor of modern pragmatism.

Berkeley's intention in all his endeavors was the improvement of human life.

In the *Dialogues* he wrote, "The end of speculation is the practice of the improvement and regulation of our lives and actions."[18] His speculations are useful to this end even as they are philosophical therapeutics for philosophical error. But more than this, he exhibits in his projects the calling of the philosopher and, more specifically, the Christian philosopher who is spiritually responsive to the Spirit of the One in whom we live and move and have our being. Berkeley was not a pedant, nor were his engagements principally academic. He wished not simply to understand the world but to change it, and when his early writings received scant attention, he devoted his energies to developing a university in America in the hope that the new world would be receptive to the new ideas generated in and from his New Principle. When this project failed for lack of the promised support, he returned to England and ultimately to Ireland, where, as Bishop of Cloyne, he faithfully served a poor diocese, addressing himself to laying bare the roots of Ireland's economic distress (*The Querist*), tirelessly pursuing the physical well-being of the people in his care, ministering directly to their needs, but also in the course of so doing producing the thoroughly remarkable *Siris,* in which he reads the Trinity out of a meditation on the humble substance tar-water.

Berkeley's goal in his philosophy was to reclaim an appetite for the good in an age in which, for all intents and purposes, this appetite was lost, and to admit again the irreducible mystery of being into science and human reasoning. He sought the evidence for his speculations in an appeal to common sense and practical application. The rigor of his work is the rigor of simplicity. Its value is in clearing away the intellectual debris that frustrates spiritual understanding.

Anne, Berkeley's wife, wrote, speaking of Berkeley's challenge to materialists, "He has taken from them their ground they stand on, and had he built as he has pulled down he had been then a master builder indeed."[19] Berkeley attacked the pseudometaphysics of his day so that a genuine metaphysics might be brought to light. He did not write that metaphysics himself. Nor did he attempt much as a theologian, content to allow the faith he received to be deployed in the intellectual space he cleared, content to practice the faith he believed, having thrown off the absurdities of matter which oppressed or diverted the theological impulse. Even in *Siris,* where he allows himself to speculate about several theological topics and the Christian doctrine of the Trinity in particular, this is done only to show how elements of this doctrine are anticipated in the writings of Egypt and Greece, and in the overall context of exhibiting the dependence of the world on God. He concludes, however, that knowledge of God is at best obscure in this life.

Berkeley is a model of theological circumspection, a theistic philosopher rather than a theologian, a thinker devoted to curbing the excesses of speculation by rooting out the causes of errors in the fields of thought to which he applied himself. This is a temperament that is much needed in the present, when fundamentalisms of all sorts abound, when the spirit of scientism and positivism persists in the beliefs and practices of those who are certain of their orthodoxies, who will deny the humanity of those who do not share their views or abandon common sense to fit their experience to the language of some sacred text or other. Naturalistic denials of the spiritual can seem like positive enlightenment compared to those sorts of flight from the world. Meanwhile, much of academic theology becomes ever more abstract, juggling yet again the old ideas as if by getting these straight once and for all the Holy Spirit will at last be cornered and forced to give up the divine secrets, or treating the will of God as an intramural affair that will be determined by doctrine or confession. A spiritual philosophy after the model of Berkeley would have done with theological abstractions of all sorts and would seek to find the presence of God in the world of glorious and terrible facts, appreciating the mystery of things while eschewing their mystification.

In the end, the spiritual philosopher is a hierophant, whose task it is to expose the divine in the sensible when physicalist enthusiasm has excluded its consideration, and to recall the sensible in the divine when spiritual enthusiasts are abdicating their responsibility to be rational agents of grace in the world. Indeed, the principal lesson that a spiritual philosopher has to teach is grace. In the language of our day, the spiritual philosopher is an "organic intellectual," a thinker who relates ideas to action for the sake of promoting moral aims among those whom the thinker understands to be his or her constituency. As Berkeley approached this task, it was a matter of relating philosophy to common sense in order to bring grace to bear for the sake of making a difference in the world, a difference that is liberating from all that would constrain the spirit and alienate it from its true home. At a time when most intellectuals were bound to the values of the New Science as enshrined in the Enlightenment and were distancing themselves from the unsophisticated world of common sense, Berkeley attacked those values in the name of common sense and the grace of God, which is known in the apprehensions of common sense. In so doing, he exhibited an approach to spiritual thinking, thinking in which grace is both point of departure and goal of intellectual work, thinking that is proved in its capacity to make thought and action in all areas of life gracious.

The thrall of modernity will not be broken by the irony or nihilism that are characteristic of so much of postmodernist thinking. These are simply convolutions of the modern "spirit," an apparent opposition to the modern which is only apparently oppositional, inasmuch as it is founded in a metaphysics that is intrinsically materialist. The way clear is to be found in the rediscovery of the primacy of spirit. Philosophers and theologians, like everyone else, have their part to play in this rediscovery.

NOTES

1. Daniel Dennett, *Consciousness Explained* (Boston: Little, Brown & Co., 1991), 33.
2. George Berkeley, *The Works of George Berkeley, Bishop of Cloyne,* vol. 1, ed. A. A. Luce and T. E. Jessop (New York: Thomas Nelson & Sons, 1948), 625.
3. John Searle, *The Rediscovery of Mind* (Cambridge, Mass.: MIT Press, 1992), 28.
4. Ibid., 55.
5. Ibid., 123.
6. Berkeley, *Works,* vol. 2 (1949), 142.
7. Berkeley, *Works,* vol. 1.
8. Berkeley, *Works,* vol. 2, 6.
9. Austin Farrer, "The Physical Theology of Leibniz," in *Reflective Faith,* ed. Charles Conti (Grand Rapids: Wm. B. Eerdmans Publishing Co., 1972), 108.

10. Berkeley, *Works,* vol. 2, 29.
11. Herbert Marcuse, *One Dimensional Man* (Boston: Beacon Press, 1968), 199.
12. Berkeley, *Works,* vol. 3, vii, 20.
13. Don Cupitt, *Creation out of Nothing* (Philadelphia: Trinity Press International, 1990), 88.
14. Cupitt, *Creation,* 195.
15. One of the best studies of the contribution and legacy of Berkeley's work is Gavin Ardley's *Berkeley's Renovation of Philosophy* (The Hague: Martinus Nijhoff, 1968). I am especially indebted to Ardley's analysis of the place of common sense in Berkeley's thinking and his development of Berkeley's distinction between metaphysics and pseudometaphysics. See especially pp. 55–143, passim.
16. This description of God from Acts 17:28 is a favorite of Berkeley's, though he applies it very differently than does Cupitt.
17. Hillary Putnam, *Reason, Truth, and History* (New York: Cambridge University Press, 1981), 126.
18. Berkeley, *Works,* vol. 2, preface.
19. Berkeley, *Works,* vol. 7, 388.

PART II

SPIRITUALITY WITHIN CHRISTIAN THEOLOGY

7

HOPE—THE SPIRITUAL DIMENSION OF THEOLOGICAL ANTHROPOLOGY

GERHARD SAUTER

Hope—A Virtue?

The French mystic Charles Péguy (1873–1914) describes hope in a surprising way—by placing it in opposition to faith and love:

> The faith that I love best, says God, is hope.
> Faith does not surprise me.
> It's not surprising. . . .
> Charity, says God, that doesn't surprise me.
> It's not surprising. . . .
> But Hope, says God, that is something that surprises me.
> Even me.
> That is surprising.
> That these poor children see how things are going, and believe that tomorrow
>   things will go better.
> That they see how things are going today and believe that they
>   will go better tomorrow morning.
> That is surprising and it is by far the greatest marvel of our grace.
> And I'm surprised by it myself.
> And my grace must indeed be an incredible force.
> And must flow freely and like an inexhaustible river. . . .
> What surprises me, says God, is Hope.
> And I can't get over it.
> This little Hope who seems like nothing at all.
> This little girl Hope.
> Immortal.[1]

This statement seems to me stimulating from several different perspectives. First, Péguy depicts hope, given by Divine Grace, as "little," like a "little girl," modest, not very self-aware or self-possessed, nearly oblivious of all around herself. Instead, in the ecumenical movement, Christian confidence has often been claimed as the "big," comprehensive hope, or as the ever and overall transcending hope, evoking and transforming so-called "small hopes" of human beings in searching for peace and justice or for achieving a better life. According to this rhetoric, "absolute hope" can be changed like a bill into coins of "small hopes," but the value of the bill is inexhaustible. Péguy, on the contrary, emphasizes the small hope as trust in the coming day, the ongoing life, the continuity of one's being, and this hope is even the belief that there will be something better tomorrow. God confesses being amazed by this small but persistent trust. Faith as confidence in the beauty and goodness of the given world seems to be natural, and in the same way as love, God expects, is challenged by the need of living beings. But hope is miraculous, even as a gift of God, given within his creation and his creatures. This hope is not related to the new creation in the resurrection of the dead (according to Paul in Rom. 4:17), but it is rooted in the promise of the creation. It is confidence in the Creator without always knowing it. This hope expresses itself as a deep trust, not limited to the motto "Life goes on" (that in itself is a lot) but striving for the new, the better. Trusting what is coming, hope awakens daily to the new.

Second, Péguy latches onto a theological tradition that interprets "hope" as a virtue, that is, as an attitude that can be acquired and developed, but which can also become stunted and deformed. This tradition recalls Paul (1 Cor. 13:13), who compares faith, hope, and love. Whereas Paul ranks love above faith and hope, Péguy stresses the inconspicuous force of hope, which seems to be supported by faith and love and yet supports both, however imperceptibly.

Protestant theology, especially when it has followed the Reformers' critique of the scholastic understanding of virtues, has been very reluctant to accept a concept of habits, which can be acquired and which bespeak an ability to shape oneself and one's destiny.

But is there not a fundamental difference between habit and virtue? Can we relate "virtue" to the question of learning? According to Alasdair MacIntyre,[2] virtue is the opposite of manipulation, and therefore it should be relevant for theology. And a "habit" may well be a sociocultural phenomenon that is linked to even deeper-rooted convictions.[3]

Yet, *the "experience" of Christian theology is the paradoxical process of learning* that faith, love, and hope are not objects of learning. Learning, by contrast, it is hoped will lead to maturity and wisdom, accompanied by "secondary habits" such as trustworthiness.

Hope, according to Charles Péguy, has its own character. Therefore it can be recognized. It is not merely a movement of attraction to the future—the not-yet existing—but confidence in uncertain terrain, confidence precisely where darkness breaks in, where worries originate, and where one wishes to break out in order to save one's self.

Therefore, it would be misleading to associate hope merely with an overactive imagination or with a passion for the possible, the not-yet-realized, with a creative dissatisfaction that propels itself along, continuously pushing off from all that has been and all that has been valid. Some of these aspects may now and then possibly be associated with the hope of faith. But it would be fundamentally wrong to conceive of hope as a basic alternative to persistence, endurance, and permanence, to define hope by mobility versus stability or change versus continuity, or to identify hope with pressing on, overtaking, and transcending. We must not confuse hope with a stereotyped attitude toward time and all facts that may be described temporally.

According to scholastic understanding, the hope granted by grace remolds all natural expectations that have been perverted radically by sin, and raises them upward to God.

The virtue of hope is endangered by our sinful and perverse presumption of all that is God's alone to fulfill. This presumption may be arrogant or desperate, and in both cases the human individual balks at his or her own true self-realization by renouncing the future granted by God.

Martin Luther argued that real presumption in anticipating the future is not manifest in temporal overleaps (so to speak), but rather results from a person's confidence in his or her own action and achievement. The person then tends to anticipate and even to grab God's judgment instead of expecting conformity of his or her own action with the work of God. Presumption is different from anticipation of the future; rather, it claims for human individuals what God alone can decide. Therefore, arrogance and desperation are impious and not merely inhuman. Luther puts the question of the certainty of salvation in a radical way. There is no certainty in settling the account of actions and omissions (including the help of God) with a credit balance—the only certainty is *trust* in *God*. With every definitive self-assessment, the person transcends humanity, gives up time and space granted to the person, and closes her or his mind to God's future. Only justification by faith enables human individuals to live toward that future: justified by faith, the human person is perfectly sound in hope, while a sinner in reality: *Ac per hoc sanus perfecte est in spe, in re autem peccator.*

For Martin Luther existing in hope means living from God's promise (justified on the grounds of the judgment and the certain promise of God: *iustus ex reputatione et promissione Dei certa*).[4] Those who receive eternal life and salvation through the forgiveness of sins no longer merely set their hope on a high goal which rules them (*sperare in dominum*); instead they live hoping in their Lord (*sperare in domino*).[5] Hope defines the location of the person before God.

The hope of faith is the certainty of being able to stand in the coming judgment of God. All human activity comes under this judgment of God. Faith emerges from God's verdict of justification. Faith emerges from God's judgment, justifying the sinner.

Hope at a Crossroads

The hope of faith changes us with respect to our wishes and apprehensions. It transfers us into God's presence and allows us to drop anchor—in fact, God's promise is the anchor, because we can only expect God's presence. It does not separate us thereby from human (all-too-human!) ideas about what will come, can come, or should come. Rather, it places these ideas under God's judgment, saving us by directing our hope to God alone. Therefore, the "accounting for the hope" (1 Peter 3:15) is the test for responsible Christian life.

I will attempt to explicate this more precisely by comparing it to two recent concepts of hope that lay claim to the special way for Christian hope. They appear to be far removed from each other, but they have in common a desire to clarify the Christian character of hope in comparison with human conceptions of behavior in the world, especially in modern times. In both cases, hope becomes a Christian virtue, which one can learn and develop—not in a paradoxical way, but as a cultural-critical or even a countercultural attitude.

"Pure" Hope?

In 1954, Friedrich Gogarten wrote a small essay titled *The Christian Hope.*[6] It is a by-product of his major publications on the problem of secularization and secularism written shortly after World War II. Gogarten analyzes the crisis of Christian faith in modern (Western) culture. In his view, and in the opinion of many exponents of cultural criticism as well, it is the illusion of rational and technical omnipotence that gives rise to that crisis: "Modern man" has reached a deadlock, because he wants to control his own history. He anticipates his own future by planning and, correspondingly, by realizing his own possibilities step-by-step. He relies on the growing and prosperous progress of history, with increasingly better conditions for human life. This confidence in historical progress, however, turns out to be the intimate enemy of Christian hope. Certainly there is a superficial similarity, because the confidence in progress orientates toward, and expects all from, the future. But with all his might, "modern man" tries to avoid being exposed to God in historical reality. This refusal prevents "modern man"—who wants to be, and to stay, master of his own history—from being open to all that comes to him, and, in that coming to him, strikes him in an unpredictable way out of a contingent mystery. This future, however, is the theological counterpart of a planned future.

Friedrich Gogarten's thesis is as follows: The Christian hope is the hope which is free from all concrete wishes.[7] (Thereby he intends to interpret and actualize Luther's sentence: Hope is *spes purissima in purissimum Deum,*[8] the purest hope in the purest God.) In Gogarten's view, Christian hope is pure as far as it intends to be utterly hope, just hope, and nothing else than hope, and has nothing to do with any desires concerning the world and itself—"hope straight." Only by virtue of this hope are humans able to encounter the contingency of God's coming and to experience themselves in a new way. The person who wants himself or herself reflected in a predictable future must be annihilated. The human individual has to be stripped of all hopes, to be nude and available, so to speak, a mere "being" in complete and unprotected openness, in order to meet the Divine incomprehensibility and to endure temporality.

Gogarten wants to fight against the disposable world in the name of hope. He confronts the planners and managers afraid of any disturbance of their well-prepared reality with the freedom that unpredictably comes to us. From this freedom alone we may expect the healing powers for our endangered (even mostly destroyed) world.

Gogarten's argument is based on the essence of humanity: the human constitution, with its basic feature of existence open to an unknown future. Human individuals need to be called back to hope, to be turned around from the danger of losing themselves in the world through the planned development in which their own wishes are extrapolated with the incessant exertion to accomplish themselves through their work, which prevents them from receiving their true character.

This global diagnosis is plausible. There is a grain of truth in the critical remark that no human individual can realize himself by any action, which can only achieve what has been anticipated and planned. But the therapy amounts to the idea that a person may repair his or her attitude to temporality by concentrating on the essentials and eliminating the disorder of *"Werkgerechtigkeit"* by radical openness and readiness for the encounter with God. In a very subtle way, hope has been changed to a virtue, and the Western problem of managing the future has been made a virtue of necessity.

Hope as Protest and Resistance?

Diametrically opposed to this therapeutic position is Jürgen Moltmann's theology. In his *Theology of Hope,* written only ten years after Gogarten's study (1964), "hope" means standing in resistance to the "reversed" world.[9] This resistance is required by God, for it is sparked by God's objection to the death of Jesus Christ.

With Easter, God has broken the spell of death paralyzing the world; God has created the new being and challenged all efforts to arrest Divine life.

Thus hope expresses itself in contradiction to the present state of affairs, to the status quo that paralyzes our thinking and acting. It contradicts all that is "reversed," where what is "reversed" has no real future but is self-perpetuating. What is "reversed" is, by definition, not allowed to have any future, because otherwise we would have to destroy it. Here hope becomes a permanent crossover of the present creatings, shapings, and existings for the sake of a better future, which, in contrast to Gogarten, is now dramatically painted. God's promises become a real utopia of the right society and life in harmony with nature.

Hope—A Household Word

In contrast to the observational category "promise," which was imported as a theological term, "hope" is not originally a word with any specific Christian coloring. And yet it has an extremely important, characteristic meaning in Christian speech—precisely as a word from everyday language.

It is remarkable that a word from everyday speech appears to be able to suffice, without any specific context, in speaking about something so wide-stretching and many-sided as God's dealings with humans and the world; about God's hiddenness and revelation; about his grace and judgment, God's Spirit and the human condition in all its tensions; about distress and happiness, temptation and certainty, death and life.

What does all this have to do elementally and basically with hope? More especially, with a hope that does not need to be annotated and commented on in order to specify it in a statement of faith? It does not have to be defined as an extraordinary hope, nor as a "greater," further reaching, higher, purer, or even absolutely "last hope." Such definition characterized later theology, which by such classifications created confusion rather than clarification. In scholastic theology, for example, hope was explained as supernatural virtue in order to classify it in the highest level of positions; God gave the human being hope to shape the human's life and to adjust it to God.

Such a pattern allows talking of a lower or higher direction of hope determining one's life. But that contradicts *the biblical way of describing hope only by marking its givenness and aim, thereby creating a consistent use of the word.*

It clearly matters, then, in different contexts to be able to say *why Christians hope and can do nothing else but hope,* without crystallizing out a "Christian hope" as an attitude and characteristic of conduct—one clearly distinct by its origin and its goals, which can be acquired, developed, and presented before God's judgment. Hope can be *described,* rather, in its theological character by pointing out God's promises, even explaining their specific paradoxical "experiences" of learning what cannot be acquired—but this cannot be sufficiently *depicted* as a habit.

Therefore, the observation that there is no genuine theological concept of hope must not induce us to infer from the hope indicated by the biblical texts an "essence" of hope. There is no general structure of hope that might include "saving hope" as a special, religious case of intentional attitude and direction to things or situations to come. Biblical hope is defined neither as opposed to "having" (according to the motto "What I already possess, I need not hope for—and what I hope for, I haven't got yet") nor as an active disposition toward matters that are open to be experienced and defined as healing, integrating, or destroying.

Hope that comes from God and is put in order by him, is first of all hope, nothing more. No other word has been specified for it that can separate it, on purely linguistic terms, from expectations in other directions. Related to the usage of the word "hope," however, are habits that must be questioned. Those habits can indicate to whom a person reaches out, to what a person directs the self, and how a person is fulfilled. People speak of hope in many unprecedented ways. This one word may connect them, but it can also definitely separate them from one another.

Hope in Conflict

Paul attempts to climb out of the theological rut of hope with the concise, closely knit sentence "Abraham believed in hope against hope" (Rom. 4:18).

Here Paul lays out the story of Abraham's faith (Gen. 15:1–6) as the biblical paradigm of hope: Abraham follows God's promise; he heads out to an unknown land, which was promised to him and his descendants.

But on his way, in the night, when he sits lonely in his tent, he feels arrested by the question of how he can achieve the blessing God has promised him, of how his physical ability will match up with the gift to come. And he asks himself: "What will happen to all that I have achieved, when I will have disappeared?"

That is a monologue—Abraham talks to himself, although he seems to address God—but God calls him out and places him before the stars in the heaven of his creation and challenges that they be numerically grasped. That is an absurd task, before which Abraham must, of necessity, be silent. And this silence, from which the forgottenness of self of the one who hopes is born, God receives as the answer of faith. He takes it as "Yes," and with this "yes" Abraham anchors himself in God (Gen. 15:6). With this spiritual gesture, Abraham appropriates the "time-space" God has given by his promise.

In Paul's view, Abraham is already transferred to the cross of Golgotha and to Jesus' tomb on Easter morning. The Christ-narrative does not outrun the paradigm of hope—on the contrary, it demonstrates how to talk of God in a new way, and thereby hope is talked of anew too, in the peculiar movement of "hope against hope." With the resurrection of Jesus Christ comes revelation of who God is, the God whom Abraham readily believed without knowing the significance of hope maintaining his confidence.

Abraham had in his mind the heir, who was to receive the fulfillment of God's promise to him. But by his trust in God, he became the father of an immeasurable number of other persons who do not belong together genealogically, but for God's sake. Abraham had no idea and certainly no precognition of the fact that he was to become the father of those faithful to God.

Ephesians 2:12 addresses the heathen Christians and their former status without God and without hope in the world, because they had been "alienated from the citizenship of Israel, cut off from the covenant of the promises." Paul's paraphrase of the Abraham story, however, makes clear that the same holds true for Abraham, the patriarch of Israel, who existed "without hope and without God in the world" as long as he stayed alone with his hope. His faith and the strength of this hope is created by the call of God, who calls him out of the prejudices of his hopes.

He must not only leave his tent to look at the heaven, the horizon of creation—he must leave himself, in order to leave himself alone in God's promise. *God places him in his promise,* in the middle of the world of his creation, yet beyond all calculable nature. What it amounts to is that Abraham "hoped against hope." Hoping here must be taken as signifying "from God's fidelity."

Abraham's future is grounded on God's promise. This statement, however, must be articulated dialectically. Hoping against hope is no self-supporting movement toward an unknown time. Faith on hope and on the strength of hope at once confronts hope and even resists hope. "Lord, I believe; help my unbelief!": this cry for help, uttered to Jesus by the desperate father of a sick child and uttered as a response to Jesus' trial of faith (Mark 9:24), must be read as: "Whenever I believe, I believe against my hope in order to trust You with all my heart!"

Abraham's relation to God's promise remains split: God allows Abraham to be involved in the promise as far as he moves away from home, but the promise has not yet seized Abraham himself.

This aspect might be underscored by the repetition of the promise, by God's starting the dialogue again and again, while Abraham, on his side, repeatedly gives expression to his hidden hopelessness. He perceives the promise, but it does not get close to him, or rather the reverse—he remains at a distance, because he assumes a wait-and-see attitude to the promise. *It is God alone who can awaken the hope in him, which makes room for God's activity.*

Thus, "faith on hope" becomes the signature of Abraham's existence, certainly not without struggle and, again and again, misunderstood by Abraham himself; this hope is often a broken one and never *Abraham's* hope without qualification. He still has to learn how to perceive himself from the perspective of his hope. Abraham believes on hope, without receiving anything else or anything more than just hope. Thus, the land he lives in will be and remain a foreign country (cf. Heb. 11:9), as a sign that he is heir of the promise, together with his offspring—which implies that they will never be without the promise and at the same time that they therefore never will leave it behind. All their hopes will be embraced by God's promise. The hope of faith is no special hope among others, but it takes shape resisting a hope that claims to judge the future on the background of predictable possibilities and tries to discern between what has a future and what has no future.

"Hope against expectations"—that is an idiomatic expression that is based on an odd, quasi-spatial metaphor: "against" hope, contrary to it, as a barrier stands against what it faces, and "from" it "to there," as if it is not yet "here" or as if faith is not yet "there."

The prepositions mark the space for a certain movement. This movement, however, is neither temporal nor spatial, nor is it spiritual in the sense of the mind's concentrating on facts or intentionally anticipating them; as Plato defined it, hope is the soul's being set on the nonpresent (*Philebus* 32c, 36b–41b).

The expression "believing on hope against hope" is an abbreviation for this extremely complex process. It has been named a paradox (Rudolf Bultmann), but that can only underline that a wonder occurs here, which cannot be brought to expression other than through a contradiction.

"Against hope," that is, not against any hope, but against hope itself—this is one side of perception; the other is "toward hope." Both are valid at the same time. The second way of perceiving does not override the first. Together they form a dialectic that keeps one moving. From the story of Abraham, Paul learns both: "My hope takes away all of my faith—I believe only toward hope!" To put it differently: "I can only hope in God—the hope which I have does not safeguard my hoping."

Both *remain* to be said: "against hope—on hope." On that, what stands *between* both, is God's promise as the ground for making this movement recognizable, but also as a call to confidence in God, not as a passage from one psychic condition to another. In this "between-ness" the wonder of faith occurs. It is *hope against expectation.* This is a hope nobody can "have." It happens against the projected demands of one's self-esteem. In this sense Abraham stands between hope and hope, that is, the hope that stands in his way and the hope, for which he exists, in which he gets involved and on which he relies.

In faith toward hope, hope that people cherish for themselves is turned into confidence in God concerning everything that occurs to them and through them.

Their hope will neither be taken away from them nor will it be replaced by some different kind of hope. Yet they are made to realize the resistance of hope when God promises them what he alone can do—and what he wants to do in their time and place, definitely not without them, but not by their exhausting the range of their possibilities. Against hope, toward hope; that is to follow God's promises, to rely on him and relinquish oneself, by fastening oneself onto the Creator and perceiving oneself as creature in the midst of the creation.

Therefore, a person stands before God, and the relationship one has with God reposes one's hope in God. The person stands before God alone as one who hopes. This relationship is brought out of prayer—in complaint, request, and thanks. Hoping in God means to call him in prayer and, thereby, to name him as he has given himself to be known.

The invocation of God in prayer does not happen in emptiness. It is rather a self-exposure to God's acting which has already seized the praying person. Therefore, prayer itself already signifies and expresses confidence, even though this confidence might not be manifest as a grateful agreement, but as complaint or accusation, as plea or intercession. The invocation of God in prayer endows hope with its unwavering certainty. Persons who set their hope in God are able to tell whom they trust. To set one's hope on God does not primarily mean to hope for something, excluding other things, but to be prepared for God.

Without hope no one can truly pray, even if this hope is hardly known to the one who prays, as, for example, in the despairing complaint and in the no-less-pressing request.

Hope in God, God himself lays out. It is, at least in its most inner, spiritual core, an event between God and the individual person, an often-presented dramatic, even turbulent, process, full of surprise—precisely "hope against expectation."

Hope on God originates paradoxically from the shock of God's presence, which widely exceeds every natural fear of God. It is a sign that God really reaches people in the prison of their self-created fates, caught in their own limiting conceptions.

God's promising presence makes hope perceptible and helps us resist the supposed clarity of our self-awareness, the ambiguity of our hopes, with their conflicting wishes and fears. Once hope has been disturbed by God, it will no longer be reducible to concepts nor can it be identified with attitudes. It rather opens up a way of perceiving that especially opposes two kinds of misinterpretation. The first one corresponds to the idea that viable human existence means being ready every time to go farther. This is a naturalistic view of a rather sublime shade. Hope is transformed into an increased capability of survival, depending on the ability to change in time, according to the password: "Whoever does not stay the same will remain in existence." This idea can also integrate death as a metamorphosis, as a transmutation into some different form of life—whether as individual survival or as being absorbed by a greater whole. There is another interpretation which locates the subject of ultimate and true hope in a different, proper world. From this view derives a yearning that cannot find rest with any aim on earth. This is an idealistic explanation of hope. It is also possible to combine both interpretations, and the result is a maxim that today seems to be generally accepted: "As long as things progress, they improve. Moving forward is to move upward."

To encounter God through hope in God does not happen to anybody who tries to overcome a distance in time and space step by step, or to climb up to higher values and qualities. If the search for God, that is, our asking after God, starts at the fact that God has given us hope in God, it will be precisely this hope which indicates why God is far away from human beings and how God gets close to them.

He gets close to them in the death of Jesus Christ, in this singular and unique event in which human beings want to speak the final word, in which Jesus Christ suffers God's will. Jesus' death confronts us with the ultimate question about God's judgment—God's judgment on whatever human beings at most bring about and religious self-assertion combined with political power can achieve—and it makes us ask about God's judgment on human suffering, especially on exceedingly unnatural suffering and dying. The answer is given by the fact that we are bound to Jesus' death, and from this our hope arises.

This hope is based on Jesus Christ's having conquered death. Not by having stridden through some ultimate twilight zone to demonstrate a hope that transcends death! Rather, God has declared Godself for Christ's dying by personally entering it and disarming death by taking away from it its power of cutting through everything. Thus, the power of sin is being denied, a power which in the face of death used to triumph after having molded with the destructive power of human *incurvatus in se* a chain of minor and major achievements.

This victory gives hope, and leads the person who starts hoping deeper into the rebellion of sin and death, which still have not been removed from this world. Time and again sin and death offer a present and a future that threaten to separate us from God's love. Human beings cannot remain in existence in the midst of this conflict unless they hold onto Christ. And God enables them by the work of God's Spirit to do so again and again. The coming of the Spirit tears open the *incurvatus in se* by which human beings move under the grip of sin and death, and leads them utterly into the conflict of their deadly will to live, making them recognize it as an abyss by God's grace (Romans 7). They will not be dragged into this abyss, for God's Spirit holds them, and this hold is their hope. Those moved by God's Spirit, precisely for this reason will realize their own weakness before God, and this will be manifest in prayer. The very fact that they want to turn to God shows that they need hope in God—yet they lack the appropriate words, and language itself fails completely. The Spirit who represents God within them has to represent, to appear for, them before God (Rom. 8:26). This happens although (or because) they call God "Father," because by God's Spirit it has been affirmed that they belong to God's children (Rom. 8:16)—and just for this reason they are longing to be finally accepted as children and heirs (v. 23). This Spirit does not leave any space for sin; those who are endowed with the Spirit now really expect their redemption, seeing themselves as members of God's groaning creation (vv. 22–25). Suffering with those who suffer, they are not allowed to balance up the present suffering and future glory (v. 18). They must neither take advantage of the future as compensation for the present—which would make suffering appear more endurable—nor must they attach importance to suffering.

Rather, they are made attentive and watchful for whatever is being given by God in a way that points back to God. It is the witness of God's Spirit joining with our spirit that opens up the view of hope. We are aroused, our senses are being changed, our whole perception is being renewed (Rom. 12:3)—this is what hope as confidence means: to be prepared for God in the midst of everything that may happen and that we might encounter.

NOTES

1. Charles Péguy, *The Portal of the Mystery of Hope,* trans. D. L. Schindler, Jr. (Grand Rapids: Wm. B. Eerdmans Publishing Co., 1996), 1, 6–7.
2. Alasdair MacIntyre, *After Virtue* (Notre Dame, Ind.: University of Notre Dame Press, 1984).
3. Cf., e.g., Robert N. Bellah, *Habits of the Heart* (Berkeley: University of California Press, 1985).
4. Martin Luther, Lectures on Romans, *Luthers Werke,* Kritische Gesamtausgabe, ed. J. K. E. Knaake et al. (Weimar: Böhlau, 1883ff.), 56, 272, 18 (hereafter cited as WA). = *Luther's Works,* American Edition, 55 vols. ed. J. Pelikan and H. T. Lehmann (St. Louis and Philadelphia: Concordia and Fortress, 1955ff.), 25, 260: "a righteous man by the sure imputation and promise of God."
5. Martin Luther, *Dictata super Psalterium:* WA 3.56, 32 (comment on Ps. 4:61).
6. Friedrich Gogarten, "Die christliche Hoffnung," *Deutsche Universitätszeitung* 9/24 (1954): 3–7.
7. Cf. Friedrich Gogarten, *Verhängnis und Hoffnung der Neuzeit: Die Säkularisierung als theologisches Problem* (Stuttgart: F. Vorwerk, 2d ed. 1958), 127: "The Hope of faith . . . leaves the future undetermined."
8. Martin Luther, *Operationes in Psalmos,* WA 6.166, 16–19 (comment on Ps. 5:12).
9. Jürgen Moltmann, *Theology of Hope: On the Ground and the Implications of a Christian Eschatology,* trans. J. W. Leitch (London: SCM Press, 1967), esp. 102–12.

8

FREEDOM TO PRAY

Karl Barth's Theology of Prayer

DANIEL L. MIGLIORE

Introduction

There is abundant evidence of a new interest in spirituality and prayer in the church today. After a period of intense activism that sometimes marginalized or even replaced serious concern for worship and prayer, theology and ministry are turning their attention to the deep spiritual foundations of Christian life without which the call to action so easily leads to burnout or cynicism. There is both real promise and possible danger in this development. The promise is that Christians will learn "to drink from their own wells"[1] as they face the social, cultural, moral, and religious crises of our time. The danger is that interest in spirituality may become a new fad driven more by popular culture and market forces than by a biblically grounded understanding and practice of prayer.

Of the resources available to the church for serious reflection on the place of prayer in Christian life, ministry, and theology, the work of Karl Barth is among the richest. No other theologian of the twentieth century took prayer more seriously or developed a more extensive theology of prayer than did Barth. In this paper I will first sketch the central themes of Barth's theology of prayer and then summarize his description of the significance of prayer for theological work. With this background I will then consider Barth's understanding of the act of prayer as a clue to the right understanding of the relationship of divine sovereignty and human freedom. In the final section I will contend that we must go farther than Barth did in including the freedom to lament and protest within the freedom to pray.

The Central Themes of Barth's Theology of Prayer

In the lectures given during his only trip to the United States, Barth challenged his hearers not to become champions of past or present theological schools, whether Thomism, Calvinism, or Barthianism, but to develop instead a theology of freedom.[2] The motif of freedom—the freedom of God and the freedom of the covenant partners of God—appears everywhere in the *Church Dogmatics*. Not surprisingly, this theme also marks his theology of prayer: for Barth, prayer is the quintessential act of human freedom before God.

1. Barth considers and rejects two standard answers to the question, *Why is prayer necessary?* The first attempts to ground the necessity of prayer in human need. We must pray, so this answer would say, because we are weak and needy, and we are thus moved to seek help from beyond ourselves. In Barth's judgment, however, our needs do not necessarily teach us to pray. They might just as easily teach us to curse, or scoff, or become resigned, or work all the harder to satisfy our needs by ourselves. A second answer to the question, Why is prayer necessary? is that we turn to God in prayer because God is the source of all blessings. If the first answer is based on a general anthropology, the second answer is based on a general idea of God. According to Barth, the attempt to ground the necessity of prayer in an abstract conception of God as source of all good is no more compelling than the effort to base it in a general theory of human neediness. The idea of God as the source of all good, far from providing a firm basis of prayer, might just as well lead to the conclusion that since God knows what we need and is able to supply all that we lack or desire, any attempt on our part to influence God would be superfluous and inappropriate.[3]

So why pray? For Barth the basis of prayer can be nothing other than the will of God, realized in Jesus Christ, that human creatures be the free covenant partners of God. In prayer human beings are permitted and commanded to come to God freely with their desires and requests. "The real basis of prayer is man's freedom before God, the God-given permission to pray which, because it is given by God, becomes a command and order and therefore a necessity."[4] As chosen partners and coworkers with God, we are invited, permitted, and commanded to pray.

While largely in agreement with Luther that prayer is based on the command of God, Barth emphasizes that this command is never to be understood as an abstract divine fiat. It is the freely gracious God who summons us to prayer. In prayer we turn to the God who has graciously drawn near to us.[5] Before we speak to God, God has already spoken to us. This is the point of Barth's claim that God is the real initiator of prayer, that God's action precedes our action, that there is always a hearing that precedes the asking of prayer.[6]

Thus the necessity of prayer according to Barth is to be found not in human need, nor in divine majesty, nor in an abstract divine command, but in God's gracious invitation and humanity's God-given freedom to pray. Only if we begin with God's concrete address to humanity above all in Jesus Christ are we able to rightly grasp the necessity of prayer. Prayer is simply "the first available use of the freedom" that has been given to us in Christ.[7]

2. If prayer is necessary because God permits and commands us to pray as those called to life in communion with and service of God, for Barth *prayer is centrally petition:* asking, wishing, desiring, expecting.[8] Of course, Barth allows that prayer is other things as well: it is also adoration, thanksgiving, praise, and confession. But unlike Schleiermacher, who saw the prayer of thanksgiving and acceptance of the divine world government as the essence of Christian prayer,[9] Barth identifies the "center" of prayer as petition.[10] He points to the fact that the Lord's

Prayer is simply a "string of petitions."[11] By arguing that petition is the center of prayer, Barth not only underscores the fact that we come to God with empty hands; he also emphasizes that we are summoned to pray in freedom. Understanding prayer as centrally petition assures that "the real man comes before God in prayer,"[12] that we do not have to hide any anxiety or desire in prayer. "All masks and camouflages may and must fall away" in the free act of genuine prayer.[13]

While we are to "come as we are" in prayer with all our anxiety, passion, and egoism, our praying will, of course, always stand in need of being ordered and purified.[14] Guided by the Lord's Prayer, our petitions will not be just any sort of asking. In the first three petitions of the Lord's Prayer, Christians pray for the honoring of God, the coming of God's reign, the doing of God's will; in the final three petitions they pray for daily bread, forgiveness of sins, and protection from evil. This order, Barth contends, is of great significance. Only as we first plead for the purposes of God to prevail can we properly plead for the fulfillment of our own needs and those of the church and the whole creation.

According to Barth, then, the appropriate response of humanity to God's gracious initiative is simply a life of invocation, calling on God freely in all circumstances. Invocation is the "normal action" of the free human creature in the covenant of grace that corresponds to the freely gracious action of God.[15]

3. In line with his characteristic christocentric emphasis, prayer for Barth is *a participation in the praying of Jesus Christ*. He is the supreme pray-er, the great suppliant, "the first and proper *Subject* of prayer" (emphasis added).[16] As the Son of God, Jesus is the divine gift and answer to human asking; as the Son of man he is the true human petitioner.[17] Representative of our true humanity, Jesus Christ "is only and altogether a Suppliant."[18] He intercedes on our behalf, petitioning on behalf of those who cannot and will not ask for themselves.[19] Thus when Christians pray to God in the name of Christ, their asking is enclosed in his asking; their petition is a "repetition of his petition."[20] In their petitionary prayer Christians participate not only in the prophetic and priestly but also in the kingly office of Christ. "Christian prayer is participation in Jesus Christ; participation, basically, in the grace which is revealed and active in Him, in the Son of God; and then only, and on this basis, participation in the asking of the Son of Man."[21] For Barth our freedom to pray is formed and disciplined by our participation in Jesus Christ.

Because our prayer is a participation in the prayer of Jesus Christ, it is sure of God's hearing. In Jesus Christ we are bound up from eternity with God, and God has bound Godself from eternity with us. Hence, "When we pray to God we have Him on our side from the very outset, and we for our part stand on His side from the very outset, so that from the very outset we must be certain that He hears our prayer."[22]

4. For Barth Christian prayer is not individualistic prayer but fundamentally "common prayer."[23] *Prayer is essentially a communal act*. "Although he prays for himself as an individual, [the Christian] does not pray private prayers."[24] "Praying for himself . . . he prays with and for all other Christians, because he prays for the service and work of the community; and in so doing he prays for all men."[25] In correspondence with the prayer of Jesus Christ, the petitions of the Christian

will be primarily intercession. "True private and public prayer will always have this particularly in common, that as petition they will have the character of inter-cession."[26] The prayers of the community are representative on behalf of all hu-manity and the whole creation; they give voice to the groaning of all creation.[27] Barth often stresses the communal and inclusive character of the Lord's Prayer. The "we" of the Lord's Prayer "are the members of this community, and behind them, not praying but groaning together with them, all men and all creatures."[28]

5. Prayer for Barth is *the primary Christian action* and thus an essential ingredi-ent in all Christian witness and activity. Prayer and Christian ethics are inseparable. Prayer is "the most intimate and effective form of Christian action. All other work . . . is Christian work . . . only to the extent that it derives from prayer, and that it has in prayer its true and original form."[29] Barth notes that the most active workers, thinkers, and fighters in the divine service have also been the most active in prayer. He thus agrees with the classical theological rule *ora et labora,* "pray and work," but understands it to mean not that prayer comes chronologically before work and is af-terward incidental to it, but that prayer is constitutive to all faithful Christian action. Barth highlights this point in his discussion of the basic forms of Christian ministry. He identifies six forms of speech ministry (praise, preaching, instruction, evange-lization, mission, and theology) and six forms of action ministry (prayer, care of souls, exemplary Christian life, service, prophetic action, and establishing fellow-ship). Remarkable is Barth's location of prayer as the first form of action ministry. "Prayer is a basic element in the whole action of the whole community."[30] "The community prays as it works. And in praying it works."[31] Barth thus describes prayer as the prototypical form of Christian action. In prayer the community becomes "an active partner in the covenant which God has established."[32]

6. Finally, Barth speaks of a definite *discipline* of prayer. While he does not make this a primary focus, it is nevertheless a basic component of his theology of prayer. He resists, of course, every utilitarian reduction of prayer, whether to ex-tol its usefulness in achieving some social program, forming Christian character, or promoting personal piety. He is especially critical of all emphases on spiritual exercises that tend to make prayer a form of mental and spiritual hygiene. Prayer, he writes, is not "an exercise in the cultivation of the soul or spirit, i.e., the attempt to intensify and deepen ourselves, to purify and cleanse ourselves inwardly, to at-tain clarity and self-control, and finally to set ourselves on a good footing and in agreement with the deity by this preparation."[33] Such exercises, Barth argues, have nothing to do with genuine prayer in which we are mere suppliants and have noth-ing to offer to God. Still, he insists that "some sort of discipline and order cannot be absent from true prayer."[34] Prayer as an exercise of Christian freedom is a formed, disciplined freedom. Thus, while a discipline of prayer cannot be imposed arbitrarily, our freedom to pray "will continually give rise to relative and concrete obligations."[35] Barth mentions regular participation in common prayer, morning and evening prayers, and prayers at meals as well-founded disciplines even if they cannot be mechanically mandated. Barth's fullest discussion of the discipline of prayer as an act of Christian freedom is found in his reflections on the importance of prayer in theological work, and to that topic we now turn.

Prayer and Theology

Although Barth considers prayer to be indispensable to every aspect of Christian life, he is especially attentive to its essential role in the work of theology. Prayer is "the attitude without which there can be no dogmatic work."[36] Discussing the relationship of prayer and theology in the first volume of the *Church Dogmatics,* Barth notes that Anselm cast his famous proof of the existence of God in the *Proslogion* in the form of a prayer; that Aquinas set a prayer for assistance at the beginning of his *Summa Theologiae;* and that David Hollaz, an eighteenth-century Lutheran theologian, transformed each doctrinal locus of theology into a *suspirium,* in which talk about God becomes explicit address to God.[37]

What is at stake for Barth in insisting on the importance of prayer for theology is whether theological inquiry will be a genuinely free science or whether it will be bound to some worldview, ideology, or set of preunderstandings. Prayer for Barth is, of course, no guarantee of successful theological work. Nevertheless, "Prayer can be the recognition that we accomplish nothing by our intentions, even though they be intentions to pray. Prayer can be the expression of our human willing of the will of God. Prayer can signify that for good or evil man justifies God and not himself. Prayer can be the human answer to the divine hearing already granted, the epitome of the true faith which we cannot assume of ourselves."[38] While prayer is no magic wand, "It is hard to see how else there can be successes in this work but on the basis of divine correspondence to this human attitude: 'Lord, I believe; help thou mine unbelief.' "[39]

In *Evangelical Theology,* written in the last decade of his life, Barth returns to the theme of the intimate relationship of theology and prayer. "The first and basic act of theological work is *prayer.* . . . [It] is peculiar and characteristic of theology that it can be performed only in the act of prayer."[40] Theological work "must be that sort of act that has the manner and meaning of a prayer in all its dimensions, relationships, and movements."[41] Barth identifies four dimensions of the inseparable bond of prayer and theology.

1. Barth speaks first of the need for the theologian to turn away for a moment from his own efforts to the object of theology, the living God. "In prayer a man temporarily turns away from his own efforts. This move is necessary precisely for the sake of the duration and continuation of his own work."[42] Prayer is for theological work, Barth suggests, a kind of "Sabbath rest." This is not to say that prayer is a substitute for work. "A man prays, not in order to sacrifice his work or even to neglect it, but in order that it may not remain or become unfruitful work, so that he may do it under the illumination and, consequently, under the rule and blessing of God."[43]

2. Another dimension of the unity of prayer and theology identified by Barth is the fact that "the object of theological work is not some *thing* but some *one.*"[44] This means that "true and proper language concerning God will always be a response to God, which overtly or covertly, explicitly or implicitly, thinks and speaks of God exclusively in the second person. And this means that theological work must really and truly take place in the form of a liturgical act, as invocation of God, and as prayer."[45] Barth again cites the example of Anselm's *Proslogion,*

which takes the form of a prayer from beginning to end. "Implicitly and explicitly, proper theology will have to be a *Proslogion, Suspirium,* or prayer."[46]

3. A third dimension of the relationship of prayer and theology for Barth is that theology can never build from past results with complete confidence but must always begin again from the beginning. Nothing should be allowed to harden, nothing taken as a matter of course from past theological work. Theological study must be permeated by the attitude of prayer if it is to be genuinely free to respond to the living word of God. "Every act of theological work must have the character of an offering in which everything is placed before the living God."[47] "Because it has to be ever renewed, ever original, ever ready to be judged by God himself and by God alone, theology must be an act of prayer."[48]

4. Finally, for Barth the work of theology presupposes that the object of this inquiry is the living and active God, who is self-revealing, and that the human beings who undertake the inquiry are capable of engaging in this work. On both counts, however, only God acting in free grace is able to satisfy these conditions. God alone can reveal God, and God alone can open our eyes and mind to the reality of God. Prayer thus belongs to theological work as a "double entreaty" for God's grace.[49] Theology must therefore proceed with the prayer "*Veni, Creator Spiritus!*" "In his movements from below to above and from above to below, the one Holy Spirit achieves the opening of God for man and the opening of man for God. Theological work, therefore, lives by and in the petition for his coming."[50]

In this essay on prayer in *Evangelical Theology,* Barth gives his fullest description of prayer as a "habit" of theological work, a distinctive human attitude that is necessary in all theological inquiry. Without the attitude of prayer, theology quickly becomes captive to forces alien to its subject matter. As Barth describes the attitude of prayer in theological work, it is characterized by such traits as: persistent attentiveness to the object of inquiry rather than to the inquiring subject; faithful acknowledgment that this object is not at one's disposal, but a living personal subject who has spoken and acted in the past and who also continues to speak and act in new and surprising ways; humble readiness to eschew arrogance and defensiveness regarding the results of past inquiry and to begin anew at the beginning; viewing one's work as an offering to God to be purified, corrected, and used by God as God pleases; and joyful waiting on divine grace as a gift that must be received anew every day. Prayer and theological work go hand in hand whenever theology intends to be a genuinely free science.

Prayer, Divine Sovereignty, and Human Freedom

Throughout the *Church Dogmatics,* and particularly in his doctrine of providence, Barth addresses the persistent problem of the relationship of divine sovereignty and human freedom. He sees the underlying issue as not whether but in what way God is sovereign, and not whether but in what way the human creature is free. Controversy about these matters has often arisen, Barth thinks, because of misconceptions of divine sovereignty on the one hand and of the freedom of human beings as creatures on the other. According to Barth, misunderstandings about the relationship of divine sovereignty and human freedom stem from our anxiety that we may ascribe too much to God and too little to the creature. This anxiety has its root in the fact that we fear God more than we are able to love God. "If our Christian perception and confession does not free us to love God more than we fear Him, then it is obvious that we shall necessarily fear Him more than we love Him. At root, this is the only relevant form of human sin. And this is the one and only reason it is so hard to grasp that the freedom of creaturely activity is confirmed by the unconditioned and irresistible lordship of God. And a reason of this kind cannot be disputed away by theological arguments. If we fear God and fear for ourselves, then we do fear. And since we all of us have the habit of fear of God, this habit will not go out of us except by prayer and fasting. All that we can say is that when and to the extent that it does really go out, the theological arguments which follow will acquire force and validity."[51]

This passage is noteworthy because it shows so clearly that, in Barth's view, successful theological work as faith's quest for greater understanding presupposes the attitude of prayer. He contends that the cogency of theological arguments does not depend solely on meeting formal criteria of truth such as the criteria of correspondence or coherence. Unless the attitude of prayer is present, unless God is approached in prayer as sovereignly gracious, as the source of human freedom rather than a threat to it, as the object of our love and trust rather than our fear, then all attempts to resolve the debate about divine sovereignty and human freedom by argument, however strong or ingenious, are bound to be ineffective.

For Barth the God to whom we pray in the name of Jesus Christ is not the God depicted by what he calls the "miserable anthropomorphism" of divine immutability.[52] In contrast to Schleiermacher, who states that the "primary and basal presupposition" in his theology of prayer is that "there can be no relation of interaction between creature and Creator,"[53] Barth calls Christian theology to eschew "the hallucination of a divine immutability, which rules out the possibility that God can let Himself be conditioned in this or that way by His creature. God is certainly immutable. But He is immutable as the living God and in the mercy in which He espouses the cause of the creature. In distinction from the immovability of a supreme idol, His majesty, the glory of His omnipotence and sovereignty, consists in the fact that He can give to the requests of this creature a place in His will."[54] Just as the triune God is not alone in eternity, so God elects not to be alone in the divine activity *ad extra*. As the living God, God is free to converse with the creature, and "to allow himself to be determined by it in this relationship."[55]

Similarly, human beings are created and redeemed for communion with God and others. They are given a share in the lordship of God, and this happens supremely in the act of prayer. The God of sovereign grace "lets the creature, in its unity with Himself, participate in His omnipotence and work, in the magnifying of His glory and its own salvation, by commanding it to ask and hearing its requests, and when He truly gives it a place at His side in the kingdom of grace and the kingdom of the world. God cannot be greater than He is in Jesus Christ, the Mediator between Him and man. And in Jesus Christ He cannot be greater than

He is when He lets those who are Christ's participate in His kingly office, and therefore when he not only hears but answers their requests."[56] God's sovereignty "is so great that it embraces both the possibility, and, as it is exercised, the actuality, that the creature can actively be present and co-operate in his overruling. There is no creaturely freedom which can limit or compete with the sole sovereignty and efficacy of God. But permitted by God, and indeed willed and created by Him, there is the freedom of the friends of God concerning whom He has determined that without abandoning the helm for one moment He will still allow Himself to be determined by them."[57]

In sum, God creates rather than crushes human freedom; God wills the "real cooperation" of human beings as covenant partners. Under the lordship of the God decisively made known in Jesus Christ, the human creature is not robbed of freedom or excluded from creative activity but is established as the friend of God, "a subject which in its own place and within its own limits has an actual voice and responsibility in the matter."[58] Genuine prayer is possible because the God of free grace wills to be vulnerable and wills the human creature to relate to God as a free subject and active partner of God.

For Barth, prayer is a correspondence in Christian life to the perfect copresence in Jesus Christ of divine grace and human freedom without confusion or separation or loss of proper order. We may thus speak of Barth's understanding of prayer as involving a very special cooperation, a singular partnership, a "double agency," grounded in the person and work of the incarnate Lord. What George Hunsinger has called the Chalcedonian pattern in Barth's theology that "posits a relationship of asymmetry, intimacy, and integrity between God and the human being" reaches its highest point in Christian life in the act of prayer.[59]

The Freedom to Lament
and Question God in Prayer

Barth's interpretation of the book of Job provides a test case of his understanding of prayer as an act of freedom, as centrally petition, and as a clue to the proper understanding of the relationship of divine sovereignty and human freedom. What can we say of Barth's analysis of prayer in face of Job's struggle with the mystery of evil and suffering?

Barth sharply contrasts the way the friends of Job relate to and speak of God with the way Job does. In a word, they speak defensively about God. They talk in abstractions and generalities; they utter timeless truths; their words are like "cut flowers."[60] Job, on the other hand, speaks out of the concrete history between God and him. Job does not have the luxury of looking over God's shoulder, as it were, or dispensing information about God. Job "simply stands before and under God."[61] He is engaged in an "eye-to-eye and mouth-to-ear encounter" with God.[62] Whereas for the friends of Job everything is fixed and predictable, for Job everything is open and in motion. He does not speak of God in well-worn phrases and old clichés. As God's living and free creature, Job addresses the living and free God. The anguish is that Job now experiences God as hidden and silent, and so he cries, argues, protests, and waits for God to speak and act again. Even in his complaint, confusion, and anger, Job thus speaks the truth in contrast to his friends, whose words are elegant and pious but false.

While the complaints and arguments of Job may not be classified as prayer according to strict definitions, they are certainly spoken in what Barth calls the attitude of prayer. However shocking, Job's witness to God is prayerful. Job knows that the deep hiddenness of God can be uncovered only by God. The truth of God must speak for itself. In the end, Job is brought to the truth that he seeks not by argument, but solely by God's own word and deed.

While his arresting exegesis of the book of Job provides impressive support of Barth's interpretation of prayer as the meeting place of divine and human freedom, the particular form Job's dialogue with God takes points to a certain deficiency in Barth's theology of prayer. More specifically, it raises questions as to whether Barth gives the prayer of lament its due as an essential form of biblical prayer. Does Barth tend to overlook or at least to subordinate the prayer of lament, protest, and anguished questioning?

For Barth, Job is a person who knows that God is free, and who has been freed by God. The free God and the freed human being are strange and incomprehensible to the defenders of God, who know only the "ignominious dependence and total unfreedom" of the *do ut des* relationship with God. Hence the friends of Job are "so very shocked by Job's obstinate protestation of his innocence, which in fact is nothing other than the freedom given him by God and exercised in relation to Him."[63] Barth clearly acknowledges the legitimacy of Job's lament and protest to God.

But does this formal acknowledgment work its way into Barth's theology of prayer? This question has at least three aspects: biblical, experiential, and christological.

1. As noted earlier, Barth defines prayer as centrally petition and sees all other forms of prayer—thanksgiving, confession, adoration—in relation to this center. While there are some advantages to this centering of prayer, the hazards become especially evident in relation to the wide range of biblical prayers that include prayers of lament. Biblical laments are not adequately described as petition. If taken seriously, the psalms of lament, the laments of Jeremiah, Isaiah, and Job, and the cry of Jesus from the cross are prayers that question, protest, dare to remind God that things are not right, that redemption is not yet accomplished, that God's justice does not yet rule throughout the creation. In speaking of prayer as centrally petition, Barth tends toward a reductionism or at least toward a perilous systematization of the irreducible forms of prayer found in the biblical tradition. On numerous occasions, Barth himself underscores the dangers of a "systematic" impulse in theology; such dangers are apparent in his own theology of prayer.

2. Barth recognizes clearly that Job, in his experience of the hiddenness of God, cries, expresses outrage, even argues with God, and that God eventually declares that Job has spoken the truth in contrast to the self-appointed defenders of God. Job's experience is also the experience of countless believers. The problem is: Does Barth allow the distinctive prayer of lament and protest, etched in the bib-

lical tradition and voiced by victims of injustice and abuse in every age, to deepen and enrich his overall theology of prayer? Is it not precisely this form of biblical prayer that is so disturbing, even stunning in contrast with conventional understandings and practices of prayer? Is not the depth of the dialogue between the God of the covenant and God's chosen covenant partner found precisely in the freedom of the covenant partner to challenge, question, even argue with God in the face of the power of evil and the still unrealized promises of God? Does not prayer that fails to make room for lament and protest as an authentic form of prayer easily decline into the masquerade that Barth himself is eager to unmask?

An observation by Alan Torrance, a sympathetic interpreter of Barth's work, is pertinent here: "[Barth's] conception of Christian experience seems predominantly to be a joyful and optimistic one which is reflected perhaps in [his] at times almost embarrassingly extravagant praise and adulation of the music of Mozart. As a result, one feels compelled to ask whether this does not reflect the fact that, although Barth suffered family tragedy on more than one occasion, he did not seem to have to face guilt, or national shame, or the humiliation of his cause in the same way that, for example, a theologian like Jürgen Moltmann had to. As a result Moltmann seems to be able to express the Christian experience of God within the depths of guilt, of despair, of disillusionment and of hopelessness in a more profound and human way than Barth could have."[64] What Torrance detects as missing in Barth's conception of Christian experience manifests itself, I am suggesting, in his insufficient attention to the prayer of lament in the biblical witness.

3. In his christocentric interpretation of prayer, Barth emphasizes that Jesus Christ is the true subject of prayer, the great suppliant and petitioner. Correspondingly, Christian prayer is a participation in the prayer of Jesus Christ. Yet Barth tends to emphasize our prayer far more as a participation in the kingly office of Christ than as a participation in the priestly office of Christ.

What remains underdeveloped in Barth's christocentric theology of prayer is the significance of Jesus' cry of abandonment as christological authorization of the cry of pain and protest by all who suffer injustice, who are oppressed, abused, tortured. Included in Jesus' representative act is his cry and lamentation on our behalf. Jesus is our representative, our great high priest, not only as the one who bears the consequences of our sins but also as one who laments on our behalf before God. He is the one who "in the days of his flesh . . . offered up prayers and supplications, with loud cries and tears, to the one who was able to save him from death" (Heb. 5:7).

Surely there has been an imbalance in many Christian theologies of prayer, inasmuch as abundant attention has been given to Jesus' acceptance of the will of God in the Gethsemane prayer but so little, if anything, has been said about the terrifying cry from the cross, precisely for our understanding of the freedom of authentic prayer. While acknowledging the uniqueness of Jesus' cry of abandonment, in which all our human cries are gathered up and presented to God on our behalf, we should also recognize that Jesus' cry is echoed in the cries of all who are abused and afflicted. The prayer of lament safeguards the fact that our prayers are uttered in the shadow of the cross as well as in the Easter hope of the triumph of God's grace throughout the creation, and that consequently room must be made in our personal and corporate prayers for "the Friday voice of faith."[65] The freedom to pray includes the freedom to petition, to praise, to confess, and to intercede; it also includes the freedom to cry out and protest against the continuing presence of injustice, violence, and oppression in the world.

NOTES

1. See Gustavo Gutiérrez, *We Drink from Our Own Wells: The Spiritual Journey of a People* (Maryknoll, N.Y.: Orbis Books, 1984).
2. Karl Barth, *Evangelical Theology,* trans. Grover Foley (Garden City, N.Y.: Doubleday & Co., Anchor Books, 1964), xi. Hereafter *ET.*
3. Karl Barth, *Church Dogmatics* III/4, trans. A. T. Mackay et al. (Edinburgh: T. & T. Clark, 1961), 91–92. Hereafter volumes of the *Church Dogmatics* will be cited by *CD* followed by volume and part number.
4. *CD* III/4, 92.
5. *CD* III/3, 269.
6. *CD* III/3, 270.
7. *CD* III/3, 269.
8. *CD* III/3, 267–68.
9. Friedrich Schleiermacher, *The Christian Faith,* ed. H. R. Mackintosh and J. S. Stewart (Edinburgh: T. & T. Clark, 1928), 671.
10. *CD* III/4, 97.
11. *CD* III/3, 268.
12. *CD* III/4, 98.
13. *CD* III/4, 98.
14. *CD* III/4, 98.
15. Karl Barth, *The Christian Life: Church Dogmatics IV/4; Lecture Fragments,* trans. Geoffrey W. Bromiley (Grand Rapids: Wm. B. Eerdmans Publishing Co., 1981), 43.
16. *CD* III/3, 280.
17. *CD* III/4, 274–75.
18. *CD* III/3, 275.
19. *CD* III/3, 276.
20. *CD* III/3, 277.
21. *CD* III/3, 282.
22. *CD* III/4, 108.
23. *CD* III/3, 283.
24. *CD* III/3, 283.
25. *CD* III/3, 283.
26. *CD* III/4, 110.
27. *CD* III/4, 279.
28. *CD* III/4, 280.
29. *CD* III/4, 264.
30. *CD* IV/3.2, 882.
31. *CD* IV/3.2, 882.
32. *CD* IV/3.2, 883.
33. *CD* III/4, 97.
34. *CD* III/4, 111.
35. *CD* III/4, 111.
36. *CD* I/1, 23.
37. *CD* I/1, 23.
38. *CD* I/1, 23.

39. *CD* I/1, 24.
40. *ET,* 141.
41. *ET,* 141.
42. *ET,* 143.
43. *ET,* 144.
44. *ET,* 144.
45. *ET,* 145.
46. *ET,* 145.
47. *ET,* 147.
48. *ET,* 147.
49. *ET,* 149.
50. *ET,* 150.
51. *CD* III/3, 147–48.
52. *CD* III/4, 108.
53. Schleiermacher, *The Christian Faith,* 673.
54. *CD* III/4, 109.
55. *CD* III/3, 285.
56. *CD* III/4, 109.
57. *CD* III/3, 285.
58. *CD* III/3, 286.
59. George Hunsinger, *How to Read Karl Barth: The Shape of His Theology* (New York: Oxford University Press, 1991), 221–24.
60. *CD* IV/3.1, 457.
61. *CD* IV/3.1, 457.
62. *CD* IV/3.1, 458.
63. *CD* IV/3.1, 461.
64. Alan Torrance, "Christian Experience and Divine Revelation in the Theologies of Friedrich Schleiermacher and Karl Barth," in *Christian Experience in Theology and Life,* ed. I. Howard Marshall (Edinburgh: Rutherford House Books, 1988), 111.
65. Walter Brueggemann, "The Friday Voice of Faith," *Reformed Worship* 30 (December 1993): 2–5.

9

TEACHING THEOLOGY
BY EXPLORING THE ORDINARY

ELENA MALITS, C.S.C.

If imitation is the highest form of praise, perhaps application is a close second. While not presuming to imitate Diogenes Allen, I have appropriated some of his ideas and attitudes, applying them to my undergraduate classes in the Religious Studies Department of Saint Mary's College. (University of Notre Dame students are usually part of them, since we have a coexchange program.) I am especially indebted to Dick Allen with respect to two electives, "Theologies of Love" and "Religious Dimensions of Musical Theater." Having now taught both of these several times, I am convinced of the intellectual and religious fruitfulness of the approach I learned, at least in part, from Allen.

In these courses I have been privileged to watch students grow perceptibly, responding to "a theology of the ordinary." My concern has been to explore the religious and theological meanings embedded in everyday human situations such as loving and being loved, the experience of betrayal, brokenness, learning to go on, heroism, suffering, death and dying, grief, hope, transformation. I have observed college students shedding immature ideas about love and friendship and learning how to evaluate the presentations of those realities they see on TV and hear touted in popular albums. I have felt these young women and men struggling with the values of the dominant popular culture and trying to gain critical purchase. Allen's book, *Love,* challenges them to do that. For me personally, my confidence in teaching undergraduates has been renewed by following their development in analyzing novels and films to discover authentic religious implications in those works. It has given me joy to experience the responsiveness of students to worlds of meaning they never dreamed might exist in Broadway shows such as *Les Misérables, Man of La Mancha,* or *My Fair Lady.* I have insisted that one can uncover theological meanings in stories, poems, plays, and films that are not explicitly religious. I invite students to allow themselves to be open to becoming renewed persons because they can and do learn to see and to respond in new ways. And I caution them to beware of what may be asked of them if they begin looking for the presence and activity of God in the ordinary schemes of human life. One student wrote on a course evaluation: "I'll never again be able just to go to a movie or take up a novel for fun. Those damn questions we asked about what we read and saw will always be in the back of my mind. I'll have to think about everything and maybe even ask myself if something in my own life should be changed!" I consider that high praise—and I pass it on to Dick Allen for teaching me what I have tried to teach my students.

As my contribution to this Festschrift, therefore, I would like to describe in considerable detail the two religious studies electives that reflect something of the wisdom Dick Allen embodies. Both classes are limited to fifteen students and meet once a week for two and a half hours in an informal lounge setting. Most of the students are seniors who, having completed many requirements, are looking for electives that are off the beaten path. I personally interview students who want to take the course, so that nobody thinks the titles suggest fun and games; a glance at the syllabus and my explanation of the work involved quickly dispels that misconception.

"Theologies of Love" is the course most directly dependent on Allen, since his book *Love: Christian Romance, Marriage, Friendship* is the central text. To supplement that provocative book we also use M. Scott Peck's *The Road Less Traveled: A New Psychology of Love, Traditional Values and Spiritual Growth.*[1] The course description reads: "Our purpose is to examine from a theological point of view the nature of love in its various forms and manifestations. We will consider different types of love: friendship, romance, marriage, the love of God, love for one's neighbor, love for the earth, love for one's work, etc. There is some reading of a theoretical sort on what constitutes love, but emphasis will be placed on how love works as shown in some novels and videos of films about the many forms of love." There are assigned readings and/or videos in preparation for each class discussion period except for the last few, when individuals present their own project to the class. This project requires that a student select a novel or film of her or his own choosing, analyzing it in terms of ideas we have already studied in the course. There is a fifteen-minute oral presentation, followed by class discussion. Evaluation of students for the course is based on the quality of weekly participation, the special project, and a final take-home examination. In that exercise students are asked to recount the story of their own learning experience about love throughout the course, with reference to particular ideas and attitudes they have encountered in reading, in the films, and through class discussions.

Along with the Allen and Peck books on love, students also read the books on friendship in Aristotle's *Ethics;*[2] *Gilgamesh: A Verse Narrative,* by Herbert Mason;[3] *The Letters of Abelard and Heloise;*[4] *The Death of Al-Hallaaj: A Dramatic Narrative,* by Herbert Mason;[5] C. S Lewis's novel *Till We Have Faces;*[6] Graham Greene's *The End of the Affair;*[7] as well as assorted articles and excerpts from classical and contemporary sources.

Videos are assigned in connection with topics and themes presented in the readings. They include *Les Misérables* (a concert celebration for the tenth anniversary of the opening of the musical), 1996; *Camelot* (the mythic love triangle of King Arthur, his wife, and his best friend), 1967; *Beaches* (the touching story of feminine friendship), 1988; *Stealing Heaven* (a somewhat fictionalized account of the Abelard and Héloïse story), 1988; *Brother Sun, Sister Moon* (a musical version of the story of the young St. Francis of Assisi), 1973; *Shadowlands* (the love story of Oxford don C. S. Lewis and a brash American woman, Joy Gresham), 1993.

Probably the idea regarding love that is newest and most fascinating to these college students (and that tends to shape class discussion after they come upon it) is Allen's notion of love as encountering and respecting the "otherness" of the other. Allen's presentation of that engages the students very early in the course and serves as a touchstone in examining other materials. Again and again we return to Allen's point in his first chapter, "The Experience of Perfect Love."

> To love perfectly is not simply to see that all else is independent of oneself and so ought to be loved as it is. Perfect love of a living thing is the recognition that it has an inside. To love it is to recognize what it is like to be that object. From the outside it looks gloriously radiant; inside it is fragile and suffering.[8]

Students are, indeed, struck by Allen's insistence on respecting the reality of the other in a genuine love relationship, but they also appreciate his balance regarding one's own needs. Especially as young adults, these students are aware of their desire and need for fulfillment. Allen moves them to see these in the larger context of community:

> All of us have a pressing, boundless desire to be loved properly. Ironically we all want so badly to be properly recognized that we ourselves are unable to recognize others. Each of us needs and desires more recognition than we are in turn able to give. What we need and seek is true community: community in which each of us is but one reality among many, paying proper attention to others and in turn receiving the affectionate attention of others. Marriage and friendship are two such communities, or at least they ought to be.[9]

Several times during the semester I ask students to watch some TV shows of their own choosing with these passages in mind. How does the notion of love in, for example, *Seinfeld, ER, Friends,* or *Melrose Place* look in the light of Allen's idea of perfect love? Some students find it painful to recognize the shallowness of characters in their favorite programs, but nonetheless they do acquire critical skills to assess the values that are projected.

Students are also particularly moved by Allen's explanation of the positive role of romance within Christian marriage, particularly after Peck's realistic treatment of the inadequacy and inevitable demise of purely romantic love. When they come into the course, "love" usually is equated with "romantic love." We read Peck and some excerpts from historical studies on the rise and dominance of romantic love in Western culture. Students usually move through several stages of reaction. At first they are in disbelief that romantic love has not been regarded as the ideal of love between men and women in all times and places. Then they feel disappointed that their own expectations and longings for romantic love may not be realized, let alone sustained for a lifetime. Some of them become painfully disillusioned. There usually is a moment in the course when most of these college students feel angry at having their boundless hopes for romantic love dashed. But then Dick Allen provides perspective and restores their youthful aspirations. He forcefully affirms the

value of romantic and sexual love, arguing (à la Kierkegaard) that the ends of romantic love may be achieved within marriage — indeed, can be accomplished only
within marriage:

> Romantic love, with its exclusive attachment to a particular person, is thus
> not unrealistic. Even should the sexual drive in its origins be utterly plas-
> tic, so that any number of objects can give gratification, sexual desire has
> intimations of more than organ pleasure, though we may refuse to recog-
> nize them. Likewise romantic love has within it the intention to love an-
> other person well, always, and faithfully, though we may refuse to
> recognize this. Sexual love in humans is a personal act, and without dis-
> tortion it can find its full expression in an exclusive attachment between
> a man and a woman.[10]

But it well may be the discussion of friendship as a form of love that turns out
to have the most relevance for so many students, both women and men. Some of
the liveliest class discussions have centered on the importance of friends in their
lives. In describing the role that friendship plays in their experience, students often talk about it in explicitly religious terms. Their quest for God is in the company of good friends. My students are also especially interested in exploring the
similarities and differences in friendships among women in comparison to those
among men. And, of course, they are fascinated by the possibilities of friendship
between the sexes. In the spring 1997 semester, thanks to my laryngitis, a graduate student who took one of the sessions on friendship had students see the video,
When Harry Met Sally and read the chapter in *The Changing Face of Friendship,*
by Gilbert Meilaender, "When Harry and Sally Read the *Nicomachean Ethics:*
Friendship between Men and Women."[11] The question of whether there can be
full-fledged friendship between men and women with no romantic and/or sexual
involvements is an important one for them and, for many, still an open one.

Allen has a brief discussion of homosexual friendship.[12] Because the issues
connected with gays and lesbians have been much discussed and hotly debated on
the Notre Dame and Saint Mary's campuses in the last few years, when I taught
the course in the spring of 1997 I supplemented Allen's cursory treatment with the
article by Andrew Sullivan in the *New York Times* (November 10, 1996), "When
Plagues End: Notes on the Twilight of an Epidemic." We also viewed a video of
Sullivan's talk at Notre Dame the previous year, "The Paradox of Homosexual
Love for Catholics." Sullivan argues lucidly for accepting homosexuals in the
Catholic community, and lays out the historical and contemporary formulations of
the problems. Andrew Sullivan comes to definite conclusions regarding the legitimacy of homosexual love and sexual expression within the context of binding and
exclusive relationships. But our class discussion remained inconclusive. Most of
my students are Catholics and remain confused about the matter. It is not so much
that they want to support the official teaching of the Catholic Church, as that they
sense how deep are these waters. We also listened to a tape of a talk by Bishop
Thomas Gumbleton, who spoke sympathetically of the plight of homosexuals in
the church. That helped, but did not resolve anything. Given time limitations and

the extent of the current controversy regarding homosexual love, I think, the best we can do in this course is to get the issues on the table and to suggest ways of exploring them.

To return to the beginning of "Theologies of Love": During the opening class session we try to identify and describe as many forms of love as students can name, attempting to distinguish one from another by distinguishing features. At this stage they are drawing on their own experience and unfocused reading. Students are advised to keep notes on this preliminary discussion and compare these ideas with ones they have developed by the end of the course. Then before we even begin reading about love, one of the first assignments is to see *Les Misérables* and study the libretto. Students are asked to come to class prepared to discuss all the forms of love they can observe in the story. That proves to be a good beginning, providing us with concrete images and richly poetic lyrics. Along with Dick Allen's conception of "otherness," the theme of the course might be summed up in Jean Valjean's dying affirmation that "to love another person is to see the face of God."

The course winds down with the student presentations that are diverse and generally provocative. This past semester, films included *A River Runs through It, The Bridges of Madison County,* and *Shadowlands* (to name a few); *Madame Bovary* and *The Virginian* were among the novels. I must say that perhaps the most interesting take-home exams I ever get to read are those that end "Theologies of Love." Students are supposed to tell me where they started and where they ended in their intellectual understanding of love in this course. They do that, and usually do it very reflectively. While it is not part of this last assignment, student writing also is often deeply confessional. Students choose to talk about what has happened to them religiously. In short, that comes down to an insight into the connectedness of all forms of authentic love. They frequently mention how Allen's critique of Anders Nygren's opposing *eros* to *agape* helps them. My students came to college carrying a lot of baggage about the dangers of human love for responding wholeheartedly to God's love. Dick Allen assists them in laying down the burden and discovering the possibilities of integration. One young man wrote that the most important sentence in Allen's book for him was the quote from St. John of the Cross that introduces the chapter "The Experience of Perfect Love": "Love consists not in feeling great things, but in having great detachment and in suffering for the beloved."[13] So there was Diogenes Allen of Princeton Theological Seminary reintroducing a senior at the University of Notre Dame to his own Catholic tradition!

The second course where I feel Dick Allen's presence shaping both the content and the manner of dealing with it is "Religious Dimensions of Musical Theater." In 1985, when I was on sabbatical in New York City, I went to Princeton once a week to teach a course at Princeton Seminary called "Biography as Theology." Dick had been instrumental in getting me there to do a course similar to the ones that David Burrell, Stanley Hauerwas, and I had developed for Notre Dame and Saint Mary's students. I remember discussions in the Allen home about the importance of the arts for people concerned about religion and theology. And I especially recall Dick's interest in the role of music in the development of any authentic spirituality. If music has the power not only to touch profoundly the emotions but to move the human soul, then it cannot be neglected in religious education. In fact, the capacity to appreciate music must be assiduously cultivated to open persons to the life of God's Spirit. The culmination of that semester for me was celebrating Christmas by going to the Metropolitan Opera with the Allen family to see *The Marriage of Figaro*. In some fashion not easy to describe, time and experiences shared with the Allens affected the course on musical theater that I eventually developed.

The description for that course, "Religious Dimensions of Musical Theater," reads as follows: "This elective explores the religious dimensions of certain musical productions, both operatic and popular. It seeks to identify and understand the theological conceptions of God, human nature, sin, grace, and redemption that may be explicit or implicit in these musicals. Normally videos of the productions will be used; CDs and librettos will be available if there is no video. Selections from theological writings are studied in connection with the religious issues that surface in various musicals."

A variety of musical theater productions constitutes the "matter" of this course; it is given its specific "form" by the theological perspectives from which the productions are viewed. The assumption is that profound theological issues can be discovered in material that is not obviously religious, if only one learns how to look for them and what sort of questions to ask. There are challenging readings designed to nudge students to think theologically about the musicals we study.

It is hoped that the mix of operas and Broadway musicals will open students to new aesthetic experiences and show them that theological questions may be examined in the settings of both popular and high culture. If it is possible to attend a live production during the term, we do so. Normally we are restricted to videos or films that happen to be around. The syllabus is adjusted accordingly. The staples, however, are *Les Misérables, Camelot, La Traviata, Amadeus, Man of La Mancha, My Fair Lady, West Side Story, Faust, Phantom of the Opera,* and *Evita*. It is recommended, though not required, that students see versions of plays that were made into movies before being adapted for the musical theater. During the first meeting excerpts from several musicals that will not be assigned during the semester are viewed during class time and discussed in order to give students some experience in approaching materials that will be used in the course. They need a simple but rigorous method that teaches them what to look and listen for, what sort of questions to pose, and what theological connections might be drawn.

The principal text used is *The Content of Faith: The Best of Karl Rahner's Theological Writings*.[14] Specific selections of relatively short length coordinated with the particular musicals are read. The Rahner material is difficult but rewarding; the anthology we use draws from his pastoral reflections as well as the theological investigations. It is startling to discover a connection between *Man of La Mancha* and a Rahner essay on "Utopia and Reality."[15] Rahner asks us to consider what "the real" is. The Don Quixote story forces us to weigh the truth and power of the dreamer against that of the realist. It invites us to ask whether beauty or goodness exists in itself or in the eye of the beholder or somewhere else. The musical *Man of La Mancha* enhances the questions raised by Cervantes, I think, by doing what good melodies and lyrics do: getting inside our heads and resonating in our feelings. Another example, Rahner's "Grace and Dying in Christ,"[16] comes alive when facing Violetta's life and death in *La Traviata*. Here is the flamboyant prostitute who embodies what Christian love is all about: renunciation and self-surrender.

In addition to the Rahner material, brief xeroxed articles on the musicals, their sources, the composers, and reception by critics and the public are assigned. Suggested readings are: Margaret Miles, *Seeing and Believing: Religion and Values in the Movies*[17] and James Monaco, *How to Read a Film: The Art, Technology, Language, History, and Theology of Film and Media.*[18]

Each week students bring to class a list of questions they want to discuss, along with a few pages of written thoughts about the assignment. Consideration should be given to the following sorts of questions: What are the key theological conceptions in the material? What happens to the story in the musical version as compared to the play, novel, or movie? Does music and dancing affect the religious character of the production? If so, how?

Sometimes it is hard going, but with practice students learn to articulate things that may not be articulated in the musicals at all. For instance, in *"Les Mis"* they wax eloquent on the God of Javert in comparison with the God of Jean Valjean. Students say things like "The God Javert believes in cannot forgive, because Javert himself cannot forgive, and he has made his God in his own image rather than the other way around." Or in *Amadeus* they readily describe the "unjust" God of Salieri and the composer's vengeful jealousy. With almost all the stories, in fact, students have few problems in identifying sins and their destructiveness. *Camelot* represents far more than a personal tragedy; there are social, even cosmic implications of the adultery. I keep prodding the students not to get bogged down in the multitude of sins we encounter, but to look for experiences of grace and redemption. *Faust* shows them the redemption of Marguerite in accepting her sinfulness and asking for forgiveness. I always challenge the students to take note of the finale. In my judgment, that exhibits forgiveness as well as anything that opera can do. Marguerite ascends to heaven singing a triumphant acceptance of the gift of grace.

The religious dimensions of *Faust* are transparent. But what is there in *My Fair Lady* that can be construed religiously without being procrustean? I usually need to supply some clues in the form of specific questions for this musical. How important is changing one's language for changing one's life? What responsibilities does someone have who is instrumental in changing another person and her or his life? Interestingly, students begin to ask themselves such questions in relation to troubled friends they have helped, or perhaps inner-city children they tutor.

As in "Theologies of Love," the last several classes are given to presentation of student projects on a musical not covered in the syllabus. Student projects have been widely different and often really delightful. To mention just a few, they have discussed *Don Giovanni, Tosca, Rigoletto, Jesus Christ Superstar, Brigadoon, The Sound of Music, Fiddler on the Roof,* and *Miss Saigon*. By the end of the semester there is scarcely a virtue or vice we have not examined in the context of human interactions. Over and over again in these powerful stories we encounter the mysterious transformation that Christians call grace. Nor do we escape confronting alternative visions of what might constitute human salvation. And, I believe, this all takes place through working with materials that are as educationally challenging as they are aesthetically enjoyable.

A final paper discusses the religious themes examined in the course as well as the student's personal learning experience. He or she is asked to address at least these questions: What kind of theology have you encountered in these musicals? What has exploring musical theater taught you about discovering the religious dimensions of life? What worked and didn't work for you in the course? What ideas, insights, questions, and emotions stimulated by the course do you take away with you? As one would imagine, the way these questions are answered are as varied as the individuals who take the course. But there are some common threads. Students say that (as Rahner says about grace being everywhere) theology is everywhere! Many observe that the ability to forgive others depends on self-forgiveness and that is rooted in recognizing God's forgiving love. They remark on the power of these stories to present the ambiguities of life: the good prostitutes, the transforming potential of dreams, the two-edged sword of power.

In their final papers, students tend not to be very articulate about what a musical production offers beyond the premusical story, but that is because none of us explains that very well. Perhaps it comes down to the fact that in a musical we feel the difference—and that is not to be lightly set aside as intellectually or spiritually irrelevant. Andrew Lloyd Webber has given us "The Music of the Night," but perhaps all music belongs to the dark depths of mystery. Do music and contemplation spring from the same realms of the human spirit? For cultured people, I suppose it would be easier to plumb the spiritual deeps of *Don Giovanni* than *Phantom of the Opera*, but who knows? A few months ago I truly surprised myself in responding positively to Madonna's *Evita*. I had never seen the Lloyd Webber stage version, and I found myself drawn into a demanding meditation on the ambiguities of love wedded to power. Good heavens, could the Hollywood Madonna be an occasion of grace for me?

When I first began talking with Diogenes Allen, I was struck by the way he probes the theological and religious implications of the stuff of everyday human life, and does so with a judicious use of literature and the arts. Through his books and lectures, but most of all in sustained conversations, I have come to experience one of Dick Allen's convictions: there is a spirituality of teaching, as there is of learning. For me these are the demands of such a spirituality: loving what you do and trying to love the people with whom you do it; respecting what is right there before you and believing that there just might be more there than meets the eye; seeking to be open to the unknown and appreciative of the known. Dick Allen meets those requirements. Others of us try in our other ways.[19]

NOTES

1. M. Scott Peck, *The Road Less Traveled* (New York: Simon and Schuster, A Touchstone Book, 1978).

2. Aristotle, *Ethics,* trans. J. A. K. Thomson (New York: Penguin Books, 1955).
3. Herbert Mason, *Gilgamesh* (New York: New American Library, Mentor Books, 1972).
4. Betty Radice, ed., *The Letters of Abelard and Héloïse* (New York: Penguin Classics, 1974).
5. Herbert Mason, *The Death of Al-Hallaaj* (Notre Dame, Ind.: University of Notre Dame Press, 1979).
6. C. S. Lewis, *Till We Have Faces* (Grand Rapids: Wm. B. Eerdmans Publishing Co., 1956).
7. Graham Greene, *The End of the Affair* (New York: Penguin Books, 1951).
8. Diogenes Allen, *Love: Christian Romance, Marriage, Friendship* (Cambridge, Mass.: Cowley Publications, 1987), 12.
9. Allen, *Love,* 13.
10. Allen, *Love,* 89–90.
11. Gilbert Meilaender, *The Changing Face of Friendship,* ed. Leroy S. Rouner (Notre Dame, Ind.: University of Notre Dame Press, 1994), 183–96.
12. Allen, *Love,* 52–56.
13. Allen, *Love,* 7.
14. *The Content of Faith: The Best of Karl Rahner's Theological Writings,* ed. Karl Lehmann, Albert Raffelt, and Harvey D. Egan (New York: Crossroad Publishing Co., 1994).
15. Allen, *Love,* 609–11.
16. Allen, *Love,* 568–74.
17. Margaret Miles, *Seeing and Believing: Religion and Values in the Movies* (Boston: Beacon Press, 1996).
18. James Monaco, *How to Read a Film: The Art, Technology, Language, History, and Theology of Film and Media* (Oxford: Oxford University Press, 1981).
19. I would be happy to send syllabi of the courses described above to anyone interested.

10

SPIRITUALITY AND ITS EMBODIMENT IN CHURCH LIFE

DANIEL W. HARDY

Introduction:
An Ecumenical Christian

I recall walking down into Princeton one day with Diogenes Allen as he told me about his family origins. It struck me as a remarkable story.

At the time when Greek people who lived in certain areas of what was to become Turkey were being expelled from their towns, those from Diogenes Allen's family's village found their way to America. As a group they settled in Kentucky. Since there was no Orthodox church where they were, with the approval of their bishop the people attended the local Episcopal church, which was happy to have them. The arrangement continued for some time, until a new Episcopal bishop told them that if they were to remain there they would have to be confirmed as members of the Episcopal Church, whereupon they thought they must leave. Later, when Diogenes was at university, he found that the most dynamic leadership there was being provided by the Presbyterian chaplain. Responding to this, he became Presbyterian and embarked on a life in the Presbyterian Church, which was consummated as Stuart Professor of Philosophy at Princeton Theological Seminary. His many years there have brought distinction to the seminary and to him—to which the present book is a fitting tribute.

What is especially interesting about Diogenes Allen may not be fully apparent from this bare biographical outline. While he has continued to enrich the life and thought of the Presbyterian Church, he has also redeveloped links with the Episcopal Church, in whose churches and conferences he lectures and teaches frequently. And his thought is richly informed not only by such a philosophical theologian as the Anglican Austin Farrer, but also by those who are normative for Orthodoxy, the fathers of the early church, and especially—it seems to me—those of the East. Even more widely, his work is enriched by the uncategorizable Simone Weil and by the attempt to trace the place of philosophy—both modern and post-modernist—in Christian believing. He is, therefore, a remarkably ecumenical philosopher and theologian. The denominationalism that so marks American Christianity has never succeeded in reducing his ecumenical spirit.

Does that mean that he is less concerned with the particularities of these different churches, as if he were somehow a generalized pan-Christian? Not at all, but it does mean that he is concerned with the possibility of being positively Christian in such a way as to include but also transcend these particularities. That, it seems to me, is a major thrust of his work; and it brings him to concentrate on the central themes and dynamics of full Christian life and believing, in order to make these intelligible and livable for Christians today. He is a philosopher in his dedication to rationality, but a Christian in the concerns to which he directs his philosophical work. My wish here, however, is not to account for his work, but to continue with Allen's concern with what I have termed "positively Christian faith" and with the question of how that may take form in the life of the churches and their mission in today's world.

Mutual Engagements and Trajectories

A central concern for Christians today must be with what is often called "spirituality," that is, how the truth and vitality of Christian faith are to be shown, in ways that are faithful to the living God and God's activity in the world and also intelligible and practicable for people whose thought and life are deeply shaped by the habits of today. How can God's truth and life, in all the profundity of their presence, order, and energy in the world, be shown to intersect with the patterns of human understanding and life in today's world? Ultimately, the answering of this question would lead to a mutual engagement between theology and all the forms of understanding by which modern life is shaped: scientific, social, political, economic, psychological, cultural, and religious.

It is abundantly evident, however, that the "Christian faith" that enters such an engagement is pluriform. Despite some progress in ecumenical conversations, we cannot presume overall agreement in "Christian faith," and still less can we suppose practical cooperation between denominations. And "theology," thanks both to its denominational connections and also to the structure adopted for the discipline in nineteenth-century universities,[1] has developed a complex pluriformity of its own. How God's truth and life intersect with human life and understanding is a major issue in ecumenism and in theology, one that always tends to preempt the engagement of faith and theology with the shaping forces of modern life.

The way forward lies in a *double engagement*, of denominations and theologies with each other on the one hand, and by them with the vitalities of modern life and understanding on the other hand. But how such engagements are to be established presents a major difficulty. If they are not to be restricted to minor skirmishes, further progress requires a coherent approach that does not underrate the differences of those involved. What might this be? It seems possible to identify certain trajectories, as they might be called, that must figure in this double engagement. If they can be identified, these trajectories might serve as the parameters within which fruitful engagements might take place.

Is such a thing possible without lapsing into "prescriptiveness" that is prejudicial to the parties involved? Given the well-developed "territories" of academic and religious life, as visible in their many disciplines and denominations, suspicions easily develop between them—to such an extent that it is thought not to be possible for any other to be more than an "outsider," or to understand or "be fair."[2] And what often ensues is a "pluralism" in which the "fair representation" of different interests is paramount, coupled with a "licensed disengagement" between them, governed by "political correctness" designed to prevent them from offending each other, which actually leaves the way open for powerful special-interest groups to predominate.[3]

If instead we seek trajectories for mutual engagement of denominations and theologies, and also by them with the shaping forces of modern life, the trajectories must preserve the "basic interests" of each participant within the development of a larger and more profound congruence of thought and practice. One such strategy is developed by the poet-philosopher-theologian S. T. Coleridge in his consideration of the constitution of church and state "according to the Idea of each," "which is produced by the knowledge or sense of the ultimate aim of each."[4] Within the overall task of providing a determinative order by which social life may preserve the inherent unity that is required for its well-being, state and church were antithetically related to each other, but might still achieve congruence in providing and reforming the material, moral, and spiritual conditions for human well-being.

In effect, this approach suggests a fundamental trajectory that begins in the *elemental life* of a people and seeks for the well-being or unity of life (social life in Coleridge's case) that is its *truth*. Insofar as all human activities presume constitutive principles and practices by which to approximate the truth of human life, even in their difference they may engage with each other in opening a larger understanding of what is the truth of human life and its well-being. They achieve congruence in following the trajectory that leads to true human life in the world.

As they engage with each other, it places an obligation on them to reconsider their thought and practice by reference to this trajectory. For Christianity, its churches and its theologies, such a thing opens a profound question—the relation of the Spirit to Christ, that is, the question of how all life is incorporated into the truth of God. And in this question are embraced the issues of the nature of creation, redemption, and eschatological fulfillment. Comparably, in forms of understanding and practice that are normally pursued without reference to Christianity, there is the obligation to reconsider the parameters of their habitual thought and practice, by reference to the goal of achieving the truth of human life in the world. And the questions raised are equally profound for them.

In focusing on trajectories that begin in elemental human life and have as their goal the well-being of life which is its truth, what we have suggested is not an attempt to find a "neutral" set of conceptualities or formal similarities (for example, between the uses of kinds of language[5]), but to uncover a trajectory that is compatible with the most fundamental concerns of those who are engaged in discussion. It differs also from the attempts of those who wish to subjugate some disciplines to categories drawn from others.[6]

The Dynamics of
Christian Faith and Life

Can Christianity be reconsidered in these terms, by reference to the movement of human life to its truth? As we have said, this raises a most profound question for Christianity, the relation of the Spirit to Christ in the work of God in the world: How is all life moved by the Spirit to its truth in Christ, a movement that is God's activity in the world?

It is clear from the New Testament and early Christian witness that the followers of Jesus are already deeply imbued with the new life that has been opened to them in the life, teaching, and death of Christ. In particular, the crucifixion of Jesus Christ is what makes this possible, while the resurrection actually opens new life to them, which is activated in them by the movement of the Holy Spirit. This is a comprehensive movement of life in them, so fully pervasive that there is nothing that falls outside it.

> For through the law I died to the law, so that I might live to God. I have been crucified with Christ; and it is no longer I who live, but it is Christ who lives in me. And the life I now live in the flesh I live by faith in the Son of God, who loved me and gave himself for me.[7]

Although the circumstances of their living remain quite ordinary, the form of their previous life—according to a divinely authenticated mode (the law)—has now been made transitional to a Christly life, through which there is a direct relation to God.

The determinative change has come about through being "crucified with Christ," in whose cross there is a reversal of the human abuse of all that is "in the flesh," and even the revocation of "nature's" corruption. To be more exact, the human abuse that is thus reversed includes the misuse of human identity, of relations with others, of relations with the natural world and relations with God, a comprehensive "missing of the mark" (sin) which culminates in the universal disorder of human personal, social, and religious life; it also includes the contamination of all the standards of reference by which such things are gauged, and even the "natural" and "truth" themselves. So convoluted do all these become that they are compounded in extreme forms of evil, whose consequences are destruction and lifelessness. It is all this for which Jesus suffers in his love for those with whom he is one, and it is all concentrated in his trial and crucifixion. But through his overriding loving and self-giving for humanity (as "Son of Man") and for God (as "Son of God") on the cross, it is all redirected to God, and a new actuality of human life is opened from and in God. And it is by the movement of faith through the Holy Spirit that this new actuality opens "true life" for human beings.

It is this new actuality, the "Christ who lives in me," by which his followers are transformed in every aspect of what they are. As a result, there is a sense in which there is a new beginning of life in them, which brings their goal of "true life" within sight. And the same applies also to the life of the world *as such:* through the death of Christ, it receives new life, moving it toward true life, by the Holy

Spirit. This is not a minor rearrangement of his people's previous religious and world perspectives, an insertion into what had been previously, but a complete expansion and transformation.[8] The issue for them, therefore, is to participate in this expansive reconstitution and to work out its meaning, not only for themselves but wherever the movement through Christ to true life occurs in life in the world.

What we have described is by no means a special Christian worldview. What makes it more than that is three remarkable characteristics: It coincides with the recognition of the fundamental trajectory of life as it reaches toward its goal of truth in the source of all life and truth, that is in God. Second, it confronts—neither avoiding nor explaining away—the radical challenge presented to this trajectory of life by sin, evil, and death; the destructive and deadening consequences of the convolutions of human life in the world that are sin and evil are confronted and overcome. Third, the dynamic of "life in Christ" into which human beings are brought by the movement of the Holy Spirit, as it opens access to the source of all life and truth in God, coincides with the inmost character of the divine life itself.

Altogether, the movement of the new life of Christ in them by the Holy Spirit is the way by which *God involves them in his truth and love,* which is also theirs. This is found preeminently in the dynamics of worship:

> Christian worship shares in a human-Godward movement that belongs to God and which takes place *within* the divine life. It is precisely into and within *this* that we are brought by the Spirit to participate as a gift of grace. It is this *enhypostatic* emphasis which liberates us from a model of participation conceived as a purely subjective—and, therefore, ultimately inexplicable—act on the part of those who are *echthroi tē dianoia.*[9]

Hence, the "expansive reconstitution" in which they participate through the life of Christ in them is the means by which God involves them in their movement toward true life by the movement of his truth toward them in love.

Contrasting Accounts

We have been exploring a trajectory that begins in elemental life and moves toward the true well-being of life. And the purpose of doing so is to develop the possibility of mutual engagement by different positions—both among denominations and theologies and between them and the shaping forces of modern understanding and life—while preserving the "basic interests" of each; and the goal is to develop a larger and more profound congruence of thought and practice between them. Recognizing that this requires the reconsideration of its position by each participant, we have seen how Christianity might be reconsidered in these terms.

That will not suffice, of course, because "Christianity" is pluriform, both in denominations and theologies, and it remains an issue how various positions within Christianity may reconsider themselves by reference to the trajectory we have been suggesting. This is an issue to which we will return shortly.

Before continuing, it is well to recognize some of the fundamental hindrances that prevent denominations and theologies, and also other construals of understanding and life, from seeing themselves in terms of this trajectory. In some cases, we will find that churches, theologies, and other positions retain within themselves such fundamental hindrances, often as the results of encounters between Christian faith and the shaping forces of life in previous eras.

Many positions show a strong preference for simplifying the trajectory, usually by appealing to basic, foundational truths from which all else is derived:

> This foundationalist approach to cognitive justification views certain the-
> ses as *self-evident*—or immediately self-evidencing—and then takes
> these as available to provide a basis for the *derivative* justification of other
> beliefs (which can then, of course, serve to justify still others in their turn).
> It is committed to a quest for ultimate bedrock "givens" capable of pro-
> viding a foundational basis on which the rest of the cognitive structure can
> be erected. . . . These initial "givens" are wholly nondiscursive and fixed
> invariants, which are sacred and nowise subject to reappraisal and revi-
> sion.[10]

A great deal of the history of philosophy and theology has had to do with the "nature" of such self-justifying "givens" and the manner in which they are accessible. Any "given" is accessible because, since it is "absolute," it follows that all understanding and life must derive from it; the "given" is available through the very process of understanding (or life itself): the process of making inferences leads sequentially to the foundation on which inference depends.

If seen in such terms, the "trajectory" that we have been considering runs only "downward" from the fullness of self-evidently true life to the lesser and needy. This has an effect also on the character of the trajectory. The result is to reduce the dynamics of the movement (from elemental life to true well-being) to an epicyclic one, in which the movement begins and ends in the Absolute.

Such conceptual patterns have proved attractive for theology, very likely because they emphasize metaphysical attributes often (and usually uncritically) associated with God. Where the "given" is considered "personal" in character, as suggested in the Judeo-Christian tradition, all being and knowledge are thought to derive from a unilateral self-conferral by the absolute source, identified as God; and even mediation through multiple human capacities or perspectives is explained by reference to a single self-conferral. Unlike the reconsideration of Christian faith presented earlier, in which there is a Trinitarian conception of divine initiative and a bilateral involvement of God and human beings, the divine "given" confers itself through a unilinear movement by which "faith" is actualized in the human being; and the Trinity of God is God's self-repetition for humanity.[11]

As the life of the world becomes intrinsically fascinating, particularly from the European Renaissance onward, these patterns of unilateral movement evoke resistance. What results is an inversion of the direction of this movement into the unilateralism of modern understanding and life, in which the reconstitution of life is derived from inner-worldly sources, eventually reaching concentrated form in the rationalism of Immanuel Kant. The most extreme form is the project of thought pursued by philosophy—culminating in Hegel—as it attempts to "know it all."

Hegel [is] the culmination of the original, evasive, philosophical passion to know it all. Hegel brings the history of the project of knowing it all into the all. With that inclusion in the system, philosophy reaches its outer limit, its perfection. The "I" that thinks, that can know it all, is the ultimate object, the last piece in the totality.[12]

In this case, the reconstitution of human life and thought is within a totality, the Absolute, which simultaneously idealizes both the human being and God.[13]

The significance of these positions for the present lies in the hindrances they provide to the reconsideration of positions in and beyond Christianity in terms of the trajectory that we have been exploring. The trajectory by which life and thought move from an elemental condition to their truth supposes the possibility, indeed the actuality, of an expansive reconstitution of the world from within, a bilateral movement involving God and humanity whereby God involves humanity in the attainment of God's truth and vitality. This is quite unlike the two unilateral projects we have now reviewed, in which the Absolute alone provides the conditions for human life and thought, and in which the state, or dynamics, of an Absolute or "Being" is discovered through human thought and life.

The Possibility of
Ecumenical Engagement

The best way to continue our exploration of the trajectory from elemental to true life is to show how it can be developed as the means of a fuller engagement between denominations and theologies, by which they may achieve congruence as they seek the truth of human life and its well-being. The other use of the trajectory, to promote engagement between denominations and theologies, on the one hand, and the shaping forces of modern life and understanding, is best left aside for attention on another occasion.

Let us first recall how the early Christians found their new life in Christ to be an expansive reconstitution of their humanness and human responsibility, by which they moved—through Christ by the Holy Spirit—to the true fullness of life:

> I pray that you may have the power to comprehend, with all the saints, what is the breadth and length and height and depth, and to know the love of Christ that surpasses knowledge, so that you may be filled with all the fullness of God.
>
> Now to him who by the power at work within us is able to accomplish abundantly far more than all we can ask or imagine, to him be glory in the church and in Christ Jesus to all generations, forever and ever. Amen.[14]

With the mutually involving plenitude of Christ and God (Christ's surpassing love *with* "all the fullness of God")[15] and the Spirit through which it is comprehended, God is involved with the Christians in their achieving true life and understanding.

In this mutually involving plenitude, there is no division between the fullness of the life of Christ and the fullness associated with God. This association is what extends the effect of the life of Christ through history past and future:

Then beginning with Moses and all the prophets, he interpreted to them the things about himself in all the scriptures.[16]

But there are also many other things that Jesus did; if every one of them were written down, I suppose that the world itself could not contain the books that would be written.[17]

Living in and from Christ therefore has the same intensity and range as the fullness of God's life that informs the life of the world.

The character of the fullness of life in Christ is coterminous with the fullness of God's righteous life involving itself with human beings in the achievement of true life and understanding. For their part, Christians are to participate in, and witness to, this fullness. The question with which we must now concern ourselves is, "How do they do so?" If we can answer that in terms of the trajectory we have been exploring, it will be evident how denominations may engage with one another while maintaining their particular "interests"; we will be that much closer to the interdenominational ecumenism that underlies Diogenes Allen's life and work.

Full Christianity

What happens when Christians live fully in the life of Christ, and thereby find the actuality of true human life and thought? One of the conclusions to be drawn is that the coinherence of life in Christ with God's righteousness in the world leads to activity that makes participation in this coinherent life both *primary* and *encompassing*. This is seen most dramatically at Pentecost, where there is for the disciples an immense change simultaneously in the intensity and the extension of life in Christ with God:

When the day of Pentecost had come, they were all together in one place. And suddenly from heaven there came a sound like the rush of a violent wind, and it filled the entire house where they were sitting. Divided tongues, as of fire, appeared among them, and a tongue rested on each of them. All of them were filled with the Holy Spirit and began to speak in other languages, as the Spirit gave them ability.

Now there were devout Jews from every nation under heaven living in Jerusalem. And at this sound the crowd gathered and was bewildered, because each one heard them speaking in the native language of each. Amazed and astonished, they asked, "Are not all these who are speaking Galileans? And how is it that we hear, each of us, in our own native language? Parthians, Medes, Elamites, and residents of Mesopotamia, Judea and Cappadocia, Pontus and Asia, Phrygia and Pamphylia, Egypt and the parts of Libya belonging to Cyrene, and visitors from Rome, both Jews and proselytes, Cretans and Arabs—in our own languages we hear them speaking about God's deeds of power."[18]

The change is real in itself, filling them with the Holy Spirit while also investing them with the power of speaking the deeds of God's power in terms familiar to the known world. The change is in the *intensity of participation* in the new life of Christ and in the *extension of its benefit*.

It has decisive effects for the Christians, in that it is constitutive for their life and thought thereafter. That is, it is a new "reason"[19] through which their life and understanding take form; it is comprehensively formative for their being and motivational for their activity. Their life and understanding become their attempt to remain faithful to this "reason" which constitutes them.[20] Their Christian life has a particular dynamic, which we need now to see by reference to the trajectory whose value we have been exploring, from elemental life to true life.

The New Intensity of Christian Life

One major feature of this dynamic is its new "intensity," or concentration. This appears in a variety of impressive ways. One is the new coherence and energy of their worship:

> Day by day, as they spent much time together in the temple, they broke bread from house to house and ate their food with glad and generous hearts, praising God and having the goodwill of all the people. And day by day the Lord added to their number those who were being saved.[21]

Their worship of God is one of intense praise expressed through the meal by which Jesus bound them to his suffering, death, and resurrection, in which they now show generosity to each other; and this spreads goodwill among all who surround them.

The new intensity also manifests itself as a new concentration on the righteousness made actual in Jesus Christ:

> "Therefore let the entire house of Israel know with certainty that God has made him both Lord and Christ, this Jesus whom you crucified."
>
> Now when they heard this, they were cut to the heart and said to Peter and to the other apostles, "Brothers, what should we do?" Peter said to them, "Repent, and be baptized every one of you in the name of Jesus Christ so that your sins may be forgiven; and you will receive the gift of the Holy Spirit."[22]

Through the witness to the cross and resurrection, a profound awareness of their sin comes upon those who hear; and entering into the life of Christ in baptism is the means of forgiveness and new life.

Likewise, the new intensity appears in their common life:

> Awe came upon everyone, because many wonders and signs were being done by the apostles. All who believed were together and had all things in common; they would sell their possessions and goods and distribute the proceeds to all, as any had need.[23]

As a result, their life in Christ binds them to each other in the closest of relations, not simply as "intentional," but also as they provided each other with the material conditions of life.

And this intensity also enters the process by which they are brought to a deeper understanding of the "reason" that is in them:

> Peter, filled with the Holy Spirit, said to them, "Rulers of the people and elders, if we are questioned today because of a good deed done to someone who was sick and are asked how this man has been healed, let it be known to all of you, and to all the people of Israel, that this man is standing before you in good health by the name of Jesus Christ of Nazareth, whom you crucified, whom God raised from the dead. This Jesus is
>
>> 'the stone that was rejected by you, the builders;
>> it has become the cornerstone.'
>
> There is salvation in no one else, for there is no other name under heaven given among mortals by which we must be saved."[24]

They were a "learning community," "pursuing *paideia,* a word which implied a full and rounded educational process, the training of youth up to maturity physically, mentally and above all, morally."[25]

These features of the intensity within which the early Christians lived—new worship, righteousness, common life, and learning—persist through the centuries. They are the means by which Christians grow toward what we have termed "true life."

The New Magnitude of Christian Life

The other major feature of the new "reason" that forms and motivates the early Christians is the new "magnitude" found to be implicit in life in Christ. Here again, a particular dynamic begins, marked by certain features: there is a *new ecclesiality* which embodies new social expectations, a new *urgency about transforming social life* more widely, even *"globally."*

A primacy is thereby accorded to social life, one difficult fully to appreciate in the context of the individualistic culture of today. This is a social dynamic that carries the most elemental units of social groupings, including their informal, political, and economic constitution, forward in the trajectory to the full embodiment of true social life. The dynamic happens through fuller personal interaction, polities that organize social responsibility, and economies that exemplify full human caring. And it is the way by which God involves Christians in the truth of their social life through "the Christ who lives in us" that is the "reason" that is formative for their life and understanding as Christians.

This new ecclesiality carries the (more elemental) conditions of previous social life to a new level, a freedom and diversity whose energies are so structured as to be productive of a more fully caring society. In interpersonal relationships, the characteristics of this true social life are social virtues such as those indicated by St. Paul (faith, hope, love).[26] In social structures, the characteristics are those listed in the Nicene Creed (unity, holiness, catholicity, and apostolicity).

> No faithful Christian will ever hesitate to confess these four attributes of the Church, which he believes to be true in virtue of that instinct for the

truth, that faculty which one may call "innate," that belongs to all children of the Church—that instinct or faculty which we call faith.[27]

As we saw earlier, however, the faith that recognizes these marks is in the church's own being as formed by the "reason," which is Christ's life in it. The actuality of this new ecclesiality rests on these marks, and without them it is inconceivable. But they in turn derive from the formative presence of Christ as "reason" of the church: "Unity" is the self-concentration of this body on its "reason." "Holiness" is the movement of the Holy Spirit by which it is thus incorporated into Christ's participation in God ("the fullness of him who fills all in all.")[28] "Catholicity" is the comprehensive coherence of the ecclesiality which is appropriate to the truth in which it participates.[29] And "apostolicity" is the active continuity of this ecclesiality in its "reason."

The four marks converge on each other in the trajectory from elemental social life to the actuality of true society. And to suggest that they are *necessary* in the new ecclesiality is not to suggest that their presence there is *sufficient* for the actuality of true society. In that sense, true society is present in the church as it is only by anticipation. Nonetheless, without their presence, either the energy that thrusts people toward each other as society remains haphazard and occasional (underdetermined) or society takes on a rigid, lawlike structure (overdetermined), where what is needed is more like a "polyphony of being" that "moves to this rhythm."[30]

This "rhythmic" movement to true society has proved difficult to sustain in Christian history. The combination of preexisting legal systems with the "structuring" of places, both geographically and politically, through which "extensiveness" is subdivided[31] has tended to stabilize movement, so much so that the underlying thrust along the trajectory toward a true society often largely disappears. The result has been a fragmentation of ideals[32] and a pragmatism in its overcoming. With the onset of modern statism, the church was relegated to its own domain; both defined themselves as the "true society." Others legitimated a dualism of state and church, and redefined the goals of ecclesiality in presocial terms, retreating from the "magnitude" of Christian life and concentrating instead on its "intensity,"[33] especially by emphasizing those characteristics outlined earlier.

New Mission

As we saw before, the "reason" that gives the new ecclesiality its basis and motivates it to move in the trajectory to the truth of society is the life of Christ by which God involves it in God's truth and vitality. The scope of this "reason" is that which is appropriate to God's truth and vitality. The new ecclesiality of Christians cannot, in principle, be turned in on itself. It must be oriented to the achievement of true society for the world as such.

What does this mean? If we imagine the world with a thin skin covering its entire surface, the "skin" comprised of all human beings related in different ways, then each individual is a dot of skin—unsustainable apart from the rest. And this skin receives the possibilities of its life from the world that it envelopes, and generates itself from these possibilities and from itself; while distinguishable from the world, it does not "stand above" it. When, then, we speak of "society," we speak of the manifold relations of these "dots"; "society" occurs when the skin is nourished through the relations of these "dots" in effective configurations which maintain the skin and will fulfill its best possibilities (its well-being). Seen in such a way, humanity is dispersed over the face of the earth, universal not simply as such but by virtue of its nourishment in effective social ordering: how humanity *is* is deeply dependent on how it becomes itself through its social ordering.

Society as thus seen is both natural and social, and highly complex in its detail. In the new ecclesiality that we have seen to emerge in Christianity, however, not only the existence but also the dynamics of this whole—in its nature and social life—are traceable in their origins, continuance, transformation, and outcome to the action of God in Christ by which they are brought to their truth. So the foundations and texture of this universality are in the life of Christ through which God involves the world in God's truth and life. It is not that these foundations and texture are somehow "outside" the natural and social world, as if abstract from them; God's work in Christ is in the same world which otherwise we call "natural" and "social," in the very existence and good—its nourishing interrelatedness—of the "skin" of which we were speaking.

The condition of social life in the world—natural, social, and graceful—is neither inert nor equilibrial. It is much more dynamic in its relationality, fragile and contingent, informed by past history and yet driven by its anticipation of the future, as it moves beyond present failure—if it does. It is never quite predictable, as each human "dot" reaches inward and outward and forward, and as they all grow, both as individuals and together, by their "mutual succumbing," through which they may learn fully humane ways of being together, such as compassion.[34] In the dynamics of this "skin," nothing is quite even or equal or predictable. Nonetheless, an indwelling is possible which will shape a growing compassion by which a new future opens. Of such a kind is the delicate universality in which we are by God's graceful "reason" in the world.

This is not to suggest that the situation is so benevolent. The social "skin" of the world is often leprous, with all sorts of lesions: a tissue of lost people who have also lost the meaning of the world, lost security, lost freedom, lost love and friendship through separations or abandonment, lost peace, lost innocence, lost homes, lost well-being, lost countries, lost lives—agonizing losses that befall people who yearn for better.[35] What are we to make of this dark side of the universality in which we exist, where the variability and contingency of the social fabric of the world brings such disruption? where we even lose faith in the meaning of life in the world?

The urgent issues of the goodness of the social "skin" of the world and of its corruption are what bring us to the deeper dimensions of the marks of the church, where the dynamic of the social life of the world is found, confirmed, renewed, and set forward in hope. And what undergirds these, as we saw, is the actuality of the life of Christ in the "extension" of ecclesiality. The gospel of Jesus Christ is social in form, and provides the possibility of movement for the sociality of the whole world along the trajectory toward true society. Seen in such a way, the gospel in the church is what confirms movement along the trajectory from elemental social life to true society.

It offers no quick resolution, but a growing consolation. It is the crucifixion and resurrection of Jesus Christ that open new life, a new intensity, a new ecclesiality and a new social life for the world; and these are realized only in movement along the trajectory to the truth and vitality of God. And even so, the confirmation, renewal, and promise occur *within* the lesions in it, in the suffering and loss with which it is marked. It is a healing through suffering and from within, from "underneath."

The Fulfillment of Church Life

We have been exploring the trajectory from elemental to true life as a means of a fuller engagement between denominations and theologies, by which they may preserve their fundamental interests while achieving congruence as they seek the truth of human life and its well-being. This has brought us to reconsider the dynamics of Christian faith and life, tracing its genesis in the Christ who lives in them as the One through whom God involves Christians, and through them the whole social world, in the pursuit and achievement of God's truth and vitality. Seen in terms of this trajectory, Christianity has a remarkable inner "reason," which is Christ's life in it, and through the dynamic implicit in that "reason" reaches, intensively and extensively, toward the fullness of truth which is God's.

If Christians have the faith that this "reason" merits, they may generate ecumenical progress and promote engagement with the shaping forces of modern life and understanding. And they may do so in such a way as to bring all human beings again to respond to God's movement to involve them in his truth and vitality.

NOTES

1. See Daniel W. Hardy, *God's Ways with the World* (Edinburgh: T. & T. Clark, 1996), chap. 18.
2. Whether a society run by the principle of fairness can be a living society, which does not come to a standstill through the need to negotiate "fairness" in every situation, is a very serious issue today.
3. "In 1891, a papal encyclical, *Rerum Novarum*, came out against class struggle and proposed a modern version of the medieval scholastic dream of perfect social order. This appeared to be a rejection of Marxist conflict in favour of 'social harmony.' In reality, it was a rejection of humanism, democracy, and responsible individualism in favour of administrative power sharing by interest groups" (John Ralston Saul, *The Unconscious Civilization* [New York: Free Press, 1997], 28).
4. S. T. Coleridge, *On the Constitution of Church and State* (London: Routledge & Kegan Paul, 1976).
5. The science-religion discussion has tended to focus on this, for example, on the use of metaphors, models, and paradigms in both. See Ian Barbour, *Myths, Models and Paradigms* (London: SCM Press, 1974).
6. Religious beliefs and practices, and not they alone, are often explained in other categories: natural-scientific, social, psychological, or cultural.

7. Galatians 2:19, 20.
8. The story is told of an Oriental rug dealer who sold a customer two rugs, a small one and a large one. When he went to the man's house to lay the rugs, he found it a huge, ornate building, built like a castle. The first rug fit perfectly, but the other one was eight feet too long. The rug dealer quickly offered to replace it with another, but the customer declined, and asked him to come back in thirty days. And when he returned, he found that his customer had lengthened the room to take the oversized rug. In the case of the early Christians, by contrast, we find nothing as simple as lengthening a room; as they live in and from it, the life of Christ expands and reconstitutes every aspect of life from within.
9. Alan J. Torrance, *Persons in Communion* (Edinburgh: T. & T. Clark, 1996), 314.
10. Nicholas Rescher, *Cognitive Systematization* (Oxford: Basil Blackwell, 1979), 67.
11. Eberhard Jüngel, *The Doctrine of the Trinity* (Edinburgh: Scottish Academic Press, 1976), 27.
12. Robert Gibbs, *Correlations in Rosenzweig and Levinas* (Princeton, N.J.: Princeton University Press, 1992), 36.
13. There is a comparable, although less extreme, attempt in Heidegger's project, to "work out the question of the meaning of Being" in a world where metaphysics is under radical suspicion, by focusing on the concreteness of *Dasein* (being-there) as the access route to Being, and making it transparent to itself as an interrogation of the essence of Being. "Our aim in the following treatise is to work out the question of the meaning of *Being* and to do so concretely" (Martin Heidegger, *Being and Time*, trans. John Macquarrie and Edward Robinson [London: SCM Press, 1962], 1). Cf. Edith Wyschogrod, *Spirit in Ashes* (New Haven, Conn.: Yale University Press, 1985), 175.
14. Ephesians 3:18–21.
15. Hence there is a much more dynamic relation between Christ's love and the divine *plērōma* than is the case with a formal analogy between them. This disallows the Gnostic division between the *plērōma* as the divine in its multiplicity and unity, on the one hand, and the *kērōma* of the present world existing outside the *plērōma*.
16. Luke 24:27.
17. John 21:25.
18. Acts 2:1–11.
19. The term "reason" is used here in the sense of that which "determin[es] that which is universal and necessary, of fixing laws and principles . . . , and of contemplating a final purpose or end" (S. T. Coleridge, *Aids to Reflection*, ed. John Beer [London: Routledge & Kegan Paul, 1993], 462).
20. "*FAITH* may be defined as = *Fidelity* to our own Being as far as such Being is not and cannot become an object of the sense" (S. T. Coleridge, "Essay on Faith," in *Shorter Works and Fragments* [London: Routledge & Kegan Paul, 1995], vol. 2, 834).
21. Acts 2:46–47.
22. Acts 2:36–39.
23. Acts 2:43–44.
24. Acts 4:8–12.
25. Frances Young, "*Paideia*—What Can We Learn from the First Four Centuries?" in D. F. Ford and D. L. Stamps, eds., *Essentials of Christian Community* (Edinburgh: T. & T. Clark, 1996), chap. 15. Diogenes Allen's *Spiritual Theology* (Cambridge, Mass.: Cowley Publications, 1997) is a "spiritual *paideia*."
26. 1 Corinthians 13:13.
27. Vladimir Lossky, *In the Image and Likeness of God* (Oxford: A. R. Mowbray & Co., 1974), 169.
28. Ephesians 1:23.
29. "There is no other criterion of truth than the Truth itself. And this Truth is the revelation of the Holy Trinity, who gives the Church her catholicity: an ineffable identity of

unity and diversity, in the image of the Father, of the Son, and of the Holy Spirit, consubstantial and indivisible" (Lossky, *In the Image*, 181).

30. Micheal O'Siadhail, "Matins," in *Hail! Madam Jazz* (Newcastle: Bloodaxe Books, 1992), 125–26.

31. Gerard Lukken and Mark Searle, *Semiotics and Church Architecture* (Kampen: Kok Pharos, 1993), 11.

32. This is what is often called sectarianism.

33. This takes different forms of self-definition. One concentrates on the church as true. Another is centered on the true confession of faith. Still another focuses on true sacramental practice.

34. In "mutual succumbing" a "lived-in music" shapes compassion. See Micheal O'Siadhail, "Quartet," in *A Fragile City* (Newcastle: Bloodaxe Books, 1995), 16.

35. "We had thought so long of ourselves as successful, liked and deeply loved. We had hoped for a life of generosity, service and self-sacrifice. We had planned to become forgiving, caring, and always gentle people. We had a vision of ourselves as reconcilers and peacemakers. But somehow—we aren't even sure of what happened—we lost our dream. We became worrying, anxious people. . . . It is this loss of spirit that is often hardest to acknowledge and most difficult to confess. But beyond all of these things there is the loss of faith—the loss of the conviction that our life has meaning" (Henri J. M. Nouwen, *With Burning Hearts* [Maryknoll, N.Y.: Orbis Books, 1994], 24–25).

NOTES ON CONTRIBUTORS

David B. Burrell, C.S.C., is currently Theodore Hesburgh Professor in Philosophy and Theology at the University of Notre Dame, and has been working since 1982 in comparative issues in philosophical theology in Judaism, Christianity, and Islam, as evidenced in *Knowing the Unknowable God: Ibn-Sina, Maimonides, Aquinas* and *Freedom and Creation in Three Traditions* and two translations of al-Ghazali. Earlier, he also published books on Aquinas and religious understanding.

Jeffrey C. Eaton is pastor of Emanuel Evangelical Lutheran Church in New Brunswick, New Jersey, and formerly chaplain and professor of religion at Hamilton College. He is the author of *The Logic of Theism: An Analysis of the Thought of Austin Farrer,* editor of *For God and Clarity,* and author of a number of articles in theology, philosophy, and ethics. He is currently trying "to make sense of spiritual theology working in an inner city parish and developing housing for homeless people and people living with AIDS."

Daniel W. Hardy has served Episcopal parishes and taught in both the United States and England. He was the Van Mildert Professor of Divinity at the University of Durham and Residentiary Canon of Durham Cathedral before becoming director of the Center of Theological Inquiry, a position from which he retired in 1995. Residing in Cambridge, England, he is currently a member of the Faculty of Divinity and of Clare Hall, Cambridge University. He is the author of numerous works in theology, including most recently *God's Ways with the World.*

Stanley Hauerwas is the Gilbert T. Rowe Professor of Theological Ethics in the Divinity School at Duke University. His earlier, groundbreaking work in Christian ethics includes *Character and the Christian Life: A Study in Theological Ethics* and *A Community of Character: Toward a Constructive Social Ethic.* Recently he has published *Unleashing the Scripture: Freeing the Bible from Captivity to America; Dispatches from the Front; Theological Engagements with the Secular; In Good Company: The Church as Polis;* and *Christians among the Virtues: Conversations with Ancient and Modern Ethics.*

Brian Hebblethwaite is University Lecturer in the Philosophy of Religion and life fellow of Queens' College, Cambridge University, and served previously for many years as dean of chapel at Queens' College. He is the author of numerous works in philosophical theology, including *The Ocean of Truth: A*

Defence of Objective Theism; The Essence of Christianity; Ethics and Religion in a Pluralistic Age; The Incarnation; and *The Problems of Theology.*

Edward Henderson is professor of philosophy at Louisiana State University in Baton Rouge, Louisiana, and chairman of the department of philosophy. He is the author of numerous articles in the philosophy of religion, including several on Austin Farrer, around whose thought he organized an international conference. He is coeditor with Brian Hebblethwaite of *Divine Action: Essays Inspired by the Philosophical Theology of Austin Farrer.*

Elena Malits, C.S.C., is a Sister of the Holy Cross and professor of religious studies at Saint Mary's College, Notre Dame, Indiana. She received her Ph.D. in theology in 1974 from Fordham University in a joint program with Union Theological Seminary. She is the author of *Thomas Merton's Transforming Journey* (New York: Harper & Row, 1980) and coauthor with David Burrell of *Original Peace: Restoring God's Creation* (Mahwah, N.J.: Paulist Press, 1997). She teaches courses on religious autobiography along with the electives described in the article.

Daniel L. Migliore is Arthur M. Adams Professor of Systematic Theology at Princeton Theological Seminary. A frequent contributor to theological journals, he is the author of *Called to Freedom: Liberation Theology and the Future of Christian Doctrine; Faith Seeking Understanding: An Introduction to Christian Theology;* and *The Power of God.* His research interests include long-standing dedication to the thought of Karl Barth and Jürgen Moltmann, and to Trinitarian theology.

Gerhard Sauter is professor of systematic and ecumenical theology and director of the Ecumenical Institute of the Faculty of Theology of the University of Bonn, Germany. He is also an extraordinary member of the Faculty of Theology of Oxford University and a member of the Center of Theological Inquiry, Princeton, New Jersey. He is the author and editor of over sixteen books in German and English, including recently *The Question of Meaning* and *Eschatological Rationality: Theological Issues in Focus.* His research emphasis has been in the foundations and theory of theology, as well as theology and science, and eschatology.

Eric O. Springsted is chaplain and professor of philosophy and religion at Illinois College in Jacksonville, Illinois, and a member of the Center of Theological Inquiry in Princeton, New Jersey. He is the author and editor of four books on Simone Weil, including, with Diogenes Allen, *Spirit, Nature and Community: Issues in the Thought of Simone Weil.* He has also written a book on higher education and is coeditor with Allen of *Primary Readings in Philosophy for Understanding Theology.* He and Allen were cofounders of the American Weil Society in 1981 and he has served as its president since then. In addition to Weil, his research interests include work on the concept of faith and its relation to Christian identity.